Music in American Life

Volumes in the series Music in American Life are listed at the end of this book.

Traveling the High Way Home

Traveling the High Way Home

*Ralph Stanley and the World of
Traditional Bluegrass Music*

John Wright

University of Illinois Press   *Urbana and Chicago*

This book is printed on acid-free paper.

Library of Congress Cataloging-in-Publication Data

Wright, John, 1941–
    Traveling the high way home : Ralph Stanley and the world of
traditional bluegrass music / John Wright.
        p.   cm. — (Music in American life)
    Includes bibliographical references (p.   ), discography (p.   ),
and index.
    ISBN 0-252-02024-3
    1. Stanley, Ralph. 2. Bluegrass musicians—United States.
3. Bluegrass music—History and criticism. I. Title. II. Series.
ML420.S8115W74   1993
781.642'092—dc20
    [B]   92-43830
                                                                   CIP
                                                                   MN

Dedicated to My Wife

Contents

Preface

Like most bluegrass fans from the Northeast, I first came to the old-time mountain music of Ralph and Carter Stanley through phonograph records. Two things about this music appealed to me from the start. The first and most obvious was its power, beauty, and integrity. The second—and for me this was almost equally important—was its autonomy. Of all the vernacular musics with which I had become acquainted, this was the only one I could find that was not weighed down by the social, political, or economic agenda of someone else from somewhere else. Not Owen Bradley's agenda or Colonel Parker's from Nashville. Not Folkways' from New York. Not Bascom Lamar Lunsford's from Asheville. This music existed for itself alone. It would be many years before I came to know what a high price its creators had paid for that independence. At the time all I knew was that it was there and I was glad that it was.

Phonograph records were still my only source of information when, many years later, inspired only by love of the music and armed (unconsciously) with a shield of blissful ignorance, I started to write a column about the art of Ralph Stanley for *Banjo Newsletter*. Fortunately I was not allowed to remain behind that shield for long. In a way that I later was to discover is typical of the bluegrass world, the fans—in this case my readers—would not let me get away with it. I soon began to receive a string of letters suggesting, or in some cases even insisting, that my column would be very much improved if it were to feature interviews with Ralph Stanley and his sidemen.

I never will forget it. There I was, for the first time, at the Stanley Brothers' old home place in Dickenson County, Virginia. I was sitting at a picnic table, a rank stranger six hundred miles from my Illinois home but already warmly welcomed by a Kentucky family who had been coming regularly to Ralph Stanley's Memorial Festival for years. Across from me was Melvin Goins, whom I had met only moments before but who readily acceded to my request to talk. The tape recorder was rolling and I asked some banal and obvious question—and then sat back and listened in awe as Melvin's rapid, eloquent, and evocative words came down like snowflakes in a Lake Michigan storm.

In writing up the results of this and subsequent interviews I soon discovered that my words and those of the people with whom I was talking mixed very badly indeed. These people, these friends as they later became, could tell their own story better than I could ever hope to. In retrospect I should hardly have been surprised: was it not the autonomy of their world that had attracted me to it in the first place? My job as a writer, I learned after a few false starts, would be roughly similar to that of a good sound man. I was to set the stage as carefully and unobtrusively as possible. I was to make sure everything was working properly. And then (in no uncertain terms) I was to disappear while the people who were central to the performance got on with the real business at hand, helped, as far as I was concerned, only by the barest minimum of suggestions and dial-twistings.

And that, in short, is what I have tried to do in this book. To be specific: I have not attempted to write a personal biography of Ralph Stanley. There were three reasons for this negative decision. First, Stanley's art, unlike that of, say, most modern country artists, is classic; it is no more dependent on the events of his life or the quirks of his personality than is the art of an opera singer. *L'homme c'est rien, l'œuvre c'est tout*, in the words (familiar to all Sherlock Holmes fans) of Gustave Flaubert. Second, the culture from which Stanley comes assigns a very high value to personal privacy. I was sympathetic to this predilection from the first and in the course of my work I came to share it to such a great extent that I could not have violated it even if I had wanted to. Third, even if I were to suppress personal details and concentrate instead on an external, purely "artistic" biographical narrative, the results would have been disappointing and perhaps even misleading. A narrative of that sort depends on change and development for its interest. But Ralph Stanley found his artistic voice very early in his career and has stayed steadily with it ever since. "He's never changed his style," sideman Charlie Sizemore used to say in his stock stage introduction of his employer: an indictment for any other artist, but in this case an encomium. For over two decades Stanley's Works and Days have been as predictable and unchanging as those of a farmer: a recording session in the fallow days of midwinter; a spring ploughing (to continue the metaphor) at the Smith Ridge festival in May; high summer in (say) Milan, Michigan, a few miles from U.S. 23, the Appalachian artery; Thanksgiving in Myrtle Beach, South Carolina (the Waikiki of the RV world); New Year's at Jekyll Island, Georgia. And so forth, year after year. A North Star, a Rock of Gibraltar. Hardly the appropriate material for chronological annals.

Despite all these disclaimers, of course, a certain amount of biographical work was inevitable and indeed desirable, and that is what the first chapter of this book consists of. The remaining chapters present a picture, a self-portrait, of the world that produced Ralph Stanley and for which he is producing his art. It is a small world, close-knit though in diaspora, which has demonstrated an astonishing ability to preserve and nourish a traditional culture while living in the midst of a larger civilization which seems almost deliberately dedicated to eradicating tradition of any sort. The culture consists not in homespun clothes or log cabins (indeed, the presence of such outdated artifacts would have been an almost inescapable sign that the tradition had been embalmed rather than preserved) but rather in a series of attitudes and memories that are best expressed, as I have said, in the words of the people involved.

Hence the bulk of the book is testimony—and I use the term not in the sense it is used in the courtroom but rather in the old-time church. The people in these chapters are bearing witness. Most of them are professional musicians, and the relevance of their testimony to the subject at hand will be immediately obvious. They provide the insider's view, and even when they are discussing the identical event (for instance, the traumatic death of Ralph Stanley's brother Carter) or the identical issue (such as the origins and explanation of Ralph Stanley's vocal and instrumental art) the different points of view they offer are invaluable for casting light on the subject. The rest of the witnesses are not musicians, some of them not even amateur musicians, and while at first glance they may seem peripheral their testimony is in fact no less invaluable. A festival vendor describes the almost religious experience that put Stanley's old-time music at the center of his life. A Midwestern welder verbally shows us (rather than telling us) how much backbreaking sacrifice was necessary to provide a professional venue for that music near his home in northern Ohio. A Michigan housewife, while describing her work as a fan club promoter, reveals almost against her will the all-consuming emotional obsession that the music can become to those who love it. An elderly neighbor and an elderly relative simultaneously describe and embody the community and family values that made the creation and preservation of the music possible. A professional student of the music gives us perspective and the long view. And so on.

The witnesses are verbal almost to a fault, but if they ramble a bit now and then, even their ramblings, in the last analysis, are relevant. A band bus crawling doggedly through the night with no illumination but its parking lights; a blind, prematurely aged ex-miner tending a mountain garden on two wooden legs; a small boy running away from an inhuman job at a cotton mill; a puzzled mountaineer encountering pizza for the first time; a farm wife riding an old gray mare to church; a cross-cut sawmill in Virginia; a Kentucky truck mine; a flooding creek in North Carolina; ginseng; chinquapins; fried apple pie—these images are as much a part of the music and the world that produced it as an account of a song origin or a description of a recording studio. And they are an integral part of the ultimate goal of this book: to let the reader hear and know, with as little interference as possible, the people of Ralph Stanley's world.

Creating the book, as its title would suggest, has been a long and delightful journey. While on this journey I have had an enormous amount of help from an enormous number of people, ranging from folklorists to filling-station owners, and I will do my best to remember them all here. The book's dedication records my greatest debt. My thanks, in addition, to Fred Bartenstein, Jim and Ruby Belcher, Hillard Blankenship, Barry Brower, Verda Cline, Hank Edenborn, Eberhard Finke, Dave Freeman, Jack and Estelle Frye, Bill and Dot Fugate, Dick Guggenheim, Bertha Hall, Willard Hall, George Hausser, Tom Henderson, Don Hoos, Mike Hopkins, Lee Kessler, Pete Kuykendall, Bill Landow, Don and Zeda Lavinder, Mason Little, Charlie and Alan Maggard, Wade Mainer, Jack Mansfield, Roy McGinnis, Bill Meade, John Miller, John Morris, Hub and Nancy Nitchie, John Orleman, Marty Poland, Curt and Hope Randolph, Gary Reid, Ralph Rinzler, Verlin Sanders, Walt Saunders, Robert Schlade, Mike Seeger, Robin Tackett Sizemore, Ron Smolka, Jimmie Stanley, Richard Thompson, Jack Tottle, Ivan Tribe, Bill and Evelyn Tussey, Miles Ward, Dick Webb, Arnie Weber, Jim Wilson, and all the people interviewed here for their hospitality, encouragement, and patient assistance. Like me, few of them could have realized what we were getting involved with when we started. But I hope they like the results.

The First Forty Years

"I've been into [this business], let's see, it'll be thirty-seven years
this coming October and I believe I can make forty more."
—*Ralph Stanley (1983)*

"This area is 'Ralph Stanley' country," said acoustic musician
Walt Michael, reminiscing recently about his extended stay as a
volunteer social worker and collector of traditional mountain music in McDowell County, West Virginia, some twenty years ago.
"Very backwoods, very unknown. . . . It was the real thing." The
phrase "Ralph Stanley country" is just as true today, and as far as
music is concerned it can be applied to any number of mountain
counties from West Virginia to east Tennessee.

A sense of proportion, of course, is in order. Big Stone Gap in
southwestern Virginia, for instance, is a relatively small town, the
sort of place where everyone knows everyone's business. But if, say,
on March 30, 1983, you were to mention to the man on the Big
Stone street that Ralph Stanley and the Clinch Mountain Boys were
at that very moment in Charlie Maggard's studio on Railroad Avenue cutting a new bluegrass album, the odds are that the person
you were speaking to would not know what you were talking about.
The local newspaper would carry no word of the session, and the
searingly powerful music on the album would stand little chance
of breaking into the prepackaged country format of the local radio
station. At the end of the session, an hour or two after sundown,
Stanley and his musicians would be able to eat supper at a local
cafeteria without attracting so much as a passing glance, to say
nothing of an autograph hunter.

But among the musicians of the area, the fiddlers, banjoists, and
guitar players who cling stubbornly to the old ways and who range
from professionals to self-confessed bumbling amateurs, it would
be a very different story. The music on that 1983 album, and doz-

ens of other albums like it, would be news from the mountain, water from the head of the stream. It, or some of it, would blend in with the oldest products of tradition so thoroughly that it would be hard for anyone to tell where tradition left off and Ralph Stanley began.

Hard even for experts. In the summer of 1959, for instance, folklorist Alan Lomax toured the South with modern field recording equipment, a tour which produced the seven-volume "Southern Folk Heritage Series" for the Atlantic Records. In southwestern Virginia Lomax recorded an instrumental called "Big Tilda," played by the Mountain Ramblers, a traditional string band which featured a young man named Cullen Galyen on the five-string banjo. Now "Big Tilda" was an original composition by Ralph Stanley; it had been released on a national label (Mercury). And Galyen's banjo style had been enormously influenced by Stanley; later he was to share a stage professionally with the Clinch Mountain Boys from time to time. But Lomax's liner notes do not even mention Ralph Stanley, and in them "Big Tilda" is identified only as "a stomp-down square dance tune popular in the Galax region."

This apparent snub is really the highest sort of compliment. It brings to mind the inevitable reaction of the visitor who sees the huge, grim, concrete crosses, inscribed with the message "Get Right With God," that dot the highway berms of Appalachia. They seem to have grown as naturally out of the culture of the region as the hills and pines grew out of its geology and ecology. But further research would reveal that they are in fact the work of a single individual, Brother Harrison Mayes of Middlesboro, Kentucky, whose life's work of constructing and erecting these crosses embodies perfectly the religious feeling of his region. So it is with Ralph Stanley and his music.

Brother Mayes had to work hard to accomplish what he did, and this has been no less true with Ralph Stanley. From their earliest childhood in rural Dickenson County in southwest Virginia, both he and his older brother Carter had set their sights on a professional career in country music. The boys' mother, Lucy Smith Stanley, provided the model for Ralph's banjo playing; from the time he was eleven or twelve the banjo would be "his" instrument. A vocal style takes longer to develop; the singing of the boys' father, Lee, the singing of other male relatives, the hymns that were featured in the Old Regular Baptist church the family attended—all were there in the background, though they would not fully emerge in Ralph's powerful brand of mountain melisma until later. The brothers' musical repertory came from family, friends, the radio, and occasional local appearances by traditional country performers. Family gatherings, school programs, political rallies, and even once or twice the local radio provided a platform and an audience for their early musical efforts.

Personally, the boys' life was pleasant enough—perhaps even as idyllic as their later songs were to suggest. A semisubsistence family economy afforded enough to eat and enough cash to get by. If their living conditions were primitive, so were those of all their neighbors. Farm chores provided discipline and order, and, for Ralph (who still is perhaps most comfortable when gardening and caring for livestock), a valuable source of solace and relaxation. Even today, and even to adult eyes, the neighboring countryside seems extensive; to young boys in the 1930s it must have been an endless playground. While the separation of his parents was surely painful to the fourteen-year-old Ralph, the shock was cushioned by a loving and supportive extended family.

Military service comes as naturally as breathing in Dickenson County (which has the highest enlistment rate of any county in the United States). V-E Day and Ralph Stanley's graduation from Ervinton High School, and with it his entry into the U.S. Army, occurred simultaneously, and after basic training the new private was assigned to service in occupied Germany. Here he learned a useful lesson in the practical value of music; the rapid promotions he received and the special privileges he enjoyed came as much from his skill on the banjo, and the effect this skill had on an audience of superior officers, as from his intelligence and self-discipline. When he was discharged a year and a half later he was mature, self-confident, and, as a musician, ready to go.

And the area that was later to become "Ralph Stanley country" was ready for the Stanley Brothers. Brother Carter met Ralph at the Bristol bus station and immediately whisked him off to a studio in nearby Norton for a performance with Roy Sykes and the Blue Ridge Mountain Boys, a group for which Carter was already working. Less than three months later the Stanley Brothers had a band and a radio program of their own; the inaugural broadcast from Bristol of the Clinch Mountain Boys' "Farm and Fun Time" was held on December 26, 1946.

The pent-up hunger of the WCYB hinterland for traditional country music had been frustrated for years by wartime travel restrictions and the drafting of musicians. The dam burst for the Stanley Brothers. "Farm and Fun Time" provided exposure and publicity;

income—an enormous amount of it in the boys' eyes—came from the seemingly endless series of personal appearances in local schoolhouses and theaters that their radio publicity generated. The entertainment the Stanley Brothers had to offer, a combination of high-spirited, raucous hoedowns and sweet, soft-spoken brother duets which can still be experienced thanks to recently discovered radio transcriptions, was just what the people of the area wanted.

The trajectory of the subsequent career of the Stanley Brothers is not easy to describe; a chart would show some rather violent highs and lows, in a rather unpredictable pattern. In 1951, for instance, despite a successful series of recording sessions for Columbia, the Brothers quit the music business and went to work for the Ford Motor Company in Detroit. This career change, as it turned out, was temporary: Carter Stanley was soon working full-time as lead singer for Bill Monroe's Blue Grass Boys—also a temporary arrangement, though a serious automobile accident suffered by Ralph threatened for a while to make it permanent. (Paradoxically the Stanley Brothers' best recording efforts, the classic Mercury sessions of the mid-fifties, took place not long after these difficulties, during what financially was one of the hardest periods of their career.) At another time Ralph and fellow musician Pee Wee Lambert were so close to establishing themselves permanently as farmers in Dickenson County that they built some rooms in the old Stanley country store to house Lambert while they attended an agricultural instruction course. And when the Brothers moved to Live Oak, Florida, in 1958, this new venue had its pluses and minuses: on the one hand, a reliable sponsor and a regular television program; on the other, separation from home and family and all the disadvantages that this entailed.

To depict the concluding period of the Stanley Brothers' twenty-year career is even more difficult. The times were hard enough for all traditional musicians, but Carter Stanley's increasingly poor health, and the denial, wishful thinking, enabling behavior, and concealment that accompanied his sickness, were taking their toll as well. Those close to the protagonists will tell the story only in off-the-record comments, but there are fans who are not at all adverse to characterizing some Stanley Brothers performances as absolute disasters, not only in 1966 (their last year together) but for several years before that. And their studio recordings during this period, to many ears, were becoming disturbingly commercialized (with the notable exception of four bootleg albums quietly released under the pseudonym "John's Gospel Quartet" by a small mail-order company in Baltimore called Wango). On the other hand the Brothers' 1966 tour of Europe appears to have been successful enough, and at least one commentator hailed their appearance at Bean Blossom, Indiana, in the fall of that year as a triumph. This, then, was an ambiguous period. But one thing is clear: on December 1, 1966, when a nurse appeared in the lobby of Bristol Memorial Hospital to tell Ralph that Carter Stanley was dead, his future as a professional musician looked very bleak indeed.

There were any number of reasons why a lover or performer of traditional mountain music might have been pessimistic at the time. For one thing, the separation of the commercial music industry from the kind of music the Stanley Brothers played was now complete. The days when old-time musicians could record for major labels like Columbia would never return; the last Stanley Brothers record to make the charts—and only as a novelty item—was the traditional comic skit "How Far to Little Rock." Something called "country music" was indeed being promoted as never before by some of America's shrewdest business people, but it had little to do with anything Ralph Stanley could ever hope or wish to do on a stage.

Live, locally produced radio programs were also a thing of the past. For two generations such shows, with the free publicity and instant, intimate audience access they offered, had been the single most important avenue to success for traditional performers with professional aspirations—including, as we have seen, the Stanley Brothers. But the Stanleys' last broadcasting contract had petered out in Florida several years earlier, and neither they nor Ralph Stanley were ever to enjoy the luxury of a regular radio or television program again.

For a while it had seemed that the folk music boom might provide an appropriate outlet. Its immediate, practical effect on musicians like the Stanleys had been minor at best, but still, the hope had been there, the expectation that traditionally based, acoustic music would become *the* art for an entire generation. But this bubble burst at Newport in 1965, when Bob Dylan took the stage with an electric guitar and a rock band while Pete Seeger wept in the wings. The young people went their separate way and to this day show no signs of returning.

But Ralph Stanley's biggest problem was personal. Losing his brother, as he said at the time, was like losing his right arm. As he did *not* say at the time (or at any other time), they had had their occasional differences. Carter's happy-go-lucky yet domineering personality was hard for Ralph to take, much as he needed the strength of such a personality to guide and humanize him. There had been fights, it is said, and insults. A former sideman recalls an embarrassing moment when Ralph told him to give Carter his notice; he remains uncertain as to the seriousness of this threat, which Carter laughed off easily.

But the violence of the quarrels only goes to prove the great depths of the relationship. In the midst of the hints and pregnant silences an investigator is faced with when inquiring into this matter, it remains perfectly obvious that the Stanley Brothers would never have split up voluntarily. Both of them needed each other and both of them knew it.

But now, involuntarily, Ralph Stanley was alone, and it was frightening. Unlike Carter, he had never been and never would be a natural performer, the sort of person who enjoys being the center of attention. And he had never been and never would be truly certain about the worth of his talent and his art. He was perfectly capable of outrageous bragging about the uniqueness of his voice, and knowledgeable observers would agree that this bragging was perfectly justified. But deep down inside, the lingering suspicion remained that his profession was nothing more than an idle pastime, that in reality he was putting something over on people. This diffidence, along with all the other problems he faced, was hardly a firm foundation on which to base a solo career.

But at the same time there were a number of positive factors operating, though almost none of them would have been evident at the time. To begin with, there was sheer necessity. Just a few months short of forty years old, Ralph was completely untrained and unprepared to do anything else but sing and play music. It was far too late for him to pursue a boyhood dream of becoming a veterinarian. He was a grown man; he had a living to earn.

The devoted crowd that packed the Ervinton High School gymnasium for Carter Stanley's funeral must have been a dramatic reminder of the fact that, no matter how hard times had been, there were plenty of fans for whom his sort of music remained important. And in later years he was to speak of these fans, of their letters and telephone calls, as a major factor in his decision to return to the road. The letters and calls did indeed come, but by the time they started to arrive his mind was already made up. The show dates, already arranged, that were there to be filled, the need to put food on the table, and (as he would state in more intimate moments) the wretchedness of sitting around with nothing to do but reminisce about his twenty years' work with his brother—these were enough to make a return, an immediate return, inevitable. There was no long, Hamlet-like period of indecision. Ralph's sideman George Shuffler recalls being summoned back to work within four or five days after the funeral.

And while George and Ralph may have been returning to work simply for want of anything else to do, the conditions for their return were more propitious than immediate appearances might have suggested. Take for instance the most mundane of factors: the road. Musicians always speak of their work in terms of being "on the road," and, by sheer coincidence, the roads themselves at this time were on the brink of a revolution. The Interstate system was improving by the hour; within a few years it would be complete. The all-important business of getting from place to place would be changed completely, for fans and musicians alike. A mobile society, apparently such a threat to traditional music, would (for Ralph Stanley at any rate) be its salvation. Driving would always be work, but now it would be predictable and dependable work.

The record business was also on the brink of great changes. Up to now, a musician had two choices: a major recording contract (with its concomitant loss of independence) or nothing. And the last record company for which the Stanley Brothers had worked, in its attempt to maintain a national marketing posture, had been floundering about for years, producing (with the other artists in its stable as well as the Brothers) a bewildering mixture of great art and commercially inspired junk. But it was soon to become clear that this was not the only route to go.

Ironically, as with the interstate transportation system, so with the recording industry: modern technology was about to come to the rescue of tradition. The invention and development of transistors was bringing high-quality sound reproduction within the reach of the small-scale entrepreneur, and the long-playing album, a much better vehicle for limited distribution than the earlier 78 and 45 r.p.m singles, was finally becoming accepted as the standard medium for vernacular as well as classical music. Hard work and dedication, rather than massive amounts of capital, were all that was necessary for a lover of any minority-based music to produce and distribute whatever artistic wares he wanted to. A sign of things to come was Ralph Stanley's second long-playing album, produced less than a year after Carter Stanley's death. Appropriately entitled *Old Time Music,* it was recorded in a basement in Dayton, Ohio, produced by a "company" that was essentially a one-man operation, and distributed largely through point-of-contact sales; it featured a collection of old, public-domain selections that would never have never passed muster with the artists-and-repertory bosses of a large record company.

Stanley was free to make *Old Time Music* because his previous recording contract was not in his name but in that of the Stanley Brothers. Though he would shortly begin a fruitful association with Rebel Records of Virginia, he would never sign a long-term exclusive contract with this company or any other. To this day the artistic control over his recording is his and no one else's.

Finally, Stanley was the beneficiary of a completely unlooked-for development which historian Neil Rosenberg has appropriately dubbed the "consumer revolution" in bluegrass music. Carlton Haney's 1965 bluegrass festival at Roanoke, Virginia, which at the time seemed to some participants to be a memorial meeting for a dying art form, instead heralded a renaissance: within five years there were enough festivals year around and nationwide to enable a bluegrass musician to earn a relatively decent and above all dependable annual income. The festivals were put on by music lovers who generally hoped for nothing better for their efforts than to break even financially, and they were attended by fans who were willing to drive hundreds of miles for the music and the music alone. The mountain had at last come to Mohammed, and all the musicians had to do to keep it there was to continue to perform in the way they had from the start.

These were some of the external factors that made the beginning of Ralph Stanley's solo career more auspicious than it might have appeared at the moment. Internally, individually, the ingredients for success were there as well. For years Ralph had been perfectly aware that his smoky, ghostly, hair-raising, and utterly "mountainous" tenor voice was something unique in the world of professional entertainers. This voice had already been the main feature of the earlier "John's Gospel Quartet" recordings, and there was no need to decide to make it the centerpiece of his solo stage performances; under the circumstances there was nothing else to do. He had, also for years, been the bookkeeper and general agent for the band; at this point there was nothing he did not know about the intricacies of handling promoters, recording executives, and sidemen. The public speaking that inevitably goes with performing—MCing as it's called in the trade—was another story. Stanley's deep shyness, what he would call his backwardness (which continues to this day), made this part of the business very difficult for him. But either out of prescience or incapacity, his brother had been pushing him forward to do a greater share of this work, and this bit of training, coupled with necessity, would prove to be enough to take care of the job.

It would be hard even for Stanley to say exactly when and how consciously he made his major artistic choice, which was to make his whole ensemble style as plain and old-fashioned as possible. In large part this had already been a major feature of the Stanley Brothers' work. But Carter Stanley, unlike his innately conservative brother, had always been willing to try out more modern material, approaches, and accompaniments. For Ralph this was simply impossible. And not for want of knowledge: he has always spent a great deal of time listening to modern country music. But it has never affected his performances. Almost as soon as his solo career began, analysts started noticing a move toward a more archaic style. With obvious reluctance he responded to their queries about how deliberate this was by saying that he supposed this style had always been in him and that circumstances were bringing it to the foreground. And this reluctant answer, in large part, is the truth.

Almost immediately Stanley made one of his smartest and longest-lasting decisions when he took on a veteran fiddler named Curly Ray Cline, who had played a few dates with the Stanley Brothers during the previous year or so, as a full-time member of the band. Cline was an excellent musician who was able without much difficulty to adjust his instrumental style, which to a certain extent had moved forward with the times, to Stanley's plainer requirements. But more importantly, his unquenchable ebullience provided a needed foil to Stanley's dour and self-effacing personality, both off stage and on. The result was a much more relaxing and comfortable show for all concerned. As the years went by, Cline was to discover a career for himself as a country comedian, to such an extent that at times he would almost threaten to take over the show, much to the annoyance of some purists in the audience. But in general the balance was kept quite well.

Not long afterward Stanley hired his other mainstay, string bassist Jack Cooke, who, like Cline, had also played a bit with the Stanley Brothers, though many years earlier. Cooke too was an excellent musician, a powerful and versatile singer with an enormous vocal range, able to handle either baritone or tenor parts in trio arrangements. He also served as record seller (and, as such, as the band's main ambassador of goodwill to the public), and for some time was the band's main driver, logging hundreds of thousands of miles without a ticket or an accident. Mundane tasks, perhaps, but essential to the work of the group.

With appropriate symbolism, Cline and Cooke stand at either end, guarding the flanks, so to speak, with Stanley in the center, as the band lines up on the stage. The loyalty that binds all three is mutual: Stanley is known in a notoriously tight-fisted business as the most generous of employers. And his generosity goes beyond money; his constant featuring of his sidemen in solo roles stands out in a musical world in which many bandleaders seem to make a point of ignoring or even publicly insulting their employees.

The lead guitar—that is, a guitar used for instrumental breaks rather than rhythmic accompaniment—had been brought into the Stanley Brothers' ensemble several years before Carter Stanley's death, at the insistence of a recording executive who wanted to get away from what he considered the band's overly rustic sound. Elaborate and very popular techniques had, relatively recently, been developed for the instrument, and of course they depended for their staging viability on modern methods of sound amplification. Ralph Stanley had disapproved of this move and will still admit that he isn't very fond of the guitar in this role. But it is an interesting measure of his musical conservatism that once the decision had been made he elected to stand by it, even after the outside pressure had disappeared. His choice was also a measure of his commercial acuity: the lead guitar had become associated with the "Stanley sound" and thus would help to identify the band. Besides, audience response made it clear that the fans loved it.

George Shuffler, who was virtually Stanley's partner at the time of Carter's death, was the best known of the Stanley Brothers' lead guitarists. He continued to work for Ralph in an on-again, off-again manner, but it was a partnership that could not last, largely because the two had, so to speak, grown up together under Carter's leadership and hence in a way were too close for comfort. After Shuffler's departure Stanley employed a series of excellent lead guitarists, among whom Ricky Lee and Junior Blankenship would perhaps stand out the most.

As the tenor voice in what for twenty years had been a duet act, Ralph Stanley naturally needed to employ a lead singer. This was clearly a vital position, and one would imagine that the process of filling it would be the result of a long and arduous series of auditions. In fact, just the opposite was true. Both initially and at the various times since when Stanley has had to replace his lead singer, he has made his choice with astonishing rapidity. To be sure, several of these singers, for instance Larry Sparks and Keith Whitley, had already worked fairly extensively as sidemen for the band. But others, including two of the best, Roy Lee Centers and Charlie Sizemore, had not, and Sizemore, who was hired after an audition of three songs, will concede that to this day he is mystified as to why Ralph chose him.

But the subsequent success of Stanley's lead singer "graduates," notably Sparks, Sizemore, and (before his untimely death) Whitley, as well as the excellent work all of them did while actually with the Stanley group, proves that however casual Ralph's methods of selection may appear he was definitely going about things the right way. We can only conclude that he had and has a perfect ear and an incredibly keen nose for talent. And of course his own teaching, which by every account is done almost entirely through example rather than precept, must have a good deal to do with his success in this facet of his business.

On the other hand, he has also had some extraordinarily bad luck with his lead singers. His first partner of course was his brother Carter, who died a painful death. Roy Lee Centers, his third lead singer, was shot to death as the result of a pointless quarrel, another lead singer died (after leaving Stanley) of alcohol poisoning, and another was sent to prison on an unsavory assault charge. It would be foolish to make too much of these unfortunate events (the "Curse of the Clinch Mountain Boys"?), but they do serve to illustrate how closely the world of traditional mountain music still clings to the elements of violence and self-destruction which make up so much of its material. They also serve to illustrate Ralph Stanley's exemplary professionalism: after each disaster the band continued its career and met its obligations without (to use the appropriate metaphor) missing a beat.

A lead singer (playing a very simple, straightforward rhythm guitar), a lead guitar player (who seldom sang), a fiddler, and a bass player, along with Stanley singing tenor and playing banjo, very soon became the standard pattern for the Stanley band. This arrangement was to become as undeviating as that of a classical string quartet; while a lead singer, for instance, might be able to play the mandolin, as long as he was lead singer he would play the guitar and only the guitar, even though there was another guitarist on the stage who could have taken up the rhythm work for a change. On occasion the band would carry one or two supernumerary musicians, who were going along largely for the experience and out of their love for the music. Most notable among these were

Keith Whitley and Ricky Skaggs, who joined the band in this capacity for a short time in the early seventies and later went on to
successful careers in modern country music. Such extra musicians
made some variation in the usual pattern possible. For instance,
Skaggs, a multi-instrumental virtuoso, would take a twin-fiddle
break on certain songs with Curly Ray Cline, both in the studio and
on the stage. But when Skaggs left he, so to speak, took those
songs with him; they would never be sung again, since the twin-
fiddle work was looked upon as part of their essence.

The artistic pattern as well as the organizational pattern of the
group was firmly established early on in Stanley's solo career. Take,
for instance, the sets he performed at Bill Monroe's first bluegrass
festival at Bean Blossom, Indiana, in June of 1967, hardly half a
year after Carter Stanley's death. (These have been preserved, as
so many early festival performances were, on private tape recordings.) It is perhaps not so surprising that in these performances
Ralph's singing voice rings with the power and conviction that has
always been his trademark. Nor does it come as a shock to hear
the surging drive of his banjo, in song breaks, in solo instrumentals, and (most characteristically to the ears of many aficionados)
in the unique backup he provides to Curly Ray Cline's fiddle tunes.
But what is most striking is that the whole show—the pace, the
material, and the spoken parts that are so vital for maintaining the
intimate connection between a traditional artist and his close-knit
audience—is virtually indistinguishable from what Stanley is doing
right now.

All the standard elements are there: the new release (an "instrumental that's called 'Row Hoe' which is going to be released in
about, well, most any day now") to open the set. Several Stanley
Brothers classics ("Rank Stranger," "Riding That Midnight Train,"
"How Mountain Girls Can Love," etc.). Showpiece vocal solos for
Ralph ("Little Maggie," "Pretty Polly," and "a real old-time solo number, one of the first songs I ever learned to sing, 'Man of Constant
Sorrow'"). Showpiece solos for the sidemen ("I Know What It Means
to Be Lonesome" for George Shuffler, "Old Slewfoot" for Melvin Goins). A more elaborately orchestrated guest slot for a fortuitous visitor, in this case Gene Duty, author of "That Beautiful Woman,"
which the band had recently recorded ("We are proud to have the
fellow here with us today from Detroit, Michigan, that wrote the
song and we're going to ask him to come out right now and do the
lead singing on [it].") A comedy routine with Melvin Goins as "Big
Wilbur" and Ralph Stanley as straight man: an antique, of course,

but personalized with references to Stanley's farm in Florida. A gracious if anonymous nod to a pick-up sideman ("Folks, I hear some awful good bass playing back there behind us. Let's everybody get together and give a great big racket for our bass player back there."). A sales pitch for albums ("A lot of you folks have asked us about where you can buy Stanley Brothers albums. Lot of people say they're hard to find and can't get them. And for that reason, why, we carry a few of them along with us. Wilbur, if you don't care, how about you coming over and telling the folks very briefly what we have for them."). And finally, a closing statement that combines an elegant tribute to Stanley's host with some adroit self-promotion ("We're real proud to be here for the first bluegrass festival at Bean Blossom, Indiana. I was talking to Bill a while ago and he is going to have this same thing every year. I believe next year he may have three days and he's done asked me if I would be on all three days, so I told him I'd be tickled to death to. We're real glad to be associated with a good friend like Bill Monroe. I consider he's one of the best friends that the Stanley Brothers ever had. And he's one of the greatest and the father of bluegrass music. He's paved the way and made the road a lot easier for just a lot of fellows you see like us and hear every day. We appreciate it, too. Let's give Bill a nice hand. . . . Curly, let's go off with an old-time fiddle tune here, one of Bill's tunes, called 'Roanoke.' And we'll see you all a little bit later on.").

This is no fumbling beginner but an assured, mature, confident professional, completely in control not only of his singing and music but of the whole self-created setting that goes with it and makes it a commercially viable art form. It brings to mind the country cliché—which, inevitably, pops up in the "Big Wilbur" routine—"raring to go but can't go for raring," except in this case Ralph Stanley definitely *can* go. And for all his diffidence he has been going along ceaselessly ever since.

Going on, yes, but going on and doing what? What was it that made the art of Ralph Stanley so special, even from this very early date? Newcomers to the music, seeing a hard-driving acoustic string band, doing their vocals in a high-pitched, intense fashion, would probably have been content to call the Clinch Mountain Boys' music "bluegrass" and let it go at that. But Ralph Stanley would not. The verbal formula he uses on the stage to describe his art is contorted: "the *old-time* style of what they call bluegrass music." The phrase is contorted for a reason: it would hardly be diplomatic to stand up before the hypersensitive audience of a *bluegrass* festival and announce, "You think that what we are playing is blue-grass music but it is not. We are playing old-time music." But old-time music is what Ralph Stanley was playing at Bean Blossom (and has been ever since).

In what way was this music "old-time"? Not, for the most part, in the origins of the material. Of all the numbers in this Bean Blossom set, only two, "Pretty Polly" and "Man of Constant Sorrow," had been learned by Stanley as a boy from his family. The rest were in no way "folk music" but were the creations of individual, relatively modern composers, such as Albert Brumley ("Rank Stranger"), Carter Stanley ("Riding That Midnight Train"), and Bill Monroe ("Roanoke"). Two, as we have seen, were specifically introduced as brand-new compositions, the instrumental "Row Hoe" and the vision ballad "That Beautiful Woman."

"Old-time," then, is a matter of style rather than chronology (as Stanley's formula suggests). The material may have been written recently but it did not and does not sound that way. It is hardly an accident, for instance, that Stanley is convinced that the ghost story in "That Beautiful Woman" was based on a true experience. Subjectively, at any rate, he is right: the simplicity, the baldness, perhaps, of that song's narrative, along with its very plain melody, embodies the voice of a believer, not a sophisticated manipulator of belief. This is why Stanley chose the song in 1967 and why he has continued to sing it for over twenty years. And, *mutatis mutandis,* similar things could be said about all his subsequent material. "Old-time" is also a matter of presentation. Instrumentally, to begin with. Casual listeners and newcomers to classic bluegrass (including, no doubt, many members of that 1967 Bean Blossom audience) have always been inclined, quite understandably, to regard it as a vehicle for instrumental virtuosity. But this has never been a hallmark of Stanley's sound. The lack of a mandolin in his band meant and continues to mean that the piercing counterpoint associated with that instrument is simply not available to him. The twin guitars are unobtrusive and largely rhythmical. As for the banjo, the non-singing banjo player, whose job it is to create syncopated melodic wreaths around the words of a singer, is a cliché in classic bluegrass. But because Stanley, the singer, is his own banjo player, this option of "playing all around it" (his own phrase) has never been open to him. Instead, using the right-hand technique known as the "pinch," he will, while singing, lay down strong rhythmic chops on the off-beat, or else create a locomotive-like continuo that will drive and guide the rest of the band. A very different sound from bluegrass.

And "old-time," most of all, is a matter of singing. While opera experts are apt to congratulate themselves at being able to recognize the voices of artists on unidentified recordings, no one who has ever heard Ralph Stanley sing would ever have the least trouble in identifying him. His is "one of the most unmistakably rural voices in country music," Bill C. Malone wrote at about the time this Bean Blossom show was held, in words that are no less true today. Paradoxically, despite Stanley's instantly recognizable sound—his "haunting, almost sepulchral voice" (Malone's words again)—and despite Stanley's continued (and perfectly proper) insistence on the importance of "feeling" to good singing, he has always been in many ways an impersonal singer, classical, not romantic. His perfect phrasing and delicate melodic twists, the product of generations of mountain vocal art, completely untouched, unlike the product of classic bluegrass singers, by the blues or any other form of popular music, are employed for the song, not for the singer. It is this stance and this artistry, more than anything else, that made and continue to make him "old-time," "probably" (to quote Malone once more) "America's finest traditional singer."

Though this Bean Blossom performance shows that Ralph Stanley had found his voice, in every sense of the word, from the very beginning of his solo career, there were in fact several important artistic developments yet to come, all of which, fortunately, can be traced in easily available recordings.

Consider, for example, the changes wrought in "Little Glass of Wine," which as a close harmony duet had been the Stanley Brothers' first hit in the late forties. Ralph Stanley rerecorded the song in 1971 on a Japanese release that is virtually impossible to obtain today, but the new version resurfaced on Rebel 1606, recorded in 1981. Here the major-key melody of the original has, very strikingly, been changed into a pentatonic modal melody, while the solo format allows for innumerable vocal slurs that were impossible in the duet. A standard brother duet has been remade into a Ralph Stanley song. The resulting sound is extraordinarily ancient, as if the newer version, though in fact produced a generation after the earlier, had been created two or three generations before it.

Modal singing of this sort was to become more and more a trademark of Ralph Stanley's style, and several examples are to be found on virtually every solo album, secular and religious, he has ever recorded. Their presentation is highly stylized: the fiddle and banjo cling as closely as possible to the sung melody, while the guitars and bass provide a major-key accompaniment, with an absolute minimum of chord changes. Stanley's arrangements of recently written songs by Randall Hylton like "Room at the Top of the Stairs" and "It's a Hot Night in August," both recorded in 1986, show how this treatment can impart a hauntingly archaic flavor even to songs which (like these two) are thoroughly modern not only in their date of composition but also in their "messages" and understated, oblique lyrical style.

One of Stanley's most influential artistic decisions was his importation of unaccompanied religious singing to the bluegrass stage. Such singing was a vital part of his Old Regular Baptist heritage, and sidemen who worked with him in the early days will reminisce about the way he would keep himself awake on all-night drives by running through his endless repertory of old hymns. (They will also, incidentally, reminisce about the way he used to read the Bible to them, thus suggesting that his motives for preferring religious music were and are something more than aesthetic or atavistic.) Though Stanley was initially diffident about the commercial viability of this sort of singing, the successful career of a Virginia a cappella group called the Chestnut Grove Quartet suggested to him that it might find an audience.

Appropriately enough, the first recording session to include unaccompanied singing (in 1971) included the time-honored "Bright Morning Star," which has been sung at mountain funerals for over a hundred years. An interesting set of comparative examples is provided by Stanley's 1967 and 1980 treatments of "Snow Covered Mound"; the first is accompanied, and smoothed out for the sensibilities of a general audience, while the second is a cappella, enormously long for a vernacular music cut, and utterly uncompromising in its primitive rawness. Stanley also re-created the old church practice of "lining out" the words of such hymns as "Village Church Yard" (1971), and archaized modern songs like "Model Church" by rearranging them without accompaniment (1983). Far from diffident about this sort of singing now, Stanley will not hesitate to challenge an audience by lining out "Amazing Grace" at the most raucous moment of a Saturday night show. And thanks to his influence, unaccompanied singing has now become a standard feature of the repertory of almost every bluegrass band.

Instrumentally, as a beginning professional, Ralph Stanley had been self-consciously modern. "As the music advanced I thought I should advance with it," he once said when asked why he had replaced the very basic two-finger banjo style which he had picked up from such old-time musicians as Wade Mainer with the difficult, syncopated three-finger style then associated with Earl Scruggs. "It was a better style and it was a better beat and all that."

The impetus for this development was commercial: Flatt and Scruggs's records were selling well, and bluegrass audiences soon came to consider what was then called "Scruggs style banjo" an indispensable part of the music. Ralph Stanley obliged by producing a sparkling series of banjo solos such as "Clinch Mountain Backstep" (his rewrite of the old mountain breakdown "Lost John"), the elaborate "Mastertone March," and the extraordinarily difficult "Hard Times." So overflowing was his creative fountain that he did not even bother to go to the studio with standards such as "Home Sweet Home," though on the stage he could and did produce a memorable version of this "evergreen" when called on to do so.

All of this was to change fundamentally as Stanley entered his solo career. Singing, after all, was his first love, so the banjo was inevitably relegated to second place. Furthermore, now that he was running the show it was difficult to take stage time off to retune for elaborate instrumentals like "Hard Times." He continued to play, of course, and play very well, but in keeping with his "less is more" musical philosophy the instrumental breaks to Stanley Brothers standards became simpler and less ostentatious.

A more positive development along these lines was his ever-increasing use of the very first method he had learned to play the instrument. This bare-fingered, percussive, down-stroking method seems to have been the original way the American (and African) banjo was played; there was no need to designate it as anything other than banjo playing and thus it had no "official" name. When other methods of play (for example, the "guitar style") evolved, this original style came to be known by a series of local nicknames, such as "stroking," "rapping," "frailing" (probably a dialectal variant of "flailing"), and "drop-thumb." Lucy Smith Stanley, and hence her son Ralph, who learned it from watching her play, called it "clawhammer."

In the days of the Stanley Brothers Ralph had occasionally showcased a clawhammer number or two on the stage or even in the studio, but always as a special novelty item. Now, however, he was to legitimize the clawhammer banjo as a regular feature of the bluegrass band. As early as 1967 he used it, in the studio, to accompany the old-time "Going round This World." In 1971 he rearranged Arthur Smith's "Bound to Ride," which he had earlier done in standard three-finger style, for clawhammer, and in 1973 did the same for "John Henry," which until then was regarded as one of *the* three-fingered showpieces. In the same year he created the deceptively antique-sounding "Old Time Pickin'" as a sort of demonstration number to emphasize the gentle sound of an old wooden banjo lent to him by Fay McGinnis, then president of his fan club.

The sources and streams of clawhammer banjo playing in the hills are many and varied; hence it would certainly be an exaggeration to claim that Ralph Stanley has saved this style from extinction. But it is still safe to say that there are many people in "Stanley country," particularly among younger musicians, who are playing this style today and who would not be doing so if it were not for Ralph Stanley's example. And not just with the secular hoedowns for which it is so obviously suited; Stanley has braved the prejudices of his ancestors and also applied the style to gospel music, as with the rousing "Traveling the High Way Home" (1977).

That classic from Molly O'Day could easily serve as a theme song for Ralph Stanley, personally as well as artistically. He came back home in a physical sense in 1968, moving from Florida to Dickenson County and the Stanleys' old home place. The reasons he gives for doing this are practical: most of his professional dates are closer to western Virginia than to Florida. But to such a home-centered man the return must have been a personal relief as well.

It was not, however, an easy move financially, at least at first. Ralph and his wife Jimmie were still living in a trailer as late as 1972, when we can hear the tape recording of a pioneering interviewer being constantly interrupted by the "contributions" of the very young Lisa Joy Stanley, later to become the mother of Ralph and Jimmie's first grandchild.

The previous year had seen the production of the first Memorial Bluegrass Festival on Smith Ridge, in which Ralph had combined a musical gathering with the old mountain custom of a Decoration Day visit to the family cemetery—in this case the Smith cemetery, which held the grave of Carter Stanley and which all too soon was to hold the grave of Lucy Smith Stanley as well. A nearby hollow formed a natural amphitheater, topped by a long ridge which made a perfect spot for concession stands. Mounting a festival can be a risky business, and Ralph was nervous about putting on this one. As it turned out, he had no cause for anxiety. The Memorial Festival was a great success from the start ("probably the largest single event in the history of Dickenson County," said the Bristol *Herald Courier*). And for years afterward Smith Ridge would be a place of pilgrimage in late spring for music lovers not only from "Stanley country" but from all over the United States. As an urban commentator later suggested, the festival was like a huge block party, or, as mountaineers would say, a family reunion. There one could meet, say, Ralph Stanley's bus mechanic, or the undertaker who was responsible for Carter Stanley's funeral, side by side with bluegrass greats from Bill Monroe on down. Harassment of Ralph's fans by the Virginia state police in the mid-eighties led to a temporary removal of the festival to Roxana, Kentucky, but soon the trouble was cleared up and the festival was returned to Smith Ridge where it belonged.

Stanley met with much less success in his several attempts to win elective office in Dickenson County. Politics is anything but a spectator sport in the mountains: not only Ralph but also Ray Cline, who follows electoral events in his Pike County, Kentucky, home very closely indeed, and Jack Cooke, who was once elected mayor of Norton, Virginia, are very much involved with it. Though all three are loyal Democrats of the New Deal sort, their motivation for this involvement seems to be not so much a wish to promote a particular governmental agenda as it is the fun of the fight and a desire for recognition from friends and neighbors. But a misspelled bumper sticker ("TEASURER" for "TREASURER") produced for Stanley's first campaign was an omen of things to come; he was doomed to disappointment, and gave up the struggle after a decade or so. "I decided I'm not crooked enough for politics," he says.

But other sorts of recognition were hardly lacking. The miraculous year of 1971, during which the Clinch Mountain Boys recorded ten long-playing albums, netted Ralph Stanley the title of Bluegrass Entertainer of the Year from the magazine *Muleskinner News*, while the album *Cry from the Cross* was named Bluegrass Album of the Year, Curly Ray Cline the best fiddler of the year, Ricky Skaggs most promising fiddler and most promising mandolin player of the year, and Keith Whitley most promising guitar player of the year. Stanley was made a Kentucky Colonel in 1973, a 32d Degree Shriner in 1974, and an honorary doctor of arts by Lincoln Memorial University in Harrogate, Tennessee, in 1976 (in recognition for giving a series of special lectures on his music there during the previous year). He performed at the inauguration ceremonies of President Jimmy Carter in 1977 and was elected to the Virginia Country Music Hall of Fame in 1978 and the Appalachian Music Hall of Fame in 1981. In 1984 he received a National Heritage Fellowship from the National Endowment for the Arts, an award which involved a visit to Washington and a performance at Ford's Theater. Meanwhile (in between endless musical dates, and the endless travel that they entail) he amused himself by hunting, fishing, gardening, caring for his horses, and, perhaps a little surprisingly, cooking—an art for which he is quite noted among his friends.

A relatively large number of people—surely many more than ever saw the Stanley Brothers—have seen Ralph Stanley and the Clinch Mountain Boys on national television programs like "Austin City Limits" or at such venues as the University of Chicago Folk Festival. These people would no doubt be surprised to learn that even today many of Stanley's appearances continue to occur at places that are much like those at which he first played: tiny schoolhouse auditoriums, accessible only by twisted mountain roads that offer a continual challenge to the band bus, for shows that are advertised only in local newspapers and handbills, before audiences that would not hesitate to describe themselves as "poor people." Is this a deliberate attempt on Stanley's part to stick close to his roots? Or simply an opportunism born out of the hungry early days, days that taught him to take every date he could get, no matter when or where? Whatever the causes, the effects are evident and valuable: the endless nurturing and preservation of "Stanley country."

The story, happily enough, continues. For our purposes 1986, Ralph Stanley's twentieth solo year and fortieth year as a professional, seems as good a point to end it as any. This year saw the departure from the band of Charlie Sizemore, who had held the position of lead singer for the Clinch Mountain Boys for nearly a decade. This was a painful business for both Stanley and Sizemore, since Charlie, who had joined the band at the age of sixteen, was almost in the position of an adopted son to Ralph. Their separation was as strained as are most divorces, and it dragged out throughout the spring and summer of 1986 because Sizemore's conscience made it difficult for him to break cleanly and quickly.

Far more cheerful was the fortieth (and twentieth) anniversary homecoming celebration, held on Smith Ridge on September 26 through 28 of 1986. On the Saturday of this extended weekend a custom-made banjo, built by master craftsman Frank Neat, was presented to Ralph by his fans; both he and the banjo made the front cover of *Bluegrass Unlimited* a few months later. And Sunday reunion visits by George Shuffler, now making a name for himself in gospel music, and Ricky Skaggs, who for several years had been a very successful performer of country music, along with several other former Clinch Mountain Boys, concluded the event. Coincidentally and appropriately, though no one seems to have noticed it at the time, the same Sunday marked the one hundredth anniversary of the birth of Lucy Smith Stanley.

A few months later Ralph Stanley, still firmly established as a leading light in traditional mountain music, celebrated his sixtieth birthday. Outwardly, at any rate, he is not an introspective man, but he may well have been reminiscing with justifiable pride, touched with no little sorrow, about the events of the past four decades when, with a chuckle in his voice, he told a friend who had called to congratulate him, "It took me a *long time* to reach the age of sixty."

J. E. Mainer

"Tell the Stanley boy I said hello"

Ask Ralph Stanley what musicians he and his brother Carter listened to most often when they were boys and one of the first groups on the list will usually be Mainer's Mountaineers. This North Carolina based string band flourished in the twenties and thirties and featured a variety of personnel, but its leader and guiding spirit was always Joseph Emmett Mainer, known universally as J. E. The style of the group was raucous and hard-driving, producing (on the many records they made, some of which are still available) the sound of a gang of rambunctious mountain boys out to have a good time on a Saturday night. Mainer's energetic fiddle-playing, full of droning sounds because of the low-cut bridge he used, was always instantly recognizable.

The "spontaneous" catcalls and pounding uptempo beat of some of the Stanley Brothers' earlier Rich-R-Tone recordings—those in which they weren't trying to produce the gentle sound typical of brother duets—and a good deal of the Brothers' earlier material as well, can be traced directly to Mainer's Mountaineers. But J. E. and his cohorts provided a pattern for more than sound. Though not deliberately, Mainer's whole life history shows us, a generation earlier than the Stanleys, how very stylized the career of an old-time mountain musician could be. It's all there: the close-knit family, the poverty-stricken childhood, the early attempts at entertaining the neighbors, the unwilling exile from the mountains, the all-important first radio contract, the off-again on-again relationships with sponsors, and the inevitable rifts and reconciliations between musician brothers.

Like his brother and sometime partner Wade, who is still an active performer, J. E. Mainer enjoyed something of a revival in his later years. With the help of E. P. Williams of Salisbury, North Carolina, Mainer recorded several long-playing albums in the sixties. One of his sidemen was a young guitarist named Morris Herbert, and it is a mark of the astonishing continuity of old-time mountain music that Herbert is the author of several sacred songs that Ralph Stanley and the Clinch Mountain Boys recorded as recently as 1980 (Blue Jay LPA 201).

But even during this revival (and in this, too, he was typical of the profession) J. E. Mainer still had to scrounge for every penny. To earn extra money he would cut tapes (at a dollar per song!) on a machine at his home in Concord, North Carolina, of any number a correspondent might request. "Everybody wants me to make tapes for them," he said at one time. "I'll do it as long as they pay me."

This habit of tape making had one very fortunate result for later historians. When Fay McGinnis, then president of the Ralph Stanley International Fan Club, asked Mainer to record the story of his career early in 1969, he was ready and willing. The results, transcribed here with Mrs. McGinnis's kind permission and with the generous and patient help of Wade Mainer, show with utter authenticity the hardships and difficulties—and the occasional triumphs— of the life of a pioneer mountain musician. They also show, with their description (completely devoid of self-pity) of Mainer's early days in the South Carolina cotton mills, why such musicians were willing to put up with these hardships and difficulties: they could never forget that the alternatives were so much worse.

A month or so after he made this autobiographical tape, J. E. Mainer was visited in Concord by his brother Wade, who had moved to Michigan and with whom he had been out of direct touch for many years. They enjoyed a pleasant reconciliation (if that's not too strong a term). J. E. Mainer died in the late spring of 1971, while making ready to go on the road, to Culpeper, Virginia, to fulfill yet another musical engagement.

I was just now thinking about the Stanley Brothers. I never did meet nary one of them boys but I always did want to. I've got a brother-in-law lives up here at Cleveland, North Carolina. They've been to his house and took supper with him, or dinner, one. I think they played a school up there pretty close. You ask the one that's a-living—the one that died's Carter, I believe—Ralph. You ask Ralph, did he ever have a meal with Flo McDaniel in Cleveland, North Carolina. Lives up there around Needmore. That's between Salisbury and Statesville.

Tell him I was real sorry to hear about his brother dying. But that's one thing I reckon that we've all got to do. It hurts us and hurts the feelings to know that we're losing some of our dear friends. I know I miss my dad and mother a whole lot. I haven't got no people anywhere around Concord here where I live at. They all live back in the Blue Ridge Mountains out from Asheville, out there where I was borned and raised at.

And it's hard to lose some of your best friends. But still, that's what we've got to do. God says we're going to suffer if we're sinners, and so I reckon that's what a lot of us has done, is suffering because we've lost some friend or some of our people. I imagine they're better off to be in the other world, if they's ready to go, than they would be if they were left here on this old earth, the shape this world's getting in.

Well, I'll get back on this story here that you wanted. I was borned and raised back in the Blue Ridge Mountains in Buncombe County, North Carolina, eighteen hundred and ninety-eight. And I stayed there till I was I reckon about eight or nine years old, and we moved out of the mountains back there to the cotton mills. Before we moved we lived in a little old one-room log cabin. They was six of us children and Dad and Mom.

And I remember they come up a rain there one night. Dad had dug a ditch around the front of the house to keep the water from running down again the house. And they come up an awful storm and I woke up way about two o'clock in the morning and I heard somebody a-pecking out there and beating and a-banging. And I raised up and looked over and Dad was out there out of the bed a-standing in water way up over his shoe tops and he had a axe there cutting a hole through the floor.

That rain had rained so hard it busted over that ditch and and knocked the front door in and was coming right on through the house. And Pa says, "You lay back down there and go to sleep." He said, "Don't you get up out of that bed now, boy, cause they's water down here." And I set there and watched him for I don't know how long while he got the hole cut through. When he got it cut through, why of course the water went on out through under the floor. The lower side of the house was a-setting I guess about eight or ten feet off of the ground. That's as how steep the side of the mountain was where we was living at this branch.

That old branch out there would get up, you know, and the water'd get so high and that branch out there would come in down that cove there so's logs and rocks would come down there and it'd make the awfullest fuss in the world. Go kindly like a freight train a-rumbling by your house these days.

Anyway, we finally moved out of that place there, moved across the mountain to a little place called the Peak Field. Moved over on an old sled my daddy had made. Had to cut a road through the woods to get over there. And Dad had a whole lot more field that he could work over there than where he was at.

Daddy never had no education in his life and he had to work hard all of his life. Back there in them mountains most people didn't make very much money. He could skin tan bark all day long, lay it out and let it dry there three or four days, and then he'd take it to town. Drive fourteen miles to deliver it to the tannery. It would take him from mighty early in the morning till that night to get back to the house and he'd only make about ninety cents. I tell you, it was rougher back those days than people think here now. So Pa finally decided he'd move out of the mountains.

Well, he went down to a little town called Weaverville, North Carolina, and bought him a little farm down there. They was I believe about sixteen acres in it. Then we had to move to the cotton mill in Union, South Carolina, to pay for it. So we went on down there and we went to work in the mill. I went to work in the mill when I was eight years old. Now you can just imagine about how it was. They'd hire you. It didn't make no difference. All you had to do was just push a box and they'd hire you. Half the mills was closed anyway on account of help. Well, I went in that mill, I learned how to doff. And you talk about a mean place, that was the meanest place ever I seed in my life. One day there we got done doffing and we had about twenty minutes' rest. And the old head doffer got Finley. That was my oldest brother. Got him down on the floor under a big old oil tub and turned the faucet on him. And boy, he just got that boy all messed up with that old cylinder oil and stuff, you know.

Finley just went down in the heating shop and told Dad about it. Dad was a-working down there. Dad come up there and he grabbed that old head doffer in the collar and boy, he hit him. I bet he knocked him fifteen feet back across the spare floor there. And he told him, "If you ever lay your hands on one of my boys again," he says, "I've just started on you. I'll just finish it up."

Then Pa, he went down to see the superintendent about it. They all stayed in the same room, back them days, boss man, superintendent, all of them. Gone on up there and he telled the old man about it. He was wicked, oh man, he'd cuss every breath he'd draw.

The old man come up there and asked the head doffer about it. Course they all stick together. They wasn't but a few words said about it so it was passed on off.

And we worked there till the next day, long about three o'clock—you see, you worked twelve hours—long about three o'clock, me and Finley, we slipped out of the mill. We shouldn't have done it but we did. They were just running over us so bad there in the mill that we just wasn't going to stay there. And the mill was five story high. We was working right in the top story and one of the section hands there grabbed Finley under the arms and held him out that window, now and him just a little wee bitty boy, held him out that window and he said, "Now boy, don't you believe I'll drop you?" Finley was crying, he was just crying his eyes out, and me a-standing back over there scared half to death too and crying, begged him not to turn him loose. And the other people standing around on the spare floor just dying laughing. Well, that fellow, he finally sets Finley back down there till the next day and me and Finley, we decided we would leave.

Well, we got out of that mill, we took up the railroad track. We didn't know where we was going. We was trying to get back home, we was trying to get back to Asheville. And it's a long ways, I don't know, sixty-five or seventy miles, and that's where we walked and we walked and the sun begin to get down pretty low.

And I looked back down the railroad track and I seed somebody coming. I said, "Finley, yonder comes somebody." Finley says, "It walks kindly like Daddy, don't it?" I said, "Yeah, it do. We just better sit down here and wait and see." And sure enough, it was Daddy, and he come up and he had them whips in his hand. He was going to whup us. He was going to give us good and asked us, "How come that you run off and leave?" and Finley he just up and told him what that section hand had done, how he held him out the window there and things. Pa just throwed his hickory away. Said, "Well, you boys come on back. I'll go somewheres tomorrow and try to get a job somewhere else." We went on back to the house and the next day Pa, he come to Glendale, South Carolina. We stayed with Dad there and holp him till he got his place paid for and after he got his place paid for, why we moved back home.

There was a boy by the name of Roscoe Banks. He had married one of my older sisters and he come from back out of what they call the Table Top Mountains. He wasn't that old at that time. He was just a young boy. They was just married and he played a fiddle and he'd bought the fiddle off of a hobo that'd come up there one time, got off the train there at Marshall and he was three days getting back there in them mountains where these fellows were working at, Roscoe and all of them.

And he sold this fiddle to Roscoe and after we moved back up home up there, why I got to getting with Roscoe. And Pa, he'd bought me a little old banjo there and I'd get up early of a morning and I'd come just messing with that banjo trying to play it. And I got to where I could play it pretty good. I'd go up to that Roscoe every once in a while and sit down, him and Jim Bailey, an old fellow that lived there that picked the banjo too. Well, I'd get my banjo and I'd play with them. So I took up banjo playing and got pretty well with it there with them two.

Well, one day there I decided I'd leave home. I went and told Ma. I wouldn't tell my daddy cause I knowed he'd jump on me. I went and told Ma that I was going to leave and she said, "Well, where're you going to?" I said, "I don't know. I'm going off, see if I can't find me a job somewhere." So I went to Knoxville, Tennessee. I went to work in the Brookside Cotton Mill.

One Saturday when I come out of the mill there, about two o'clock, about two hours after the mill had stopped, they was a whole crowd of people out there standing around the railroad crossing. I decided I'd walk down there and see what it was. And when I got down there, they was an old man a-standing there on the railroad track. He was playing this fiddle and the poor fellow was drunk. And he was just a little fellow. I was standing back there watching him and I always did love a fiddle.

So he played a tune there—now this was in about 1913, '14, something like that. But anyway, he played a tune there that I've never forgotten. I don't guess I ever will forget it because when he got done playing this tune he turned around and started to cross the railroad tracks and Number Eleven hit him and killed him. And it just tore him all to pieces down that railroad track. Course the old fiddle busted and kindly went in the ditch, in the weeds. I went on back there to the boarding house where I was staying at.

The next day I decided I'd go back down there and maybe some—maybe they didn't find that fiddle. And I went down and got to looking around and I found it. Well, I went right to the mill and put in a week's notice and I worked the week's notice and I come back home. Hadn't been there too awfully long and whenever I got back home I was showing it to Roscoe and it was busted up pretty bad. Roscoe says, "That thing ain't worth fixing." I said, "Well, I believe I'll fix it anyway."

By the way, I didn't tell you what tune that old man was playing. He was playing an old tune called "The Drunkard's Hiccups."
That's the tune he was playing. And I took that fiddle and had it
fixed up and I've still got it today and I wouldn't part from that
fiddle at all. Cause that was a real fiddle.

But anyway I came on back to the house and went back to playing my banjo with Roscoe and them. And we'd play around at
square dances, we'd go out and visit people and play till away in
the night, be entertaining people around, you know. Never did
charge them anything for it. Just old country folks back there in
them mountains. And there I got round to knowing my mind again.
I decided I'd leave home again.

Well, sir, I caught a freight train—this was six years later, in
nineteen hundred and twenty-two—I caught a freight train and
come to Concord, North Carolina. Got off of the bus at Salisbury,
walked through Salisbury and caught the train at a little old place
about five mile this side of Salisbury and come on into Concord.
And whenever I got into Concord I was broke. I didn't have but one
twenty-five cent in my pocket's all I had and I was starved half to
death.

Went up to a fellow's house there and asked him where I could
get a boarding place at. "Well," he said, "I'll tell you. They's a lady
right down here about the fourth house on the right." Says, "She
runs a boarding place down there. If you'll go down there and see
her, you might get a place to stay all night." I said, "All right, I believe I will." So I went on down there and knocked on the front door
and boy, there was the biggest old stoutest looking woman come to
the door you ever seed.

I introduced myself to her, told her that I was a-hunting for a
job and I was broke and I didn't have no money. But if she'd let me
stay all night with her, why, when I got the money I'd send it back
to her. She said, "Well, you talk like a pretty honest boy. Come on
in." So I went in around in there and set around a while and they
asked me if I ever worked in a mill. I told them, "Yeah." I told them
I was a good doffer. So I went in the mill next morning and it just
happened that I got a job.

This old lady's name was McDaniel. Flo McDaniel's mother,
that's who it was. And she had a daughter there and I fell in love
with the daughter and she did me, so about a year after I come
there we got married.

And I'd took up playing the fiddle through all that time and I
wired to Asheville, didn't wire, wrote up there rather, and told Wade

to come down there and get him a job in the mill and bring my banjo with him. And he did. So me and him, we went to playing together and after that, why, here come Daddy John Love along and he wanted to play with us. And me and Wade and Daddy John Love got to going to fiddlers' conventions. Yessir, we won just about every one that we went to. Just the fiddle and the banjo and the guitar. John Love was one of those types that sung kindly on the style of Jimmie Rodgers. He was a yodeler. And he was a good one, just like Jimmie Rodgers was. He was an old-timey.

They was a program started here in Charlotte called the Crazy Water Crystal program and they heard about me and Wade and John Love. So they sent one day for me to come over there and I went over there and they wanted me to take a job over there and broadcast, advertise for them, over at WBT in Charlotte.

Well, I come back and I tell the boss man about it and I told him, I said, "I don't want to leave my job." I said, "I might not make it, and if I didn't, I'd be out of a job." And he says, "J. E., you go on and take that. If you can't make it, your job will be here when you come back."

So I went on. And that was where we got started in, J. E. Mainer and the Mountaineers. They booked us out and we traveled just about everywhere. We traveled North Carolina, South Carolina, Georgia, Alabama, Kentucky. Played some in Tennessee, Virginia. Well, we went on that way for I reckon about thirty years. Playing nothing but schoolhouses. Didn't have nobody booking me out. People'd write in to me a-wanting us to come and make these personal appearances.

And I'll tell you, it was every night. Every night we was out somewhere or another. It didn't make no difference how it was a-raining or how it was a-snowing, anything like that, we was always on the road. Driving an old A-model Ford. You know about how one of them was. No heat in it and nothing else, snow on the ground, we went right on anyway. Well, I could tell you a lot if I just had time to, but I ain't got the time to, so—

Wade and Zeke Morris, they got to giving me a lot of trouble. They gone off and leave me and poor John there, we was on that fifty-thousand-watt station. Wade, I reckon he was like me, he'd get homesick and he'd want to go home. He wouldn't tell me where he was going or nothing. Come program time Wade and Zeke'd disappear. And me and John would have to take the program by ourselves, just the fiddle and the guitar. But we carried it on.

I went and told the boss man about it in the office down there.

"Well, J. E., just find you somebody else," he said. "Where did they go to?" I said, "I don't know where they went to." And that was on one day at Saturday at dinner time. And I says, "I'm going up to Asheville tomorrow. Maybe Wade's up there." And sure enough, he was there, down in a well, helping Roscoe dig a well up there. He was pretty glad to see me, but he wouldn't let on like he was. So I brung him back to Charlotte with me. And we hadn't been on the air but a day or two, Zeke walked in the studio. And it was a sight in the world.

I can't think of all right now to tell you what really did happen. But anyway it was a sight in God's world how they worked us boys. I had a contract in California to go out there and make a movie with the Fox film company and I was tied up with the Crazy Water Crystal Company contract and they wouldn't turn me loose. So we left Charlotte and went to Raleigh, WPTF, and stayed up there for, I don't know, probably a couple of years together.

And you know how people is when they get—think that they're doing it all, why then, they just think that you ain't—they ain't got no more use for you. So that was the way Wade and Zeke was. See, I put them boys right on top. I held them up there for, well, all the time they was with me, and they got to where they thought I wasn't in it at all.

So I just decided one day I'd just quit them and leave. And that was where me and Wade and them boys split up at. I come back home here and stayed back here for three or four weeks. Decided I'd go back on the air. Well, I went to Harris, North Carolina, and got Snuffy Jenkins, went back to Old Fort where I got Zeke at and got George Morris, his brother, and I went down here at Richfield and got Leonard Stokes and went on the air over in Charlotte, over on WSOC.

We stayed there about two months, I reckon, and I got a call from WSPA in Spartanburg, wanting me to come down there and take a program. I went down there and took a program and we was getting along fine. People found out I was back on the air down in there and they got to writing in, wanting me to come out and put on a show. Well, I was booked up there, I don't know, oh, I'd say over a month ahead every night and I'd think to myself, "Well, it won't be long it'll be like it was before. I'll be on the road every night somewhere or another."

And I come off the air one day at 12:15 there and old man J. W. Fincher, the boss of the Crazy Water Crystals program from Charlotte, was out there in the yard sitting out there in his car. He says,

"By golly, J. E., they just can't hold you down, can they?" I said, "No, I'm still going." He says, "That was a good program you boys had on in there. I really enjoyed you. I set out here and listened to that."

And he wanted me to go to Columbia, South Carolina, for him, down there on WIS. And I asked him, I said, "When do you want me to go?" He says, "I want you down there Monday morning." This was on Saturday at 12:15. "Well, Mr. Fincher," I said, "we are getting all the work we can do here. I kindly hate to leave here." I said, "They're so good to me, I hate to leave here." "Well," he says, "I'd sure like to have you down there. If there's any way of getting you," he said, "I'm going to get you. I'll give you sixty dollars a week. You take everything that you make on your personal appearances, sell your songbooks."

"But," he said, "I do want you to take the Old Hired Hand with you." That was a fellow that worked for Charlie and Bill Monroe. He was doing announcing for them and they had had a wreck in Blacksburg and I think a couple of them had to go to the hospital. Byron Parker was one of them, the Old Hired Hand, he had to go. Well, the others got out before he did and so they left Byron down there and Byron was out of a job and he got to wanting to go down to Columbia with me down there if I'd take him and he'd do my announcing.

Well, that's where I just played you know what. Anyway, I took him on down there. He had a good education. He'd studied for a preacher and a lawyer both. Well, he got down there and we were just a-going fine. We was making plenty of money, booked out every night. And he got to rooting in ahead of me, rooting in ahead of me, and I seed he was going to take over the band down there and I just said, "Well, you can have it. I'm just quitting. I'm pulling out." So I come back home.

Went to Greensboro. Hadn't been up to Greensboro but about a week I reckon and got a long-distance call from San Antonio, Texas. Bensington Doyle from out of Chicago called me up and wanted me to go out there and take the program for them. So I asked them what they would pay me, and they said they'd pay me five hundred dollars a week and I could have all the money on the side I'd make.

But I didn't have as good a band as I'd been a-having. Them old-time musicians was hard to find. But I had one I thought that I could get by with out there. They was playing my records all over the United States. You could be a-riding along at night and hear

J. E. Mainer and his Mountaineers just most anywhere. And I went on out there and worked for them there in San Antonio, Texas. Worked for them out there six months.

And after the six months was up they sent me to KMOX in St. Louis, Missouri, and I stayed out there six months, and I decided then that I'd come home. So I come home here and they wanted me to go on WBT in Charlotte. So I went over there to see them about going on the program over there for Bensington Doyle from out of Chicago. And that man said to me, he said, "Have you got their address?" I said, "Yeah, I've got it." And he said, "Give it to me, will you?" And that's where I made another mistake. I give him Bensington Doyle's address from out of Chicago.

Well, this fellow over there, was over this station, he had a string band on there called the Briarhoppers, Dick Hartman and the Briarhoppers. No, Tennessee Ramblers, that's who it was, Tennessee Ramblers. And they had to handle every program in the hillbilly line that the station took on over there. Well, he wrote this company a letter, Bensington Doyle from out of Chicago, and told them, says, "Ain't no use bringing J. E. Mainer and the Mountaineers over here, when we got musicians right here can handle it just as good as he can." Then he says, "It won't cost you not nearly as much it would if you'd had J. E. over here because they have to handle the program that we tell them to handle." He said, "We could just pay them a certain salary."

Well, you know what that done. That knocked me in the head going to Charlotte. But it wasn't long after that Bensington Doyle, he went off the air. I don't know what ever happened to him. He sure was a good company to work for.

I just about forget to tell you, Bensington Doyle sent me to Monterey, Mexico, one time. We crossed the Rio Grande down there going over from San Antonio, Texas. And we didn't have no pass. We got on the other side, they arrested us, put us in jail, for not having a passport. I told them, I said, "Mister, I'm supposed to go on the air up yonder in the morning, 6:15, for Bensington Doyle from out of Chicago." And I said, "I can't stay in this jail." "Oh yeah," they said, "you will too." Course they didn't talk like that. They talked in a different kind of a language but I understood most of it. I knowed what they meant.

But anyway, I told them, I said, "You call the radio station up there and see if I ain't supposed to go on the air in the morning." So they did. They called up there and they told them, Yeah, that J. E. Mainer was supposed to report there between 9 and 6:15 in the morning. So they said, No, they wasn't going to let J. E. Mainer out of jail.

Well, the radio station, they called Bensington Doyle in Chicago and told them about it. So Bensington Doyle told them, he says, "What's the phone number down there?"—where we crossed the Rio Grande at—and they got it and Bensington Doyle called up down there and told them to turn us boys loose. We had to go on the air up there the next morning. So they did. They turned us loose. And we ran on up there.

We didn't stay down there but about three weeks. Boy, I didn't like them Mexicans a bit no way. You couldn't turn around but you was scared to death of something. Afraid one'd throw a knife through you or something. Get one of their girls out there on the floor, sweetheart of a boy, and go to dancing with her, you sure were going to have a fight. That's all there was to it.

I've been on a hundred and ninety different radio stations throughout the United States. Been on the British Broadcasting Company across the water. In fact, I'm just known what you might say all over the world. And old J. E.'s going to quit before long. He ain't going to follow it up very much more. I'm getting too old to. Can't take it like I used to be any more.

Well, I'm going to say so long. If there's any more that I can do, why you let me know and I'll be mighty glad to do it for you. Wish you all the best of luck in the world and hope you uns have happy new years all the way through. And tell the Stanley boy I said hello when you see him.

3

Ruby Rakes Eubanks

"They're just my brothers"

The name of Ruby Rakes is familiar and yet mysterious to fans of the Stanley Brothers. Familiar, because the name appears in the composer credits of many of the Stanley Brothers' best-known songs and tunes. Mysterious, because the person behind it is so little known that many people probably believe the name is just a pseudonym, like Bill Monroe's "Joe Ahr." But Ruby Rakes Eubanks is very much a real person, and, though an elderly lady, she is very much alive.

Lucy Smith's marriage to Lee Stanley produced a complicated extended family, since they were widow and widower with children from their previous marriages. The couple's numerous brothers and sisters added up to a sizeable clan. Though Lee Stanley was clearly a powerful personality (and, through his remarkable singing ability, a great influence on Ralph Stanley), emotionally speaking Lucy Smith Stanley was the center of things for the boys, and especially Ralph.

Ruby, or Sister Ruby as she is sometimes called, is Ralph and Carter Stanley's older half-sister, their mother's only child aside from the two boys. This unique relationship in itself would have made her important to them, but there was much more to it than that. She was and is a warm, generous, loving person. Already a teenager when the boys were small, she was more of an aunt than a sister to them. She spent many hours caring for them, a duty she remembers as a joy rather than a burden.

Ralph and Carter were the only two members of their generation to carry on their parents' musicianship—their father's singing and their mother's instrumental skill. Ruby followed their career with interest and devotion from the very beginning. In the usual mountain pattern, she migrated to the area of Detroit in later years, but she never stopped thinking of Smith Ridge as home. She remained very close to the Brothers, and was assigned the rights to a number of their compositions for personal financial reasons in the late fifties and early sixties. In later years she attended every one of Ralph Stanley's annual Memorial Festivals at McClure, and she shows up at all his Michigan appearances whenever her physical condition permits it.

Ruby Rakes must have heard "Hills of Home" a hundred times, but she still weeps whenever Ralph Stanley performs this recitation in memory of his brother. For everyone who knows her, she is an irreplaceable link to a distant and idyllic past.

Noah Smith, that was my grandfather's name, and Louisa was his wife, my grandmother. I'll be seventy-one next month. Well, now my father died when I was fourteen months old. And Mother, she stayed a widow about seven years, I guess. And then she married Carter and Ralph's daddy. We had the same mother, but a different father, you know. My father was a Rakes.

Well, they lived down on, they called it Big Spraddle. And then they moved up on the mountain where they lived in the house that burnt. It was an old-timey house, and it had a porch all the way around. Just one end, the end down there that didn't have no porch on it. It was nice, you know.

They lived on a farm. They didn't sell anything, you know, they just raised their—like they would raise the beef and the hogs and chickens, had their own chickens and things like that.

They had no electric, not down on Big Spraddle. And then they didn't have any electric in the old house until it burned and they built the new one, there where Mother lived when she died. They used kerosene lamps. And we had a spring down at the foot of the hill and we carried water up to wash clothes. Washed clothes on a board and we carried it up the hill to wash and everything.

But the old house burnt and when they built the new one why Mother had—well now, we finally had water in the old house, you know. And I can't remember, I don't much believe that they was lights in it. Now they could've been. It's been so long I've just about forgot, but I don't believe they was. But anyway, she had electric and everything in the new house. It's still there, that house. Ralph sold it after Mother died.

It's pretty country down there. It really is. And up there on that mountain. They used to be chestnut trees there and chinquapin trees and everything, you know. You may not know what that is, chinquapin. They're a little round thing and you'd break them open, bite them till they open, some people can, and eat the inside. They're good. Something like a chestnut. Little round black things. And the end of them was kind of yellow like, where they'd come out of the burr. They had burrs, just like chestnuts.

I didn't live there. I was married then. But I was there, you know, in and out and things, but I never lived there. Because I was married. I married when I was seventeen years old, you know. Crazy.

We took care of the kids. Ralph was the one I looked after and my step-sister, Georgia, took care of Carter. She's, I don't know how many years older, she's a few years older than I am. But we grew up together. We never had a short word or anything. And us just step-sisters, you know.

A lot of people say Ralph and I look alike, and a lot say Carter and I was turned alike. But I don't know. I can't see that me and Ralph looks alike but a lot of people say we do, you know. But we took care of Ralph when he was just a little boy. Mother would go with his father, you know, and me and Georgia would take care of the kids.

Ralph was tow-headed. His hair was real light. But Carter's hair was dark. It was brown, dark brown. And he had brown eyes where Ralph's got blue eyes. Lot of people says Ralph looks like Mother. And he was closer to Mother than he was to his father, Ralph was.

Oh, he was mischievous, you know, naturally. They are, into everything. Like all of them. He done so much I can't remember what he did now. I can't think of nothing right off, you know. It's been a long time. But he was good, you know. And I always said he was my boy and Georgia said Carter was hers.

So much has happened that I've forgot a lot that did happen when I was a-growing up. I'm getting so forgetful now I can't remember from one day to the next. But one time Ralph come down to plough for me. I was going to plant some corn. And he says when he come, "Ruby, I could eat a whole chocolate pie if I had it." I said, "Oh you could?" He said, "Yeah." Well, while he was ploughing I made it. He ate the pie before he left, but not at one time. But he ate it. Yeah, he sure did.

Mother, she played the banjo, the clawhammer style. And Ralph and Carter takes after her. When they was growing up they liked to play music. And we had a mail boy, Woodrow Owens, and he would show Carter how to play the guitar, you know, when he'd be carrying the mail. Carter'd watch for him. And he showed him some things on the guitar.

I don't know, maybe I'm prejudiced, but nobody'll ever play the banjo like Ralph, to me. My cousin, Carrie, it's her mother that they bought Ralph's first banjo from. You see, her mother and father lived down the road about a half a mile, I would say. Down the road there from Mother, the old home place, now, you know.

They took their music after Mother. Their daddy couldn't play. And the church. They'd sing those old-timey hymns. The Old Regular Baptist church. They'd take Mother to church and back then people would get up and sing the old-timey hymns and everything. I like them.

I believe they had to go in the service before they got their diploma but they finished school. When Ralph was in service why I wrote, I'd walk and go to the post office to see if I could hear from him. Now, me and Ralph's always been close. And Carter too, when he was living. Like I say, I didn't have a brother or sister, you know, but till Carter and Ralph come on. After Mother married their daddy why—people say your half-brothers. I say, "Them ain't half-brothers. They're just my brothers. That's all I've ever knew."

And when they first started out, why I'd cook for them. I was married. Hadn't been married too long. We lived at Bristol the last time. And they'd come over and eat and I'd fry these apple pies. I don't know if you know what I mean or not. Fried apple pies? Well, you cook your apples and you put spice and sugar and then you make your dough and then you roll it out. And then you put your fruit right down here and then you turn it over and pinch it up together. And I'd fry them a bag of them to take with them to work, I mean, on the road, you know. But I'd cook for them. I used to like to cook but no more.

When Ralph and Jimmie was first married they had a trailer right there at the house, you know, right there by the house where Mother lived. And then he built the house where they live and they moved from there, let's see, I believe Mother died before he got the house finished. I believe she did.

We used to see Mother sitting on the porch with her bonnet on when we'd go home. I used to call her and tell her when we was coming, but I got so I didn't. Jimmie told me, she says, "She just walks the floor if you're not there by the time she thinks you should be," so I just quit calling. And I'd always fix her something to eat. I'd have enough till she wouldn't have to cook when we got home.

We'd go once a year, on vacation. See, I worked in a hospital fifteen years and, let's see, I think I got three weeks. I worked over fifteen years and I think it was three weeks that I got and we'd go down home and stay two weeks if I got three. Or if my husband just got a week we'd just stay a week, you know. Just according to how things was. She was something, Mother was. You know, Carter, a lot of songs he wrote was about Mother.

I used to go to the studio at Bristol and watch them on "Farm and Fun Time." And every time Ralph's in Michigan and if it's where I can, I go to see him. I did down there too, when I'd be home, you know, and could go. I've been to a lot of his shows. And I didn't miss a festival at the old home place. I was there all of them. People I don't guess expected them to go and be like they are today. I guess they didn't realize.

Now I like to go down home, but seem like I'm not interested in that festival in Kentucky. It's not the same, not to me, it isn't. I missed—I was sick that I couldn't get to go to Ralph's fortieth year in music, but Vergie's car, something happened to it, so we couldn't go. And I didn't have a chance to try to get somebody else.

Carter's second son, or next to the baby, the youngest son, Bobby, he was my boy. When we'd go down home he'd come up to the gate and holler Hi. I'd go let him in. He'd stay all day with his mother. He was just a little fellow too. But he was my boy.

Ralph and Carter was in music twenty years when Carter died. But I miss Carter when I go down home. He loved chicken and dressing. And every time I'd go, he says, "Ruby, we'll have chicken and dressing, won't we?" I said, "We sure will." I made it with hamburger, and that's the way he liked it, you know. I made it for him, you know. Oh, I miss him, when I go home.

4

Benny Steele

"It's all come to pass"

When we consider that Ralph Stanley celebrated his sixtieth birthday in 1987, and the tiny size of the community he lived in as a boy, it is surprising how many witnesses survive who have first-hand knowledge of his childhood and that of his brother Carter. Gaining real insight into that period, however, can be a tricky business. An old neighbor once remarked, for instance, that he and the other boys he knew used to make fun of Ralph and Carter, calling them sissies because they spent all of their spare time with music. But this is not the sort of comment that will ordinarily be made to an outside investigator who is looking for public testimony. Mountain (and family) solidarity, awe at the later achievement of the Stanley Brothers, and a well founded distrust of scandalmongers instead combine as a rule to produce a romanticized and unfortunately rather bland picture of those early years.

The late Benny Steele of Wise County, Virginia, knew the Stanley family well when the brothers were boys, and remained a close friend ever since that time. This connection eventually became the center of his life. Thanks to it he became a public figure in his old age, almost a professional mountain patriarch; he was interviewed countless times for radio, television, and print. He traveled with Ralph Stanley in the Virginia and eastern Kentucky area, and was often called upon to sing a song or two with the band on stage. He was a tomato gardener, and in a way that seems almost feudal to an outsider it was one of his proudest boasts that he supplied Ralph Stanley with all his tomatoes. He was a true and loyal friend and an enthusiastic fan, eager to do nothing more than heap praises on his idols and the world that produced them. But in the midst of his continually reiterated statements that the brothers were nothing more than plain country boys one or two rather more

hard-edged observations emerge that show us, in memorable fashion, some of the obstacles Ralph and Carter Stanley had to overcome to achieve what they did.

———————

My daddy was Reuben Steele and my mother was Nichotai
Steele. I was borned in Wise County, Virginia. Nineteen and eight,
that's when I was born. I married when I was about seventeen
years old. Me and my wife went to school together, took our school-
ing together. And she was a good woman and we got hooked up
and got married. We raised twelve kids, eight boys and four girls.
They're all married and gone. I still live in Wise County.

I always liked music, listening, you know. I'd go to old apple
peelings and bean stringings and we'd dance and have clawhammer style banjo, them days. Ralph Stanley and Carter, they was a
little relation of mine. I knowed them ever since they's little bare-
footed boys. And I just liked them. Me and my family always went
for Carter and Ralph. I went up where their daddy had a little store
at the side of the road. And I went up there to get me a job off of
him, a-cutting timber. But the boys wasn't big enough to work.
They was a-going to high school then.

They was kindly getting started in the music business then, but
they had a hard time a-getting started. Well, I hung to the boys. I
went to their little shows everywhere in Wise County and Dickenson County. The little church houses and schoolhouses and courthouses and theaters. I'd go to where they was making music at the
high schools, you know, and they'd get up on an old flat-bedded
truck and stand there and pick, and I'd pitch 'em up there dimes
and quarters to them. They was just old-timey country boys.
That's all you can make out of them. Just old-timey boys. And Lee
was that way, their father. And their mother, Lucy, she was that
way too. I went to see Lucy before she died, way before she died, I
went back and forth to see her. She didn't stay on the road none.
She just picked at home. She told me before she died that she
learnt the boys how to make music and the first tune that she ever
learnt Ralph was "Shout Little Lulie," and "Little Birdie" and all
such as that, you know.

They liked the boys' going into the music business. Their father
got them a few show dates at the courthouses and around, you
know, and he'd go around with them a little bit. I've seen him with
them some. He tried to help the boys, but Lucy helped them more
than their daddy did.

They raised corn, they hoed corn, worked the sawmill, and just worked on the farm around there. Last work I seed the boys do, they was a-working the sawmill. And I didn't like that much to see them boys work, thinking they was good music players as they was, you know. Well, Carter, them big logs, he'd get down under them and roll them up for his brother to saw in the skidway there, and Ralph, he was out there taking lumber from the big saw, him and brother Doc. They was half-brothers, Doc and Ralph was. And Lance, their half-brother, was a-doing the sawing. And they'd roll them big logs up there and they'd shut the mill down to file the saw.

Big Lee, their daddy, was standing there. He said, "Boys, get to moving them slabs out of there." He never let them stand. They had to keep on the go. And I sat there on the rock. I never will forget it. Sat there on the rock and shook my head in shame that them boys had to do a hard work like that and was good as music players as they was. But that's the last work they ever done. They wound up at that.

Carter was a good talker. He had the altitude. He was really a better talker than Ralph. Ralph never was a talker much. You can tell that. Old Carter, he'd get up and he could think of things what to say pretty fast. He was a good fellow, Carter was. Great man.

The last time I saw Carter was at Culpeper, Virginia. He was there. He was looking bad then, his jaws sunk in. But I talked with him, got an album. I believe he went to Indiana and played one more show. I was a-working in Fairfax when I heard Carter died, but I was about four hundred and fifty miles away from home then. I couldn't come in for the funeral.

I was afraid that Ralph'd quit, you know. Maybe he wouldn't play no more music, he'd come back to his home. Maybe get him a job or something or other. But you know, he got about a thousand letters in the mail just to keep staying on the road. They was stronger behind him than they ever was, since Carter died. That gave him something to go by right there, didn't it? So he kindly continued on, and played on, and I just kept going, listening to that Ralph. And up there at his festival I asked him one day, "Would you let me travel some with you, make a trip?" "Oh yeah, I'd be glad to have you." So I got took up with Ralph and I've been on the road with him about eleven years now.

I made that song, "Pretty Woman Blues." I just kept putting it together, how it would run and everything. If you ain't got a tune of a song you ain't got nothing. Well, they ain't nobody sings that song. They don't know it. And it's a hard song to sing. You can tell it. And it's got a lot of verses in there, too. You notice that? I told Ralph—he tried to sing that "Pretty Woman Blues," you know, he can't hardly get it. I said, "You fellows are going to have to learn that cause I'm going to be gone some of these days." But they got us on television. They're trying to get it all off of me while I'm a-living so they'll have something, my dancing and singing.

My 'matoes, I've got out about two hundred and fifty vines this year. I stake them. Put big high stakes in them. Sometimes they'll grow eight foot high, if you got stakes that high. I've got about ten or twelve different kind out this year. I furnish Ralph his 'matoes. He comes down just when he gets his out, I call him and tell him I got him a box of 'matoes.

They's going to be some people at my house before long to interview me. I don't know how many of them's a-coming, but they're going to come and interview me. And they're going to put it in the papers and put it on radio. And I'm glad to get to tell the people about Carter Stanley and Ralph. Wouldn't they've been somewheres if Carter'd been a-living yet? He never lived to get to see much of it. If Carter could raise up out of that cemetery up there and look on top of that hill and see what Ralph's a-going on, wouldn't that be something? And see that big fine home he's built. See all them horses he's got, that white fence around there. When I pass away I want Ralph and the boys to sing over me.

I've been practically in Wise County all my life. But I'd never thought back then I'd ever see a festival and I didn't think I'd ever get to travel with Ralph Stanley and get on the bus with him and get on the stage and perform on the stage like I have. But it's all come to pass.

5

Ralph Stanley

"It's the hardest music in the world to play"

Ralph Stanley has been asked to tell his life story by over half a dozen serious interviewers in the last twenty years. He is not known as an easy subject. He is, to be sure, cooperative, patient, and generous with his time, but the thought of speaking for posterity, or for a wide audience, appears to unnerve him. "He will answer your specific question very politely," one writer has said, "and then stop." It is very rarely that he will spread himself when asked a question of fact, and unlike so many people in this psychiatric age he is even more reluctant to respond at length to a question that demands self-analysis.

All of his interviewers have probably gone away disappointed, to one extent or another, in their encounters with him. But interestingly enough, when all of these interviewers are taken as a group, Stanley has in fact done a very creditable job in relating his history to them. This is proven by the following monologue, which is a composite of seven interviews, five published, two unpublished, extending in time from 1966 to 1987. Originally assembled for a souvenir book to be sold by the band on the road, it is an "authorized" autobiography in the sense that Stanley has declared, in hawking it from the stage, that he wrote it—certainly a true statement as far as celebrity autobiographies as a whole are concerned. Aside from a very few insignificant editorial adjustments, all the words in it are his own.

It is, of course, a public statement, from a man with old-fashioned ideas about what a public statement should contain. Domestic crises and professional quarrels are glossed over or ignored. Above all, it contains nothing whatsoever that could reflect adversely on the reputation of Stanley's family. In this it adheres to the code of the mountains as well as the mores of the Victorian era to which Stanley, whose mother was born in 1886, is so directly connected. It inevitably begs several important questions—unfortunately enough, not only because of the gaps that are left in the story but because a complete answer to some of these questions would demonstrate very creditable, in fact even heroic, aspects of Stanley's character and behavior over the years.

On the positive side, the basic facts are there, except for a few minor slipups. And the voice and the thoughts and the words are there. If we listen carefully to the silences as well as the words recorded in these pages, we can emerge from them with as clear a portrait of the real Ralph Stanley as we are ever likely to see in print.

———

I was born on what they call Big Spraddle Creek, about three miles down from the home place. Post office was Stratton, Virginia, a very small place right close to McClure. I was born on February twenty-fifth, 1927. We moved to where I lived, where the festival is, when I was about nine. That was my mother's old home place, where she was raised. She was a Smith and they call it Smith Ridge. It was a little farm. We used to get up early, way before daylight, and light an old lantern, you know, burns kerosene, and go to the barn to do our feeding and milking, to get ready to go to school. We used to keep two or three milk cows, two or three head of horses, and things like that. And we used to raise tobacco. We had a acre of that, one acre's about all we had. We used to walk two or three mile to catch the school bus, down the mountain, so we had to get up and start preparing early.

See, we lived on a country dirt road, and we had to walk out to the paved road, which was about two and a half mile. And we'd leave away before daylight and I know we'd catch the bus about daylight. We'd see it coming and turn the lights off about the time it got to where we got on. They got a bus up there now, but they didn't have one then. It's steep. Sometimes people go off the mountain and wreck. They's been two or three starved to death before they reached the bottom.

Carter was the only full brother I had; my daddy was married before and my mother was married before. Her husband died and his wife died. He had six children and she had one girl by her first husband. He had three boys and three girls. That was three half-brothers and three half-sisters, and a half-sister by my mother. None of them played music.

We didn't hear too much around home except this old clawhammer banjo playing. My mother used to pick the banjo, you know. She didn't do very much singing but she played the banjo. I call it the clawhammer. A lot of people call it, I don't know, frailing or something, I guess. Actually, drop thumb I guess is what she did. Tunes like "Chinquapin Hunting," "Shout Little Lulie," "Walking in the Parlor," and "Going up Cripple Creek," things like that.

She had I reckon eleven brothers and sisters and all of them played music. She told me a lot about that. They had these old-time dances back then and things like that. Banjo, fiddle—they wasn't any guitars. She told me she played all night a many of a night for square dances—until the sun was coming up the next morning.

And then there's different people like my uncle that used to play one on the banjo sometime. My daddy didn't play, but he sung a lot around home. He knew a lot of songs. He sung "Man of Constant Sorrow," "Pretty Polly," "Wild Bill Jones," "Omie Wise," and "The House Carpenter." And one called "The Brown Girl," I believe. Really where we got some of the old ballads was from our daddy. And he sang in the church. He sung a lot of them old church songs. "Tarry with Me O My Saviour" and "Village Church Yard" and "Amazing Grace." My daddy was a great singer. He had a voice. He had a lonesome voice.

We attended the McClure Church, Primitive Baptist. As kids we didn't sing very much in church. A little bit. Daddy and Mother always did. They didn't use instruments in church. They all sang, I guess, the same part. Everybody actually sung lead, but there would usually be three or four men and three or four women, and the women would come in higher, just an octave higher or something, and they really blended well. But no music. They don't believe in music in the church. Just a cappella. That's where they line them, see. That's where I learned that. Maybe they wouldn't have but one songbook. They didn't know what to sing there and the old preacher'd get up there and line them and spit that tobacco juice right out and that was doing something. And they had the feeling to it.

I've saddled an old gray mare I used to have called Old Patsy a many of a time and my mother'd crawl on that mare and ride to church. I'd walk along with her. Just us two. Carter was in the army. I was in high school.

I recorded some and lined some, like "Village Church Yard." The only change that we made is that we use the tenor, baritone, and use the parts of harmony singing. That's the only difference. It's the same singing that we learned to do in church.

And of course the mail carrier that used to come through there, why he played the guitar and the harmonica and I heard him play some. He carried the mail on horseback. He'd always carry his harmonica especially with him. You'd hear him a-coming every day, about a half a mile or so.

Not too many musicians right around that part of the country where I was raised. Performers came by. There were a few to the high school there. I believe the first show I ever saw was Clayton McMichen and his Georgia Wildcats. And the Delmore Brothers was on that show. Then they started coming to maybe fifteen or twenty mile of where we lived and we went out and saw some from Bluefield, West Virginia. Molly O'Day. Back in them days she was called Dixie Lee. She played out of Bluefield and it was sort of headed by a fellow named Gordon Jennings. I believe all that was with her was her brother, played the fiddle, name was Skeets Williamson and Gordon played the guitar with her. I always liked to hear Molly sing. I think she sings it just the way she was raised.

Then Uncle Dave Macon and Bill Monroe, he came through the school we went to, and I think we saw him the day that Clyde Moody started with him. He'd got Clyde Moody in Bluefield and he had Clyde and Art Wooten and Stringbean, I believe, with him. I don't remember exactly but I'd say it was '39 or '40.

And the radio. I think we got our radio in about 1936, I guess, and while we was waiting on breakfast we'd have the radio on. They had this program at Knoxville, Tennessee, and at Bluefield, West Virginia, and people like the Bailey Brothers and Bailes Brothers and Molly O'Day. I used to hear the Carter Family and Mainer's Mountaineers, but I don't remember where they came from. And you know, Grand Ole Opry, Monroe Brothers. Arthur Smith and Sam and Kirk McGee. And they used to be two called the Poe Sisters in Nashville. Whatever happened to them, I don't know. But they could really sing the old-time. They sort of sang the bluegrass style. I don't know what ever happened to them, that's just all I know, the Poe Sisters.

But we had hopes, you know. When I say "we" I'm speaking about Brother Carter. We'd listen to the Grand Ole Opry stars and we'd listen to the people on the radio and we would just think in our mind how we would like to be people like that. Back then we had an old-time wood stove in our living room and part of the time just a grate, you know, like a fireplace and we'd have to cut wood, kindling, to start the fire with and we'd listen to the radio. I know we was about the first family in that area that ever had a radio and a lot of people would gather around on Saturday night to listen to the Grand Ole Opry and we'd get those kindling sticks, you know, like we had a fiddle or a guitar or something, and we'd play on them sticks with the music we heard on the radio like we had instruments and the neighbors that come in, they enjoyed it. But when we first started now, Carter never did mind too much but I was so bashful that when anybody would come in to hear us, they would be in the living room and we'd go in the kitchen and play. I was too bashful to play before them.

I'd say I was eleven or twelve when I started to pick the banjo. I first learned to play the clawhammer style from my mother. My aunt, Roxie Smith, had a banjo and they raised hogs and this sow had a litter of pigs. She had a pretty sow pig I wanted. I wanted to raise some pigs, you know. So my mother said, "Now I can't buy the both of them, so do you want the pig or the banjo?" I took the banjo. We had a little grocery store and I know she traded out in groceries, I believe it was five dollars worth, for the banjo. That's how I got started on the banjo.

I think the first tune I even learned was this "Shout Little Lulie" and my mother tuned the banjo the first time I ever had one in my hands. And she played that tune and I think the first time I ever tried I could play it a little bit. I never did play the clawhammer much after we got started together. I played with one finger and thumb until after I got out of the army and everything. I sort of picked up that style from maybe Wade Mainer or something like that. When I first heard it I couldn't figure out what was going, that fifth string was ringing away so much. When we started playing professionally I started playing, or trying to, with three fingers. It was in about '47, I guess. The first three-finger I heard was Snuffy Jenkins and I heard Hoke Jenkins play it. And I heard another boy—I can't think of his name right now—in North Carolina. And then when I was discharged why I heard Earl Scruggs play it. I'd never heard Earl until after I was discharged from the army. On the radio, with Bill Monroe. Snuffy and Hoke, I heard them before I heard Earl. But actually, what decided me was Earl, because Earl did take the three-finger and really do something with it, I think. He improved it so much, you know, than what Jenkins or any of them had. I really liked his way of playing. And still do better than anybody I've ever heard.

You know, when Earl first went to Bill they hadn't heard much of that style banjo playing down there. I mean, Uncle Dave Macon was really, he was *it* at the Grand Ole Opry. And when they did go down there why they—I was told this now by Bill—they went in the dressing room that night and Bill called Uncle Dave in and Earl played "Cumberland Gap" or something and Bill said, "Uncle Dave, what do you think about that kind of banjo playing now?" And Dave said, "Well," he said, "I'll tell you," he said, "he's a pretty good banjo player but he ain't a damn bit funny."

Anyway, as the music advanced I thought I should advance with it. It was a better style and it was a better beat and all that. How I learned it? Well, I don't think I could put that in words. I just played it the way that my fingers led me and I just—I really couldn't explain that, I don't guess. Couldn't play it any other way. Tried to copy a little bit here and there, but I never could. And I'm proud that I didn't because what I do know is mine.

Carter got the guitar when he was about thirteen or fourteen year old. He started about the same time I did. He didn't play banjo, not to amount to anything. He just played the guitar. He did fool with the banjo a little bit and he played it enough to beat me in a contest one time. That was in Grundy, Virginia. When we was grown, after we'd been playing professionally. I guess they just wanted to have a joke on me. But Carter could play a tune or two on the banjo. I think he used his forefinger and thumb.

We used to play at home a lot, on Sunday, you know, and of a night before we'd go to bed. And our daddy, he usually had business to take care of. He worked men, in his job, and he was a little nervous and he'd usually run us out of the house. Couldn't stand that noise. We'd go to the woodshed or the woods or the barn or wherever and practice. We'd go anywhere we could get to play and sing a little. Carter got a guitar before I did the banjo and immediately after we got them I'd say we was trying to sing some together. I always sung tenor.

Jewel Martin played some with us. He played the mandolin a little bit. We played some with him in school. He's about ten miles from where I live. And there was a boy that played the fiddle by the name of Richard Nunley. He played some with us. We just played wherever we could, under apple trees, whatever. No pay. Just a apple or two. When they'd fall off.

We'd just play around home and around the neighbors' houses and at school. They would have a junior play or senior play or something and between acts they'd pull the curtains and we'd step out in front of the curtains and do a number while they was making the next setting for the next act. Things like that. We did "Hills of Roane County," "When I Lay My Burden Down," "I Called and Nobody Answered," "Roll On, Buddy." Just a lot of old-timers like that. We played a few dances, not too many. I never did like to play dances. It's hard work, for one thing. They'll dance sometime for twenty-five or thirty minutes and you get tired, you know. And then they usually had the dances from maybe like eight till twelve or one, you know.

I think the first song we ever sang on the radio was in Elizabethton, Tennessee. It was a Saturday morning show that they had there called the "Barrel of Fun" and I believe the first song we sang was "When I Lay My Burden Down." And way back then Carter, he always liked to cut up a little bit, you know, and holler maybe during a song. And I know the first time that we played on the radio, why he tried to holler and it wouldn't come out. He was scared so bad it wouldn't come out.

The first time we ever really played in public was at a Republican convention at the Greenwood Grade School in Greenwood, Virginia. That's the first public gathering we ever played before. It was just for the county, see, and these county officials, they come by and got us, and I think we rode in the back of a pick-up truck and went to this school where they had their meeting that night, you know, and played and they brought us back home. Just the two of us.

My daddy worked at the sawmill—logged—and I worked there a few days, not very much. We sawed some for the mine. Timbers, collars, cross-ties and just regular lumber. There used to be a lot of sawmills around here, but you don't see it any more because all the timber's gone. They didn't have buzz saws back then. They had these old crosscuts, you know—one man on each end. That was a job. But I didn't do that part of it. The job I worked at always was rolling dust, they called it. The dust that they saw from the logs. A lot of dust comes from it. And you roll that off in a wheelbarrow. And then I worked some in the woods where they used horses to haul the logs out, you know, and you had to have what they call a swamping road. Somebody had to cut that road out for the horses to go get them. The timber cutters would cut it and you had to cut a road out to get your team to it. So I done some of that. I was about sixteen, I guess.

I went to school at Big Oak, down the ridge about three miles, the first we went to. And then I went north, where the high school is. Carter left and went to the army about two year before I did.

Well, during that time why, I don't know which one, me or Carter one, sold some of these seeds, garden seeds and so forth, and as a premium for it we got a fiddle, you see. And while he was gone, why I tried to learn the fiddle a little, which I never did do much at. But anyway my mother played the banjo and I'd play the fiddle and a lot of neighbors would invite us in on weekends and we'd go around and play some. We played "Cindy" and "Old Joe Clark," "Boil the Cabbage Down," "Cripple Creek."

I graduated from high school on the second of May, 1945, and went in the army the sixteenth of May. To the infantry. Did basic training at Camp Gordon, Georgia, and then I went to Germany. I had it pretty good in Germany. The war was over when I got over there but we done a lot of disarming. We went through a lot of the villages, you know, and disarmed the houses and got guns and things like that. I brought one back. One's all you was allowed to bring back. See, they inspected you. It was a .32 Walther pistol. But anyway, they'd break in them houses and just take everything they had. I've seen them take them rifles and just knock them men and women down in the corners and just take what they had and everything.

But I didn't do that very long till I got an old banjo from the—what do you call it?—Special Service. I began to play that and one night about four o'clock in the morning a fellow by the name of Lieutenant Henry, he was from Beverly Hills, California, and he was a lieutenant in our battalion, he come by my door in the room there and I was up picking. He knocked on the door, him and a captain. They liked the sound of that. I was a private at that time. And they knocked on the door and asked me to play them a tune or two and I did.

Well, about two days later they called me and made me a mail clerk and about two weeks later I was what they call a T-5. That's the same thing as a corporal, only a corporal is over men and a T-5 is office duty. That way they put me in a private room, no bed check, no reveille of a morning, no nothing. I had it made. About, I guess, about three months they called me one day, wanted me to come in, said, "Would you be interested in taking a job in the head-quarters?" And I took it. So they made me what they call a S-2 sergeant, intelligence sergeant. Just as soon as somebody went home they brought me in and I took that over. That was a tech sergeant, that's the same as a master sergeant. Master sergeant's over men and a tech is office duties. So they made me that. As fast as I could I was a tech sergeant. I had it made.

I'd play the banjo a little for them now and then. They really liked me and I know the old colonel, his name was Lorenz, and I was in the office one day and Lorenz hollered out and said, "Hey, Sergeant Stanley! You know what?" I said, "No, what?" He said, "Orders just come in that all soldiers that's served eighteen months overseas is eligible for discharge." You know what I said? I said, "You're a God-damned liar." To a *colonel*, now. He said, "No, sir." Well, he called me in. He said, "We don't want you to go. We want to send you to Officers' Training School. We'll make you a second lieutenant in three weeks and just as fast as you can go up you'll become a first lieutenant. We'll just move you just as fast as you can go." I said, "I'm not interested. I'm going home." He said, "Okay." But now I was in that good with them. I could talk just like that to him. Now anybody else they'd've went to the brig for thirty days.

Oh, I had a good time in Germany. I was there about thirteen months. I learned some of the language. But I'd rather spent three years there as two months in the States. Yes sir, I had it made, buddy. Anything I wanted, I got. They said, "The sky's your limit. We'll see to it. We'll put you in there."

How I got home, well, we left, let's see, I was in Bad Aibling, Germany, that was out of Munich, and we rode a train to Bremer-haven. Got on a ship in Bremerhaven and sailed to New York. And they brought me out to Camp Shanks, New York, stayed there a couple of days and discharged me there. Caught a bus then home.

Carter was discharged from the army about six months before I was. He was discharged in March and I was discharged in October of '46. And before I got home he was already a-singing with a group that Pee Wee Lambert was in, Roy Sykes and the Blue Ridge Mountain Boys. And him and my dad met me in Bristol in the bus station and I went on the radio before I got home. They were playing at Norton, WNVA. They had a daily program somewhere around three o'clock. So I sung a song with Carter before I got home. I played a show that night before I went home and been into it ever since. Didn't even go home.

Well, I played with this group that Carter was playing with about, oh, I guess three weeks and I didn't like it. You see, this fiddle play-er, Roy Sykes, that Carter played with, he also played the banjo. Well, I'd play the banjo on the songs and then if they was a banjo tune featured he'd come and get the banjo off of me and take it and play it. I'd stand back and watch it, see. So that was one thing. Anyway, I didn't like it. I told Carter if I was going to play, if we could start a band, okay, and if not, I was going to go to school and be a veterinary. Do the G.I. Bill. I told him, I said, "If you want to organize our own we will, and if you don't, why I'm just going to step out and you can do what you want to." And he said, "Well, you're not going to do that. If you're not satisfied, why, we'll give our notice right now." Pee Wee Lambert, mandolin player, he said, "Well, wherever you boys go I'll go too." Pee Wee was from Thacker, West Virginia. So we just turned in our notice, two weeks' notice, and started our own group. We got us a program on the station there in Norton. I believe we were sponsored by the Piggly Wiggly company and we played maybe two or three weeks there.

And I believe the first fiddle player was Bobby Summer from Vicco, Kentucky. Bobby was a boy you couldn't depend on. He was a good fiddle player but he'd come and he'd stay with you a week or maybe two weeks and then he'd slip off in the night and leave you. We couldn't have that so we got Leslie Keith. I call him my first fiddle player. He was in Harrisonburg, Virginia, and we drove up to see him and got him. Course later Bobby recorded I believe on our first session on Columbia that we made, played the fiddle. He was with us three or four times. He'd come and stay and then he'd slip off. Anyway, we worked WNVA about thirty days and then Leslie joined us at Bristol.

We heard about this new station going on the air in Bristol and our daddy went up there and talked to them one day. They were planning to start this hour program, and they didn't have any talent to start it with. It just went in in that fall, sometime, of '46 and they had about thirty minutes that Curly King was there, that he played on Saturday. And we heard him. And it was a larger station than what we were on and we decided to go see if we could get with them. They was interested in starting a daily program, an hour a day, and Curly, he was afraid to chance it. He worked, you know, and just played on a Saturday, and he said he didn't think he wanted to fool with it. So we started ourselves. It was known as "Farm and Fun Time." An hour a day. They said, "We won't promise you a thing. If you want to come and play the hour by yourselves with no pay or anything," so that's what we did.

That was WCYB at 12:05, right after the news for fifty-five minutes. We had handbills made up with the call letters of the station, and the name of the program and the time it was on. The first appearance that we played there were four of us. I think it was the day after Christmas, the twenty-sixth of December. And we split, and we made, I believe, $2.25 a piece.

And the next night we played a fairly good-sized school. It was between Big Stone Gap and Appalachia, no, between Big Stone and Pennington Gap. I don't remember what we took in, what we made, but anyhow we had two shows—two full houses. And from then on we just couldn't hardly find buildings big enough to hold the people. That was about a week after we started at Bristol.

And we hadn't been playing over two or three weeks till we started getting, oh, from five hundred to a thousand letters and cards a day, you know, and in that bunch why we'd get anywhere from maybe one to twenty-five letters a day wanting us to come to a school or to a church or to a theater or something. And we got so many that we couldn't take care of them. We just had to throw a lot of them away. All we had to do was just answer a letter. They'd say, "When do you want to come?" We'd send them a date and there wasn't enough days in the week to take care of them.

Now Leslie Keith, he was a old-timer and he knew how to make money. He had a tune called the "Black Mountain Blues" that was real popular. He'd put out the notes to that and a picture of himself. I believe you paid ten cents or a quarter or something but he really sold it. That gave us the idea to put out a songbook. We couldn't mail them out fast enough. We got to carry the orders home in a box or a basket or something.

We did real well. They wasn't anything, see, they wasn't all that kind of music. People wanted it, I guess. We just happened to hit at the right time. They wasn't many radio stations. WCYB in Bristol and they was one more in Bristol, WOPI, but other than that why it was maybe a hundred miles before there was another station. It was clear channel, 690, and they could really get it.

We left Bristol a couple of times, but we never did stay maybe over two months. We went to Raleigh, North Carolina, once, but we didn't stay in Raleigh too long. And, let's see, I imagine the next place we went to was Huntington, West Virginia. That was about I guess '49 or '50. Anyhow, it was about the time the television station started there and that was among the first TV stations to ever start and we did television there about six months. So we played there about six months and then we went to the Louisiana Hayride in Shreveport, Louisiana.

Well, we didn't like that much and anyhow, why we got a call there from Lexington, Kentucky. They had a Saturday night jamboree and they offered us a good thing. We wanted to get back close to home so we left Shreveport after three or four weeks and we went to Lexington and stayed a few months. And we moved from Lexington to Oak Hill, West Virginia, WOAY, and played several months there and then we moved from there to Pikeville. And we went to Versailles, Kentucky. But we didn't stay long. We'd always come back to Bristol. And we played maybe a year or so until other groups started coming in, like Mac Wiseman, Charlie Monroe, and Flatt and Scruggs was there a while in '48. We were on there off and on for twelve years. Left there in '58.

We started recording just after we went there. I believe around February or March, in '47. We recorded for Rich-R-Tone. This fellow by the name of Hobart Stanton had this company in Johnson City. I guess he heard us on the radio station and he contacted us, and we made some records for him. We recorded in WOPI radio station in Bristol. First session was Pee Wee Lambert, Leslie Keith, Carter and myself. And that time we didn't know A from B. We didn't know about things like that. And he didn't pay us anything; just promised us some royalty on the record. We were glad just to get some records out.

I was told by a fellow the other night that Hobart told him that the record of "Little Glass of Wine" sold 100,000 copies. I know we were sponsored by a store over in Honaker, Virginia, called Honaker Harness and Saddlery and the "Glass of Wine" version was released. They got us to come one day, one Saturday, and play at their store and they bought a thousand of this record. And I know they sold that thousand out that day. People came out of the mountains, and different places. They advertised us on the radio, you see. They sponsored part of our shows on the radio and they got us to come down and play and advertised that they would have that record on sale. And they ordered a thousand copies of it and run out before the day was over. The first time we recorded, I guess, two songs: "Mother No Longer Awaits Me at Home" and "The Girl behind the Bar." We recorded some at WOPI and some up at Pikeville, Kentucky, at WLSI radio.

We stayed with Rich-R-Tone about a year. We did I imagine around sixteen or eighteen songs for them. "Little Glass of Wine" was the most popular. After Rich-R-Tone we recorded for Columbia. Art Satherly, the A&R man for Columbia, called us one day on the telephone and said he wanted to sign us on Columbia records. We signed, I believe, with Columbia in 1947, but I don't remember exactly what it was, some kind of ban on the union, you couldn't record at that time, and we had to wait until that was settled. I believe it was 1948 when we first recorded for Columbia. We were playing in Raleigh, North Carolina, WPTF, at that time and Art Satherly flew down and signed us to a contract. At that time we had Pee Wee Lambert, Art Wooten, Carter, and myself, and Art Satherly rented a room or two in the hotel there and we went to see him there and we signed the contract. And I think he pulled out of his coat pocket a couple of hundred dollars and said, "You might need a little money." He said, "I'm gonna give you this." He said there's three songs they needed real bad that we'd been doing—"Pretty Polly," "Little Maggie," and "The White Dove." Yeah, and "The Glass of Wine." There was four. And if we could cut that four for him on a session and we did. Cut them in Nashville, Tennessee, in the Tulane Hotel.

At that time Pee Wee Lambert played the mandolin and he had a high voice, he liked to sing like Bill Monroe. And I guess at first we sort of tried to follow him, because he did most of the tenor singing at the start. Actually, we weren't too happy with the sound. We were looking for more of a style of our own. But we had a good trio with Pee Wee. Now as far as I know—I may be wrong but I don't think so—we were the first to put out a high trio in that style. Like "Lonesome River." That was good material we had on Columbia but I think some of our best recordings were some of the Mercurys. But for the first couple of years I guess we tried to follow in Bill's footsteps. Pee Wee stayed with us till about 1950 and after he left, why, I think that's when Carter and me started doing all the singing that we sort of styled our own at that time. We just sung it the way we felt. We got down to doing the Stanley style. Curley Sechler worked a little while with us on the mandolin, and Bob Osborne worked a little while with us on the mandolin. Then Bill Lowe and Jim Williams. Then, for a long while, George Shuffler was with us on lead guitar.

Bill Monroe didn't want Columbia to sign the Stanley Brothers. He thought it was too much on his kind of music. I was told by Art Satherly that Bill said if they signed the Stanley Brothers he would probably leave. And so they signed us and he did go to Decca. As for Lester and Earl, I think they always had their aim set on Columbia, but at the time maybe they couldn't get on, so they took Mercury and waited until they could get on Columbia.

About '48 I think's when Flatt and Scruggs come to Bristol and about all we was doing then was Bill Monroe tunes. Well Lester, he didn't like that, so he tried to ground us, see, he tried to stop us from doing any of Monroe's tunes, and—which he didn't do much good. But there was some words over it, you know, and Carter, he stepped out more than I did and he just decided and he started writing. And I'd say in the next year's time he had fifty or sixty songs wrote and that's when we began singing Stanley Brothers. So I guess that was a help to us after all.

Way back then Bill didn't want us doing his songs, but he was misinformed a lot and I guess we were too. About us doing his songs and everything. I mean, he felt like we was trying to ride on his coattails, I think. Bill was about the only artist in the field at that time, you see, and when someone else come along to getting a little of the attention, that might've hurt a little bit. But after we learned Bill and met Bill and he met us, I don't think we got a better friend. I think it was all just rumors and things that caused all of the ill feelings to start with.

We just worked around in reach of this radio station. Parts of North Carolina, Kentucky and West Virginia, Virginia, Tennessee. But when we started doing our singing ourself you know we decided that we'd never get anywhere trying to copy anybody. We'd just be ourself. If it sold, all right, if it didn't, why we'd do something else.

We were with Columbia five years. Along before that, we quit a while and went to Detroit and worked at the Ford factory. I worked about eleven weeks, I believe. Carter worked more than I did, three or four weeks more. Then Carter went and worked with Bill a while. That was about '51, I guess. And by that time, I guess we was with Columbia three years. Anyway, I was in a car wreck, and when we started back on our own again why our contract had run out with Columbia and we signed with Mercury.

Pee Wee Lambert was the one that was driving when we wrecked. Pee Wee and me were together. We were driving out of North Carolina, going through Tennessee and home and had the wreck in Shouns, Tennessee. Pee Wee wasn't hurt to amount to anything. Now, actually, Carter was already with Bill when I was in the car wreck. Rudy Lyle played the banjo with Bill, and he was called into the service and I was helping them out on the road on some personal appearances until he could get a banjo player. And Carter was with them, see, with Bill. But I didn't want to go with them regular. And Pee Wee just went along with me on the week, ten days, whatever it was. And so we were coming in is when we had the wreck.

One time before that, business got a little bad in the winter time and then Lester Woodie, he was playing fiddle, he got his call to the army, and we went home and Carter built him a house on the old home place. Naturally I was single at that time and I stayed with my mother. And our dad and mother used to have a little country store there, so we fixed it up and put partitions in it and fixed Pee Wee a place to live. And Pee Wee went home with us and lived there. And so, me and Pee Wee, we farmed and signed up on some kind of a farm school and went to it for a couple of months. And Carter, he worked some at the sawmill. We wasn't off very long and I just don't remember where we went to from there, but we started, probably Bristol I guess, back somewhere.

Well, we signed with Mercury. We called Dee Kilpatrick. He was A&R for Mercury at that time, and signed a contract with him. We did our recording in Nashville. Most of it was at Owen Bradley studios. We stayed with them five year. We had different people on Mercury. I believe Pee Wee Lambert helped. He wasn't with us, but he went along and cut one session with us. And Jim Williams was on some of it. On the mandolin. Bill Lowe was on some. And Joe Meadows played the fiddle on some. And Chubby Anthony and Ralph Mayo and just different people like that.

Jack Cooke started with the Stanley Brothers when he was about sixteen, seventeen years old. I think we had some contests there in Norton, and him and his brothers come in to enter the contests. He called me and asked me if he could go with us one week, up at Watermelon Park. That was the last time. I don't remember how we hired him the first time. But Jack's a real handyman. He can fill in several things. He can drive, he can sing tenor, he can sing baritone, play a bass. He can do a lot of things on the show if you need it.

Tom Ashley, he contacted us at the radio station in Bristol and Tom played a lot of shows with us. He played the old blackface comedian, Rastus Jones. And Fiddlin' Powers. I knew him very well; he was with us a lot of appearances. He'd come and stay a week or ten days at a time with us. He was from Castlewood, Virginia. His real name was Cowan Powers. We sang at his funeral in '54 or '55. He was seventy-five when he died. The last seven or eight years before he died, he'd come about once every month or so and stay a week with us. He come to know us by hearing us on the radio and that's how he come to play with us on shows and on the radio too.

Now at that time you know this type of music it was hard to make it. It was hard to sell a record of this type. And most of the people, you know, had to quit. And I guess Mercury got so they couldn't sell any. So they done away with all of their country music. We were with them and several more.

We were still going pretty good on personal appearances. They's places in Kentucky and West Virginia and places that we could go just every month or every six months, whatever we wanted, and still have good crowds during all the bad days. We managed to survive and stay in the business. We were playing just schoolhouses, some outdoor parks around in the summer time, little homemade places, but we had good crowds.

We were still on WCYB. We were on noon each day, five after twelve till two o'clock. We started an hour, you know, and then after three or four year, why, they put more time, from 12:05 to 2:00. We played most of them live. We transcribed some of them. They didn't have a tape at that time. It was on just disc. They would transcribe them and lay them back and then if we had to be gone, why they would just use them. We didn't put any dates or anything on them.

We just played short dates, you know. Went in and out every night. We'd get in by maybe midnight or one or two o'clock or something and then we didn't have to get up, you see, until nine or ten o'clock because the radio show was about twelve or one. There's times when we played six nights a week. We'd have three months ahead, six nights a week. Carrying a full band. We usually had a car. Traveled in a car, most of the time.

I think the first car we had was a '37 Chevrolet and we played, I don't know, we'd been playing maybe six months and we paid cash for a brand new Cadillac after about six months. We traded the '37 to a '39 Cadillac, kept it a couple of months and then bought the new '47 Cadillac.

There's a lot of time to pass in the car, and of course when we had George Shuffler with us, me and him, we traded a lot. Now George could make pretty good company with most any kind of a crowd he was in and we'd just trade. Like horses, you know. We'd exchange horses and so forth. If we saw three or four in a pasture going along, why we'd stop and look at them and find out all about them and everything and maybe sometime buy one.

Horse is about the only game we'd play, except car. Now we played car some, you know. Like every car you meet, maybe one will take a Chevrolet and one will take a Ford or something. Chevrolet and a Ford's the most popular, you know, of all the cars and whichever one you meet—the game goes to eleven and if you see eleven Chevrolets or eleven Fords, why that's the winner, see. Or horses goes the same way. Now a gray horse counts three and a spotted horse counts two and every other horse counts one. We used to count a white mule as a game until we got to arguing so much that if there was one little black hair, you know, on a white mule we wouldn't let him have it. We'd have to stop and go see if we could find the black hair. So we ruled that out, just started counting him as three.

We'd rehearse at times. Not too much but sometimes. We didn't discuss too much business. Really all the business that was to be discussed was between Carter and myself, see, so we didn't discuss it too much. I mean, everybody'd understand everything before we'd start, you know, and then if there was any business to be discussed, why it was usually between the two of us and we'd usually get to ourselves to do that.

We continued on Bristol till about 1958 and then we moved, went to Live Oak, Florida. Started Suwannee River Jamboree. We needed to move somewhere, you know, because we felt like we was wore out around the Bristol section. And we talked to Cas Walker some and he wanted us to come to Knoxville and start but we decided to try Florida and if it didn't work out, why we'd go to Knoxville, see. We just heard that they'd been having some playing down that way and just went down there. So we wound up in Florida and after we'd been there a few months we got on television circuit and worked it a little over five years, with the Jim Walter Corporation, shell home builders. We had a circuit there about five years—five nights a week—television. All over Florida, Georgia, and part of Alabama and some of Mississippi. For three or four years, why we had about all we could do, playing television and Sunday open houses and so forth like that. I'd say that from '57 to '61 was really about the best we ever had financially. When we quit doing the television, why, we still lived there and traveled out. Then from '63 to '66, why we just maybe went in there once a month.

We signed with King in 1958, Syd Nathan. I guess we stayed with them ten or eleven years. And Syd was most responsible for us starting to use lead guitar. He wanted something that the Delmore Brothers had used. They'd been successful with the guitars. They thought we ought to get away from the mandolin because nearly all the bluegrass bands used a mandolin. And they wanted us to get the lead guitar in and get a different sound, which we did. Bill Napier was the first we played the guitar with. He was on the first session. After that George Shuffler done the lead guitar playing after the first album.

I think the way we discovered George, we played a little school about fifteen or twenty miles from his home in Valdese. Let's see, Salem School, I believe right out of Morgantown, North Carolina. And of course, I believe at that time—no, we didn't either, we hadn't got Lester Woodie. Lester Woodie come from the same place George did and George and all his brothers was out that night and all of them's musicians, and that's the way we found him. And then the others, why, you'd just hear of them here and there or they'd call you or write you wanting a job, you know. So you'd tell them to come in and you'd listen to them and you'd like about one out of ten you'd hear.

But after '61 or '62 we didn't carry a full band. The reason was that maybe we'd play two weeks and off two or something and not keep anyone on a regular salary except George, of course. We'd pay George a regular salary whether he'd play or not and if we'd play two weeks out of the month why he'd draw his money, see. We couldn't afford to do a full band that way. But we could take George and just about serve as a full band, you know.

But we was having some hard times. We went places where we'd have to play the show before we could afford to eat supper or buy gas to get home with. But Carter, I couldn't tell a bit of difference in him than if we'd had a million dollars in our pocket. Carter was a showman. If it affected him, he didn't show it. I would have given up I guess several times if it hadn't been for him. He'd hold me right to it.

His health had been failing him, but I didn't think it was that bad until about six weeks before he died. Carter was a wonderful MC. He could please any kind of crowd. I was always backward about MCing. But, you know, about a year before he died, he seemed to want me to do a lot of talking. I don't know whether he knew that he might not be around. Sometimes I'd say "No" and he'd just walk off the stage. I'd either come up and talk or it'd be blank. The same way on radio stations when we'd guest. So I done a little of it, and the way it turned out, it was good that I had.

But he wouldn't give up. He just said, "I'm gonna make it. Don't worry about me." One time a doctor told him he'd give him about another year. The doctor was older than Carter and Carter told me, "I'll be around long after he crosses the line." He felt like nothing could conquer him. The night before he died we made plans and called to buy a bus. He always wanted a bus to travel in. That night he hemorrhaged. He had cancer, I guess, of the liver.

At the time he died, I really didn't know what to do. I didn't know how the people would take to it without him. And there wasn't too much else I was really qualified to do. I didn't know much else to do, except going down to labor and hard work and I never did like that. It was about three weeks until we had anything else booked.

I didn't know how sponsors would feel about showing up without him.

Then I started getting all kinds of cards and letters from fans saying, "Don't let us down" and "If you quit, why you've let us down and you've let Carter down." They encouraged me and everywhere I went, they were right behind me. I just don't know how to thank the people for it.

Of course, that helped me up. I just made up my mind that was all I could do and I was going to do it. About six or seven months after Carter died, I went to Syd Nathan and told him that I would like to record, and I asked him if he wanted me to stay on with him. And he said, "Why not? The Stanley Brothers have really done well for us and who knows, you might do better."

Now I really wanted someone maybe not necessarily to sound like Carter, but I wanted him to sing the same style. So Larry Sparks, well, Carter and me went up that way in Ohio and Michigan a few times and Larry played the lead guitar. He played two or three shows with us. But he didn't sing any songs. I didn't know he could sing. But when Carter died, why, we played up that way somewhere and Larry called me and said, "I'd like to audition as a singer for you." I didn't have any idea that he could sing or anything like that but—I don't remember where it was but he met me somewhere and sung and I hired him.

He says it was Dayton? Well, I'd say it was cause we used to just nearly live in Dayton and Cincinnati and Columbus and Middletown and around those places. We just mostly played them clubs, bars and things. That's about all there was to play. Yeah, I call them clubs. It's like Roy Acuff, I was listening to the Ralph Emery show a while ago, "Nashville Now." Roy Acuff was on, and his first band name was Roy Acuff and the Crazy Tennesseans. And Ralph asked him, he said, "Well, how come you changed your name?" And he said, Well, when he went to the Grand Ole Opry, was it Jack Stone? Who was it? Some Stone. He said since Nashville was a big station he thought that was sort of a slur on the state of Tennessee, Crazy Tennesseans. Said, "You're from the Smoky Mountains. Why don't you call yourself the Smoky Mountain Boys?" He said, "I agreed and that's why I changed it." And so that's why I say clubs instead of bars.

Roy Lee Centers, I'd known him for a long time. Carter and me, we played up in Ohio where he was at. Him and another fellow had a little group they called the Lee Brothers and they made some records and sung together, and Roy always admired Carter and would say that in his opinion Carter was the greatest lead singer that's ever been in this kind of music. Roy would always come out to our shows and I knew Roy real well.

So after Larry Sparks left, why I knew about Roy so I just gave him a call and he was ready to go. And that tickled me very much because in my opinion I wouldn't have traded Roy Lee for any other singer in bluegrass at the time.

I really don't know whether he tried to sound like Carter or not. But he did sound a lot like him and I don't know, it just seemed like it fell in place, that he'd do a song just exactly like Carter. And there were so many things in Roy's actions and in Roy's ways that he'd do that I can remember Carter doing. I don't know why it was. You know, I guess a lot of things are meant to be and I guess maybe this was.

About 6:30 or 7 o'clock one morning I was in the bed and the telephone rang and it was beside the bed and I answered it and it was Roy Lee's little boy, Lennie. I don't remember how old he was then, but he was real young. He just said, "Daddy's been killed. A fellow shot him last night."

Now Keith Whitley and Ricky Skaggs had already been with me while Roy Lee was with me. And when we went to Roy Lee's funeral, why Keith and his mother and dad was there. Keith wasn't doing anything. He was washing dishes, I reckon, at a place there somewhere, at a restaurant. Well, the funeral all went through and everything and there wasn't a word mentioned. And I knew all the time I'd like to have Keith and I thought Keith wanted a job but neither one of us didn't mention it.

So we left and we stopped up at a restaurant in Jackson to eat and Keith and his daddy and mother was there. Well, they invited me over to the booth to sit with them and while we were sitting there why Elmer, Keith's daddy, said, "If you ever need a lead singer I know where you can get one." I said, "Well, I need one right now." So he started the next week. That's how it happened.

That was on—let's see. Roy's funeral was on a Sunday, I believe, and we was playing somewhere in Mississippi on Saturday the next week and I had to take my Shriner's degree in Roanoke, Virginia, on Saturday. That was on the same day, the same day as to be in Mississippi. So I went to Roanoke and took my Shriner's degree. Caught a plane. Boys left and went on. And I landed somewhere in Mississippi and Carl Jackson's daddy met me at the plane and took me out to the place about fifteen minutes before we was to go on, the festival. I got out of the car and walked up and they already had their instruments on, tuned up with them and I got on the stage and done the show. Keith knew everything that I did. I wasn't afraid, I wasn't a bit afraid to call on something. I knew he'd know it. That's the way it's always been.

Now, that Shriner's degree, a Shriner is a thirty-second degree. That's what I went to take, when we had that date in Mississippi. The highest degree that you can make in a Shriner is a thirty-third degree. But you've really got to be somebody, I mean, somebody. You've got to go overseas to get that degree. And Harry Truman, President Harry Truman, and Colonel Sanders is the only two people that I know of—I know they's a lot more but that's the only people that I know that had a thirty-third degree. You see, a Mason's is a third degree, and you got to go through twenty-nine more degrees, which I did, to get the Shriner. See, the Masonry is a secret organization. You can't let none of it out. But most of it is based on things from, you know, other countries. Strictly, the Bible. If you live a third degree Mason it's as good as any church you ever walked in the door. If you lived it. That's all it is. It's strictly religious. I wouldn't take nothing for it.

How I met Keith and Ricky? Well, we were playing a little club in Louisa, Kentucky, and we were late getting there. The man that ran the place knew Ricky and Keith. We got there and they was on stage, filling in for us. And they sounded identical, I thought, to the way Carter and me sounded when we first started. They had it down better than anyone I've ever heard. And they knew more of our old songs than I did! They wanted to get started in music, so I took them on the road with me. I didn't pay them much—I paid them all I could, but I had a full group. I wanted to get them exposed, and to show people that there was more people who could do that kind of singing. Some of these days—in the next forty or fifty years—I'll probably be through and I'd like to see the young generation keep it going. And they could.

Emmylou Harris recorded one of our songs, "The Darkest Hour Is Just before Dawn." She recorded two or three that we put on record, like "Going up Home to Live in Green Pastures." Ricky Skaggs told me that they had recorded "Vision of Mother"—him and Emmylou and Dolly Parton, I believe. He was wanting me to come in and dub a vocal part. Now that Ricky's left Emmylou, I don't know whether it's being released or what's happened to it.

John Duffey told me one time he'd like to sometime record a song or two and sing the high baritone. And I think John Duffey is a wonderful entertainer, a good singer and a good mandolin player and is one of the fellows that started the original Country Gentlemen. I think he's got a fine sound. So we recorded two songs with him, "The Fields Have Turned Brown" and "Lonesome River."

About a year after Carter passed away, I decided it was just too much traveling and I'd get a little closer to where we had been playing. So I just moved back to Virginia and been here ever since. I moved back in '68, I believe, April '68. We stayed with my mother there a little while and after that we had this house trailer about two year and a half. I thought about building a house right on top there, where the cemetery is, until I bought six acres between there and Coeburn out on the highway. It was lonesome for my wife Jimmie for a while but I think she's used to it now.

Now Jimmie, let's see, I met her at a show. Her and her sister and her brother-in-law come out to a show in Cincinnati, Ohio. And I saw her and I thought she was the prettiest thing I ever saw so I began sort of making little passes at her. But she just said, "Why, who's that? Why I wouldn't fool with him." Course she told me this later. Said, "Why Lord have mercy, I wouldn't have him." Anyway, I got down to talk to them. I went down to the table to talk to them. Asked them to come back the next night. And her sister and brother-in-law, they was real good fans of ours, you know. They wanted to come back, but she said no, she wouldn't come back at all. Well, she said that night she dreamed I kissed her. So she said when it come to the time that next night to come back she just couldn't stay away. So that was her undoing right there. We played up that way a lot, so every time we'd come out why she'd, I call her, she'd come out. That's the way I met her. There she is, stuck.

Anyway, all our work is up this way. I was staying away from home three or four weeks at a time. I just decided it was too much traveling. Here, you see, anywhere I go out, it's handy. I keep the bus at Coeburn. When we go out to a show, we just meet wherever we are. If we're going through Kentucky into Ohio or that way, why we meet down that way, and if we're going the other way, then they meet me in Coeburn. And they all come together and pick each other up along the way. Jack Cooke's closest. He lives in Norton. That's about twenty-five miles, I guess. Well, Curly's about that close the way the crow flies, but you have to go around some curves and mountains. Curly's actually about forty miles.

I signed with Rebel in 1970, Charles Freeland. I've recorded for several of them but I like to record for a company that, if you feel like you want to record a certain song, you can do it. In other words you can sort of do as you please, you know. They more or less leave it up to me to select all the material and, well, most of the time—oh, about all the time—I go to the studio and record it and they never hear it or know what it is till I send it in. And I'd rather do it that way because a lot of times the record companies puts things on you that you actually can't do right and I'd rather pick out my own stuff and do it the way I want to.

We used to record them on two tracks and that way they really sounded natural, you know. They sounded just like you was up there doing it. We'd go in and record them and that's the way they came out. Right there to be pressed and put out. Now, I wouldn't want to leave my tracks open for the engineers or somebody like that to mix them because I think that I know more about how my sound ought to go than they do. Used to, back when we recorded for Columbia and Mercury and so forth, I don't know how many tracks they had but they left them as we recorded them. But now, the bigger companies, they get their engineers and they go in and they suit theirselves. A lot of them don't know what they're doing, I guess. The tracks are all right if you can get in and mix it right, and engineers, if they'll work with you, you can get them the way you want them.

After I moved back to Dickenson County I run for Circuit Court Clerk and I run for the Commissioner of Revenue. And I didn't get it, cause both times the party swapped me out. Do you know how they do the swapping? There're three or four hundred of them in the county that does that. The Republicans and the Democrats get together, see. You vote for my man and I'll vote for yours. Well, Clintwood is the county seat, and in order to win you've got to go into Clintwood with about seven hundred majority, and I never could go into Clintwood with over five hundred majority, which I done every time. So that way, they fouled me up. For clerk I got beat by about ninety-some votes. And they swapped me out that many votes. My own party done it.

I run against a fellow by the name of Teddy Bailey for clerk, see, that's a eight-year job. He done served one term and he's the most popular Republican in the county. I believe he beat me about ninety-nine votes. And he come to me afterwards and cried. He said, "Now Ralph," he said, "you know and I know that you're the most popular man in the county." And he said, "You know how I won. But when you're in politics you're out the window." Then another fellow, I went in his office one day after the election and he said, "Why, they swapped you off. One of these days I'm going to come to your house if you'll let me and I'm going to tell you exactly how it works." And he said, "You won every election you ever run but you didn't get it." There's about three or four hundred of them in Clintwood, Virginia, that swaps it out. They can get on the telephone in two nights and change it.

So I got on "Hee-Haw" and saluted Coeburn as my hometown. Well, I went over to the courthouse to pay—I believe I was getting my dog tags. I went in the treasurer's office and the treasurer run out and talked to me. He said, "I saw you on 'Hee-Haw.'" He said, "Judge Phillips said to tell you when I saw you that he was going to disown you for not saluting Clintwood." And I said, "Paul"—his name's Paul Moore—I said, "You know and Judge Phillips knows exactly why." And I said, "I'll never salute Clintwood. You can tell him I said so." And I said, "He knows exactly why. And I'll salute Coeburn the next time."

Now our festival—I just thought that Carter had done a lot for bluegrass music and you know he was buried there where I have the festival. I wanted to keep his name alive and give a lot of people a chance to come and see where Carter and me were raised and where Carter was buried and everything, and that was the main reason. Just as a respect to keep his name alive, because I think he deserves it. The only thing I've hated is that Carter done so much to pave the way for the success I'm enjoying now, and the success a lot of other people are enjoying now. It hurts me that he can't have some of it.

Why I stopped the festival? Well, I've never said too much but most of the reason I stopped it is because of the state police. They always harassed and give me a lot of trouble. And actually I never really tried myself to do too much about it. Governor Robb was governor and I had blanks filled out where a lot of people wrote him. I know that he got a thousand or more letters from the people a-telling him what was happening and he never would do anything about it. Well, the last festival I had, Governor Baliles, he was lieutenant governor then, he called me the day before the festival, he said, "If you ever have another one, you let me know and you won't have no trouble." Well, the next year he run, see, Governor Baliles did, which he's governor right now. Well, my congressman there in the ninth district is Rick Boucher. He's a good friend of mine. I played shows for him and helped him get elected and he wrote me a letter and said, "If I can ever help you, you call me at midnight or whatever and I'll help you." So about three months before the festival, in 1986, I called Rick Boucher. Told him what I was a-doing. I was having my fortieth year. He said, "Don't you worry one minute."

He said, "As soon as we hang up, I'll call Governor Baliles. Don't you worry." And he stood up to his word. I didn't have any worries this past time. And he said, "If you ever have another you let me know."

That's why that I quit having it. Some of these days I'll have another one. But actually I don't care anything about having it every year. I'd like to have it when people's really anxious and when they'd really enjoy it. Every five year, that's what I'm a-thinking. I said ten year, but I'm thinking now about every five year. It's a different sound there, different something, I don't know what. You get on one of the points up there, up there where the cemetery is or somewhere, and listen to a lot of the songs Carter wrote and figure where he got it. "White Dove" and all that. He was writing about those mountains. And it's the best sound I've ever heard on any festival. You wouldn't believe it, how it rings.

My doctor's degree? Well, this professor, Doug Gordon, at Lincoln Memorial University, he believed in this style, and he got me to come down there. He hired me two or three times to come to the university and we had classes on it. We had classes that I taught on music, you know, and he advertised it and had people to come in from several states. Let's see, I don't know, he had thirty-five or forty, maybe from Georgia, maybe from North Carolina, maybe from New York, and they stayed during that session. And I taught them all that I knew. And when I finished they gave me that degree. But I could've told them in three minutes all I know. What would I have said? I don't know nothing.

I'm not going to brag, but I'm going to tell you this little story. Like I was saying before, we went to Live Oak, Florida, in 1958, to try to hunt some new territory. Well, Carter, he went to the Chamber of Commerce in Live Oak, Florida, fellow by the name of Aubrey Fowler. He liked music and he was interested in bringing music to that part of the country. And together they set up the "Suwannee River Jamboree" which we started in 1958. Well, after we got down there and stayed a year or two, one day I was talking to Aubrey Fowler. He done a lot for us to get us down there. He said, "Ralph, I want to ask you something. Why do you stay back in the background all the time?" I said, "Well, the reason I do, I feel like Carter is much more qualified to head it than I am." "Well," he said, "I'm going to tell you something. Carter's a lot better talker than you are. But," he said, "two words from you means more than a hundred from Carter." I never forgot that. I didn't—that didn't mean it was true, you know. But he told me them words.

Junior Blankenship and Charlie Sizemore? Well, I met both of them when they were very young. Junior, he's a close neighbor of mine, maybe twenty or twenty-five mile, and I saw him about when I first started my festival in 1970. He was a very young boy then but he was playing and he was about ten years old. And he had played the first festival, I think, with his daddy, Hillard. They had a group called the Rocky Mountain Boys and I saw him every year. I judged a contest or two that he entered in school. And of course, Charlie Sizemore, he's from Kentucky and we knew his daddy from away back. That's Henry Clay Sizemore. He was principal of some schools there in Kentucky and we played some of the schools. And couple of times we went home with his father and stayed all night with him. Charlie was a very small boy then. He was so small that he'd sit in Curly Ray's lap and try to play the fiddle a little bit. And then we saw him around personal appearances and everything all up through the years, you know.

And he'd play rhythm guitar and do the lead singing and do a lot of business for me when I wasn't around or not available or felt bad or something. I sort of called him my business manager. And of course Junior, he still plays the lead guitar and sings a solo now and then on stage.

I'm real proud that I was able to carry on but there's a lot of difference from when Carter was around. Now I have everything to see to and I realize that he did help me a lot, you know. I realize what a burden he had on his shoulders that I didn't have.

I do most of the booking. Now and then they's an agency—well, they's two or three agencies in Nashville, Tennessee, that book me some. They call in, and if I don't have it booked, why, I take it. But I'm not exclusive with them. I do my own booking.

The shows are the way you make money in this particular kind of music. They might be some of the big country stars now that really get a hit record that gets them way down in the number one class, you know, and keep right on and on, they's good money, but bluegrass entertainers don't receive too much royalties.

My sound, I guess it just changed without me knowing it. I wanted to keep as near as I could the same sound, but I guess maybe it didn't. Sort of getting more of a, I don't know what you would call it, a lonesomer sound. I don't know. A mountain sound, or something. It might have just happened, and then seems like, in the last few years, I've tried to make it as natural as I could, the way I felt it. Back in earlier years, I guess it takes a fellow a while to really get till he don't care to let himself just come out the way he feels. It might have been at times that I held back a little bit, maybe just didn't put it out exactly the way I felt it, and in the last few years I've done that. I'd say that's about the way it is.

I never tried to copy anyone on singing tenor. Just like I'm talking right now, the way it comes out is the way it's coming. I'm one of the very few—well now, I'd say Bill Monroe does too—I just about lead the lead singer with my tenor. There's not many tenor singers that does that. I can sing tenor on any song that I know without the lead, with every turn and everything in it that I do. I don't listen to the lead; I just sing it and they're usually in with me.

Where do I get material? Just here and there. Sometimes I write one; sometimes one of the Clinch Mountain Boys will write it. Or people's all the time sending in songs and things. I guess I've got ten thousand that I'll probably never get to look at. Maybe a hit song buried, just laid up somewhere. And people, you know, might know some old songs and maybe send me one. I always like to learn any of the old stuff that hasn't been put out by other people. I like the old songs. Now, "Going round This World, Baby Mine," I believe I first heard that in Renfro Valley, Kentucky, played by Lily May and the Coon Creek Girls. "Jacob's Vision" I learned from Enoch Rose; he was a Free Will Baptist preacher from Caney Ridge, Virginia. "Village Church Yard" we learned at the McClure Church. Our dad and his brother, Jim Henry Stanley, used to lead that one. He worked for Dad; used to drive a team of horses for him in the woods logging. And he would come home with Dad now and then and they would set up late at night and sing a lot of the old songs like that.

"Arkansas Traveler" or "How Far to Little Rock," we learned that from a fellow by the name of Fletcher Moss. He was from Pike County, Kentucky, and one of our older brothers had a house built and he was a carpenter and he built the house for our brother. And on weekends when he didn't go home, he would come up and stay with us because we was trying to play a little bit, you know. He'd bring his fiddle and he would come up an play some and he would do that "Arkansas Traveler" and he would ask the questions and answer them too, you see. And he had a banjo with a guitar neck on it. It had six pegs up on it, you know, keys, but still it just had five strings. I bought that one from him and that's about the second one I ever had.

Now "Little Glass of Wine," we heard a fellow do a little bit of that. He had the melody to it, and we wrote a lot of the words to it. This fellow worked for W. M. Ritter Lumber Company; his name was Otto Taylor. That was back in '37 or '38. He played the banjo—used one finger and thumb. Didn't learn any other songs from him. "Drunkard's Hell," that's a song we heard our daddy do. If I hear a song I like and feel that I can put it in our style, you know, I do it. I can sort of feel how I can do it the best, clawhammer or finger style; I can just sort of feel it.

Back home, you will find some of the best singers, maybe musicians, that's never played off their back porch. Sometimes you see them in jam sessions but sometimes they don't even do that. They just play for their family.

I like to sing gospel. I believe in it and a lot of people I think do too. We've always sung gospel. We were raised in the churches, you know; we were raised to sing gospel and respect gospel music. I'm not necessarily trying to convert people with it, but it would tickle me if I knew I did. And which, I have got letters and so forth from people that said it had, you know, and I feel good that they do.

Singing is the weak spot in bluegrass. Now, I feature singing more than I do instruments. I've always liked it better. If I sing a song I think people want to hear the song. Course, it's good to have some music to take a break, but the song is what they're interested in. The instruments are there to bolster up the singing.

What do I listen for in a song? Well, mostly the feeling. Course the words are important too. It's hard to say. Me, I like it just as lonesome as you can get it. Something that'll bring tears, sweat, this that and another. That might be the difference in the sound I've gotten since Carter. Carter didn't like them as lonesome as I did, I guess. He always wanted to experiment. He still liked to keep it right and keep it down simple, but he would experiment if he could add a little something. And we're doing more of the Old Baptist songs now. More of an old-time sound to it. I guess the material has a lot to do with it.

I like to sing better than I do to play. I know you need the instruments, but I enjoy singing the most. That might be one reason that we've done a lot of a cappella songs—without music. But I might write another banjo tune, if I can ever get up enough energy to just start fooling around. That's the way that I wrote all of the banjo tunes that I've put out, is just be a-messing around with it and just something come to me. I don't think I could just sit down and go right into one.

As far as I'm concerned, I like pretty plain picking myself. A lot of entertainers will notice you more if you put in a lot of hot licks and play here and there and play all around it. But I've found out through my experience that the entertainers don't pay to get in, pay to see me, you know. And I don't make too much money off the entertainers. I make my money off of the public, the people that likes to hear it the way it is.

When I play the banjo, I do my best to make them strings sound just exactly like I'm a-saying it. Like I'm singing it. You know, Curly Ray Cline, he plays the fiddle sort of like I play the banjo. He plays it the way he feels it and he tries to play it as near to the melody as he can. I heard a lot of people come up to him one night and request a certain tune, you know, and say, "Well, we heard some-one play this but he left this out of it, and he left that, and we want to hear you play it, because when you play it you play every note of it."

Curly's a good singer. I tried to get him to sing a couple on his gospel album. And he wouldn't do any. But I made the remark just a while ago that I could sing a lot better with, could feel a lot more, singing with Curly Ray than I could a certain fellow that traveled some with us and was supposed to be a lead singer. And I mean that. Curly ain't a bad singer. I like playing with him. I recorded one or two with him. I helped him with those albums. He was afraid to risk—you see, he recorded his own and had them released him-self. And I told him to go ahead and record the album and make five hundred of them. And I said, "What you lack in getting your expenses back, why I'll buy the rest of them." That's the only way I could get him to record. I said, "That way you can't lose. I'll pay your expenses, take the albums."

That National Heritage Award, well, this fellow Joe Wilson called me and asked me if I would accept it and I didn't know what it was all about. I said, "What is it?" He began to tell me. And I said, "Why, of course I will." He said, "It'll pay you five thousand dollars in cash." And all expenses to Washington, back. And I said, "Why, cer-tainly I will." Bring the band and everybody. Which we did. Took the family. They got us rooms and treated us real well. We went to the Capitol, met some of the senators, went to the Mike Mansfield room.

One senator, he was a Republican, which, now I've always been a Democrat, but Senator Warner from Virginia. You've heard of him. He married Liz Taylor. He brought his camera crew and all his people and come out and hunted me up and told me how proud he was of me. And you know what I done the next November the second? I voted for Senator Warner. And I will again, too. He took pictures of me and Jimmie and the family and sent me some of them and buddy just treated me right at home and some of the Democrats didn't. He made me a follower of him right now.

We performed in the Capitol some but the award was at the Ford

Theater. And the president was supposed to award it but somehow he was out of town or something happened. He was afraid to come or that was sort of during a critical time or—and he didn't present it but he was supposed to. But anyhow, he wrote me a letter after that and apologized and signed, him and Nancy, and told me how sorry he was that he couldn't be there to present it and how proud he was of me and all that stuff.

I'm not especially a Reagan man but I'm going to tell you, everything that I've ever received has been through the Republican administrations. I'm still a Democrat, but when I got the Virginia Music Hall of Fame a Republican, Governor Dalton, was in, and when I got the National Heritage Award Reagan was in. And a Chevrolet dealer, Bartley Chevrolet in Haysi, Virginia, give me a big award a little while ago from the county of Dickenson County, a Republican, stating what I had done for the county and had never been recognized like I should have been by the officials. That was another Republican. Everything I've ever got's been through the Republican administrations.

How the Stanleytone banjo got started, I met Frank Neat I guess twenty-five or thirty years ago up in Indiana, Bean Blossom, and he come around and talked to me. I was playing this old Mastertone and he said, "That's the best sounding banjo I ever heard. I'll tell you what I'd like to do. It's a long ways off, but some day I'd like to make you a banjo and give it to you, one that'll sound just like it. If you'll let me take that old banjo home with me and go through it, look it over, I'll make you a direct copy of it."

Well, he did. I let him take it. He took my old one. And years later, why he made that banjo and give it to me. So then we just come up with the idea. He said, "Why don't you let me make you some of them and sell them?" So that started the Stanleytone. But the one he made me, he put my name on the neck, got "Ralph Stanley." Oh, it was a pretty thing. But I couldn't play it. I'm dumb, I couldn't find the positions. And I told him I couldn't and I said, "I'm going to sell it and then I'll just pay you for another one." He said okay. So I sold it to a boy I believe in North Wilkesboro, North Carolina. He's got it now. Got "Ralph Stanley" in great big letters.

Eighties compare with the fifties? Well, they's been a lot of changes. Used to, back in the fifties, we played several nights during the week, like drive-in theaters, indoor theaters, played more schools and so forth. And the festivals—you know, the first festival I believe was in 1965, and that changed bluegrass music all around. I don't remember when we played the first colleges, and that changed things some, too. But the bluegrass festivals have been highlighting just a whole new era I think for bluegrass music.

And the audiences are different now. Bigger all the time. Carter and me stayed together a long time and recorded I reckon around forty long-play albums but people have come up to me every day and say they never heard the Stanley Brothers, that the first they heard was me, as far as the Stanleys was concerned. And I have so many that say that they never saw the Stanley Brothers together.

I think it's changed now and I think it's gotten much better in Nashville. A lot of the younger folks are coming to the festivals, a lot of college people and right on up to the grandmothers and grandpas. All ages like bluegrass music. And a lot of the people that live in the cities and suburbs now are from the country, maybe used to live in the country and moved in. And I think enough of their teaching and so forth for their children that they raise up now will rub off on them enough to keep it like that, you know.

And it seems that the young people are doing a good job. There's a lot of good bands coming on now but in my opinion there's not really enough of the young ones that's doing the old-time traditional bluegrass. I believe the ones that are playing the old sound in years to come will reap a better harvest. The Wilson Brothers is a good group that's doing it traditional. And the Johnson Mountain Boys, I'd say they're traditional. But there's really not too many that don't jump in there and tear it up a little, somewhere.

There'll be some that'll hold in the old sound, course I'd say the majority will go to the more modern type. They's not too many people that can really play the old-time way. You've got to feel the old-time way to play it. And they's a lot of people don't feel it any more. I really think that bluegrass if it's sung right and done right and the proper feeling put to it is the hardest music in the world to play.

I believe it's a gift that you have. You know, people can go to college and learn to do things and they can sit down and learn to play the banjo and the fiddle after hearing somebody else do it, and catch on to that. But actually I believe to play what I call real down to earth music, it just about has to be born and bred into a man and be a gift from God for him to really feel it and do it in a proper way.

I'd like to be remembered as an old-timer that put forty or fifty years, the best years of his life, into the music business, and a fellow that believed in respecting it, and not—in other words, when I go on the stage I like to be well dressed and when I get off the stage I don't like to be out swapping around with the general public a-drinking and rip-rapping and things like that. I believe a man ought to hold himself up and respect it. I do, because everything I've got, the music has given it to me, and I respect it, and it would hurt me real bad just—I know I'm not going to abuse it and I'd hate to see anybody else.

Mother would play banjo when I'd ask her round home, you know. She died in May, 1973; she was eighty-six. She was always in favor of us playing. She liked it herself, you know. Daddy died in 1961; he was seventy-three. After we got on the radio he booked for us and helped us. They were real proud of our music. They always felt that religion had its place and music had its place and neither didn't interfere with the other. They believed that it depended on the individual. My music? I don't know what you'd call it. I think it's old-time mountain music.

6

Joe Wilson

"I can't even contemplate being the kind of singer that Ralph is"

Many of the older generation of bluegrass musicians are apt to imagine that they are surrounded by secret enemies. In Ralph Stanley's case the fact is that he is surrounded by secret friends. Joe Wilson, currently director of the National Council for the Traditional Arts (NCTA), is one of the best of these.

Wilson's life reads like a latter-day Jack London novel. He came from the easternmost tip of Tennessee, from Trade, Johnson County, in the heart of the Appalachians. He pieced an education together for himself here and there, and worked at various times as a union organizer, civil rights worker, journalist, and advertising agent, from Alabama to New York City. It was a strange odyssey for a boy from the hills, but when he describes it, it seems the most natural thing in the world.

As Wilson says, traditional music was always in the background, and often in the foreground, of what he was doing during these years. He worked in Nashville during the time—a nightmarish time for lovers of bluegrass—in which what was then called country and western music was being transformed into a broad-scaled medium of popular entertainment. It was this transformation, he maintains, and not the growing popularity of rock and roll, which caused such great damage to the cause of traditional music during the period. The eye with which he viewed this phenomenon was wise and sophisticated, and we have to take seriously his contention that, despite the contrary views of many fans and entertainers, there was no nefarious conspiracy behind it.

This calm, nonparanoid stance is refreshing and no doubt correct. Great events are seldom as well organized as they appear to be in retrospect, and from the outside. Still, his case as a whole, if only because it is so well put, deserves a response. Older bluegrass artists continue to maintain that it was the advent of rock and roll that virtually put an end to their business, and it must be admitted that they have a point. After all, the commercialization Wilson speaks of had been going on for a very long time, all the way back to the days of Vernon Dahlhart, a trained light-classical singer who had a huge success selling pop-style covers of such traditional songs as "The Wreck of the Old 97" as far back as the twenties. And old-timer Carl Sauceman recalls how record distributors were pushing the popularized recordings of Eddy Arnold in 1947 (much to their surprise, the people in the area Sauceman was working—"Stanley country," in fact—preferred the Stanley Brothers).

Commercialization, then, was nothing new. But in the early fifties country singers and bluegrass musicians could comfortably share the same stage, as the Stanley Brothers did with Webb Pierce and the Wilburn Brothers on the Louisiana Hayride program. Unfortunately all that was soon due to change. In August, 1954, the Brothers recorded "Blue Moon of Kentucky," and Bill Monroe, who was present at the session, encouraged Carter Stanley to hew as closely as he could to the style of Elvis Presley in making the cut. The same session produced Ralph Stanley's great banjo instrumental, "Hard Times," and Stanley's later explanation of the tune's title is succinct, and its implications inescapable: "We were having some *hard times*." The Brothers' Mercury contract soon expired; they were never again to work for a truly major label. And all this was years before the coming of the aural-wallpaper "Nashville Sound."

It is much harder to quarrel with the other major points Wilson has to make. Bluegrass is indeed a "genuine national folk music"—always remembering that by "folk music" he does not mean the sort of thing produced in counterculture coffeehouses but rather a traditionally based music guided by a group aesthetic. And recent years have indeed seen one of its richest, most creative periods. It is difficult to convince some fans of this. Romanticizing the past—in the case of bluegrass the "past" is the late forties and early fifties—is an inevitable part of the traditionalist mentality. There have no doubt been times when even Ralph Stanley, to say nothing of his fans, believed that the glory days of the Stanley Brothers' Mercury sessions reached a height that will never be equalled, even while he was in the act of producing the masterpieces that led (thanks in no small part to Joe Wilson) to his receiving the proudest honor of his career, the National Heritage Fellowship of 1984.

———

I've been around a long time. I heard Carter and Ralph when they were on 'CYB, Bristol. I was raised between Mountain City and

Boone. I saw them in that period, too. I guess I was literally at their beginnings.

I've got a story for you about that car wreck when Ralph got hurt. My home is in Trade, Tennessee, and that accident happened in Shouns, Tennessee, on the old 421 which has now been replaced, the curve where it happened. I'm from the next wide place in the road further on. Trade and Shouns are both between Mountain City and Boone, North Carolina. In fact, Mountain City has extended its city limits so that it now takes in Shouns.

Anyway, some time after World War II there was this fellow from Damascus, Virginia, whose name I don't know, but we called him the Old Prospector because he was sure that there was gold on top of Long Hope Mountain in North Carolina. Long Hope is a plateau that runs along there. It's nearly six thousand foot in altitude. It's a vast tract of land that was owned I believe at that point by the Vicks Chemical Company. The Old Prospector had a surplus World War II jeep and he would work very hard at what he was trying to do. Every morning he'd come up the road from his home at Damascus, beyond Mountain City, about fourteen miles. He'd come on up by our house into North Carolina about six in the morning. And he'd work until 2:30, and 3:30 he'd come back down the road heading home. He was very regular. But his driving was a little bit, ah, offhand, shall we say. He had one of those tendencies to swing wide on the curves. Well, it was him that the Stanley Brothers were dodging when they rolled their car on that curve out there. And they also hit the jeep, though they tried very hard to avoid it. Tore it up considerably. Didn't hurt the Old Prospector none. Banged Ralph up rather badly. But the Old Prospector was not put out of business by that.

But for years thereafter, if I was going to town—we were living on a farm then, I didn't have a car and it was nine miles and too far for my bicycle. If I was going to town I'd go over and hitchhike a ride. And usually in the summer time I was through work by 3 or 3:30, and I'd be over and the Old Prospector would always pick me up. And the conversation was always the same. I would get in and he'd say, "Hello, son." "How do you do, sir." "You going to town?" "Yes, sir." "Well, I guess we'll make it if we don't run into the Stanley Brothers."

I don't know that Ralph even knows that it was the Old Prospector that sent him to the hospital. I never told him.

It was Pee Wee Lambert with Ralph in the car? Well, you know, there was always a question of why Carter and Ralph weren't working together at the time, and I think at one point it became convenient to say that Ralph wrecked and therefore—whereas probably something else was the problem. That gets into the complexities of relationships between brothers and bands, you know.

Anyway, my family was interested in music. My father sung in a gospel group at one point, sung in a quartet, Baptist church of course. One of my uncles was a fiddler, my father's older brother. One of my maternal great-uncles was a fine guitarist. I grew up right square in the middle. Tom Ashley lived six miles down the road. Frank Proffitt lived four miles across the mountain.

I played bass in a band when I was in high school. I came to Nashville in '59, stayed through '62, and those were tough years for traditional music. A lot of that's been blamed on rock and roll, Elvis, those folks. I don't really think they were so much the problem as it was that the industry had decided that it was going to make country music palatable to the great American middle class and it was going to take all of those rough edges that it imagined offended those people off. So the banjo and the fiddle had to go. Owen Bradley at one point—I worked some at Bradley's place—he just wanted no fiddles. He was putting doo-wah choruses and lots of guitar and all kinds of things to soothe the fevered mind of the middle class, you know. If you ask me to cite a meeting devoted to this, a conspiracy, there wasn't one. Just the consensus.

And you have to say that it worked. If you have no aesthetic sensibility about the music it worked just fine. It made it one of the major musics. This is industrialized art, you know. Nashville makes records with roughly the same set of sensibilities that General Motors makes hubcaps. The question is not whether it's good or beautiful but will it sell? Will the people buy it? And you have a formulaic way of figuring out where the world is going, getting there just a little ahead of it. That's all.

They're mainly nice people in Nashville, you know. I don't have anything bad to say about them. It's an industry. That's the way an industry's supposed to operate. They're corporations, there to maximize the profits of their stockholders. But unfortunately I came from another place. I really liked that other music that was getting dumped in the waste can. I loved it. And I thought that something could be done with it. And if I was going to evangelize, I was going to evangelize it.

I know how to evangelize. At one point I ended up working for seven years on Madison Avenue. I wasn't selling music there but I found out I could sell stuff. And in doing that kind of work you have kind of a detached view of it, you know. Doesn't have anything to do with anything except making money. And if you're satisfied just to make money, if you want to spend your life just making money, it's a good place to go. And I guess a lot of them felt that way.

I met a lot of nice people in Nashville. I liked Marty Robbins. I worked for him for a little while. Great guy. I knew Willie Nelson, think he's a fine guy. Roger Miller was there at the time and he's a crazy, nice guy. And I still have friends there. I like Skaggs a lot and I worked with him a number of years. I think he's good for Nashville. And I like the Whites, they're really great people. And they're good for the town, too.

But there came a time in 1962 when I said the hell with this. And I went my own way. Went down to Birmingham for the steelworkers for a while, working with advertising, fundraising, that kind of thing. I was the editor of the *Southern Steelworker.* Traveled some for them for a little. Wound up after that on Madison Avenue in New York. I never quit monkeying with the music. I kept on working with records, most of it just for my own amusement. Then I met people like Dave Freeman and the Rounders in the early seventies. Got involved with making records. I've done about fifty albums, in one way or another. Either done everything with them, or written notes. Mostly it was just finding people that needed to be recorded and getting them to somebody who would record them. I'm still doing that.

The NCTA? No, it's not government. Private sources. 501 (c)(3). Tax deductible. We do a lot of work for the government, though. Those tours a lot of those guys have been on and things. I was serving on the panel for the National Endowment for the Arts, advising the United States Information Agency as to what it ought to send abroad to represent this country. In 1980 I joined a little advisory board. We've been able to change to some degree what was being sent. We've managed to get some of the things I feel are a little more representative of the country sent over.

That cost me a lot of hours, largely free time. They pay me seventy-five dollars a year. We're supposed to have one meeting a year when the recommendations get made, you know. I've probably had a conversation with those folks once a week. So it's really my work as a citizen. Everybody needs to do a little work as a citizen. But there've been a tremendous number of bands that've been abroad now. Johnson Mountain Boys, Jim and Jesse, Thomason and the Dry Branch Fire Squad, Bluegrass Cardinals, Buck White, Ricky Skaggs, Quicksilver, Byron Berline, David Holt, Red Clay Ramblers. That's all since then.

But that's not the NCTA's work, you know. That's just me. The

NCTA was a contractor for the USIA on a Caribbean tour earlier this year, Jamaica, the Bahamas. But mainly it's just been me as a volunteer, and a committee member, trying to be a good citizen of the country as well as a friend to some of the better people who play our music.

A few years ago we did these cowboy tours, working cowboys, not Hollywood cowboys, people that had spent their lives on horses, working wild cattle. It was a great experience, and I began to wonder why the horseman through history had been romanticized. What was it? And it was an idealizing of the past. There's an antiquarian bias that affects, afflicts a lot of us. You know, the real heroes are always back there somewhere. You can find that in Moslem history, you know. You can find it in—hell, you can find it in Jerusalem when Christ was born, because the people who were really honored were the shepherds. They were up in the fields. But it was not the publicans, the innkeepers.

If you look at that through the filter of a folklorist it tells you something about people. Now I know that there're people who look at it very reverently and I was raised near the Cross, you know, but I've learned to look at things other ways, too. It's okay to look at it very reverently. I don't have any problem with that. But there's this romanticizing—and I think that's always been true of traditional music in this country. And you can see it in a lot of other things other than bluegrass music. All that says, again, all that screams at you, is you're dealing with tradition, buddy. You're dealing with the way people keep tradition in order. You're dealing with a group aesthetic.

What other goddamned music is there in this country that you can find all over the country that has a group aesthetic? Any group aesthetic for country music? Hell, no. You can do anything, and the audience won't care. It'll either buy it or it won't. But you float something into bluegrass and people get indignant about it. You see it in the letters to the editor of *Bluegrass Unlimited.* That's group aesthetic. This fighting of tradition, non-tradition in there, that's group aesthetic. So by definition deeply folk music. Now a lot of my bluegrass buddies, they think of folk in terms of Pete Seeger and Joan Baez and they don't know what the hell I'm talking about. But you know about that. Yeah.

So the funny thing about bluegrass is that it's not an industry directed music now. It's a genuine folk music. It's probably the closest that there is to a genuine, honest-to-God national folk music that we have. I believe that, and I've worked on folk music things either for fun or for my living for the last thirty-five years. It's been a great period, this recent period. Very richly productive of style, repertoire. And it's been guided by some real hard-headed aesthetic. I think it's been a fabulous period. Anyway, I kept on doing the records, kept on working on things, putting on the fiddlers' convention back in my hometown. The people who ran the NCTA found out about me through that kind of work. Dick Spottswood was on the board. He'd met me. They just called me up one Sunday afternoon and asked me if I'd like to apply for the job. So I took a terrible salary cut.

But in the sixties I was still in Nashville. I was around and very much alive in all that period and following those guys, the Stanleys I mean. I saw them in Nashville when they were doing their Florida shtick, you know, a couple of times. Sort of kept some idea of what they were doing, you know.

Course in the sixties the folkie thing hit, but it didn't really change much for those guys. For bands that were accustomed to working a hundred seventy-five, two hundred shows a year, that was not a big thing. Because what are you going to get out of that? You're going to get maybe a dozen shows a year at most at colleges. And the pay is cheap and the only thing you really get is a little recognition, though it's a type that's very important to folks like them. Being invited to play at Harvard is a real validation if you barely finished the eighth grade.

But I remember seeing them and talking to—the last time I saw them when you could really kind of talk to Carter was in Nashville. I remember where I talked to them. They must have played the Friday Night Frolic which was then in Studio C, WSM. I remember we were standing out on the porch there in front of WSM where the landing is, and it was the last conversation I had with Carter that kind of made sense. And that would have been '60 or '61. And when I saw them after that, he was—maybe I just caught him in times when he wasn't in a talking mood, but I'd always been able to talk to him before and he knew who I was. I'm not sure that Ralph did, though Ralph was always courteous and nice.

When I talked to Carter at that time he always remembered one thing about me. He remembered where I was from, and that was where Gilliam Burton Grayson was from. G. B. Grayson, Grayson and Whitter. His name was Gilliam, not George. Named for General Alfred Gilliam, a Civil War general. Not George. I corrected that on the Grayson and Whitter County notes ten years ago. I pulled his death certificate and his pension records—he was visually handicapped and his father was a Civil War veteran, so here are all these documents in the archives that are filled out by his mother, and they had his right name.

Any rate, Carter Stanley knew where I came from, that county, and Grayson came from there. And he used a lot of Grayson's melodies and songs. Obviously had been exposed not only to all the Victors but all the Gennett records. One of the things we talked about was how we could get them, who had good copies of them. I gave him a tape. I don't think it ever affected anything he recorded, it was after he had recorded some of the early things that had—he used some Grayson and Whitter tunes, melodies, and he recorded some of the songs.

Everybody's parlor in the mountains had one of those old crank-up phonographs. I don't know whether the Stanleys had one at home or not. But Carter knew Grayson and Whitter. He knew the records. He knew not only the records. He knew that there was the Victor, he knew the Gennetts, and that means that he—the Gennetts were not distributed at all. Virtually nobody in the mountains knows about the Gennetts. It's a record label, Star Piano Company. Richmond, Indiana.

And Carter remembered that Grayson had his train start from two different places on two different records. Terminal Station in Atlanta, and the other one's New York City. Now, I'm not sure when Carter did that "Train 45." But he was eager to have all of that material. I remember we sat down and took an envelope and he wrote down the names of all of the songs he knew that Grayson and Whitter did and says, "Now if there are any others that you could give, that you got—" and I responded to it by giving him a little reel tape that had probably ten or twelve more songs.

And he was curious about Grayson. He knew that he was the fiddler and the singer and he really had an intense dislike for Whitter because he missed all those chords, and he thought it was just a pity that Grayson had to record with a guitar player that bad. But then I told him, I said, "Well, but for Whitter he would never have recorded. Whitter was the guy that got him in the studio." So he says, "Well, I guess we'll have to forgive him then." Think better of him than we otherwise would.

And Carter was interested in Mainer, J. E. Mainer, and those people. But he was not as interested in Mainer as he was in Grayson. And he was also aware of the fact that Mainer had got a lot of material from Grayson, had come to the same recordings, but he thought Grayson's were better. And I guess they were. Musically, on the balance, though there was obviously more of an ensemble sound with Mainer. And the Stanleys really were patterned after Mainer when they first went to radio much more than they were after Monroe or any of those people. That came later.

They knew Tom Ashley very well. I guess it was Tom that had filled them in first on Grayson because Tom played with Grayson a lot. He played with Grayson far more than Whitter did. Whitter was from way over in North Carolina, Ashe County. But Tom had lived nearby and had performed with Grayson for years and years. Never recorded with him.

Tom worked his Rastus Jones from Georgia act with the Stanleys. Tom was a great entertainer. He had the kind of sense of humor that tickled the hell out of Carter, which was the kind—we think of blackface stuff as being real rough, pie-in-the-face kind of stuff. It really wasn't, not in the way Tom did it. I've seen them. He had Carter doing straight man stuff on that. He had the whole band involved in some of those things, you know.

I never saw him do the full act but there's one point I saw him do it with Charlie Monroe, where—I can remember one joke with Carter and Tom. Tom has on these pants that're just a little bit short, and his galluses, you know, and he had a great mimicry of black voice. Carter says to him—this is standard in the whole act, Charlie Monroe did the same thing—Carter did it real well. "Rastus, is your pants too short?" Tom would look up and say, "No, they not," he says, "I'm just down in them too far." Light stuff like that, you know, for a long time.

Then there was part of the act where the bandleader's real busy and he hires Rastus to be a guard at his door, to keep people from bothering him, and then the band members start coming in, and each one finds some kind of reason they need to see him and Rastus puts them off with various excuses. It's a very delicate situation because he's black and they're white and he has to invent various kinds of lies, which he proves very adept in.

And Carter really liked that, but even if the racial mores hadn't changed I can't see Ralph carrying that kind of act. He was much more intently musical. Even then. Though there's a lot of humor in Ralph's act, it's more of a country boy on the store porch kind of humor, with Curly Ray and so forth. It's not that minstrel situation kind of thing, which is really a little more from the head, a little more worked out.

But Carter really liked that and he liked Ashley. I'm sure it was Ashley that told him where Grayson was from. I mean it's not very far away, one county over—Washington County, between Dickenson and Johnson County where Grayson was from. But Carter always talked to me about it and he appreciated that tape.

He knew all of Grayson and Whitter's stuff. He knew some of Tom's stuff with the Carolina Tar Heels. He knew the Mainers' stuff. He wasn't interested in the Georgia string band stuff. He was only half interested in Stoneman, he thought Stoneman was a rough singer. But that old melodic stuff, that droning fiddle, that's really the string band style from that area, you know.

With Ralph it was still the Stanley Brothers sound. That part of it was still alive. So I wasn't surprised when he continued. The only thing that he ever said to me about it, and this was six months after—I saw him in a show, and he said a lot of people had told him they wanted him to continue. He said, "I appreciate that and I'm going to." And I said, "Well, did you ever consider doing anything else?" He said sort of aside, with a grin, "Well, not for very long."

If you listen to some of those John's Gospel Quartet things that Ray Davis recorded, Carter's barely singing in them. That's Jack and Shuffler and Ralph. They were carrying the Stanley Brothers for a long, long, long time.

That was the cross Ralph Stanley had to carry. It must have just been pure hell, but that's part of being a family. You have to put up with it. You come from a place where family ties, where even an extended family will remain together a lot longer than it has in other parts of the country, you know, where extended families don't count so much any more. Brothers now are people that you grew up with and not brothers. I mean you can't even have the brotherhood ideal politically or in unions or other things because you don't have brothers any more in this society. Ralph Stanley was a brother, so he put up with a lot from a brother. And never a harsh word has fallen from Ralph Stanley's lips about his brother. I never heard him say a thing bad about Carter.

You know these contradictions that exist in hillbillies. It was at the Old Home Place, a bunch of the old boys from over on the edge of Kentucky. I was sitting there one night, one of them picking a banjo and the other one a guitar. I've forgotten these boys' names. They're always there. They'd been doing their Stanley Brothers style stuff. They sung a verse of a Stanley song, maybe it was "Rest on a Peaceful Mountain." And he does a little recitation where Ralph says he's going up to the graveyard, you know. He'd do a great imitation of Ralph. He says, "I'm going up to the graveyard and I'm going to pray and see if I'm doing the right thing." So he goes out on the grave and he's praying. He says, "Now Carter," he says, "you know it's been six or seven years since you went away and left me and I've tried to carry on the Stanley Brothers sound and I've done my best, and I just don't know whether what I'm doing is right and whether you'd want me to do it this way," and he goes on for a long time and he says, "Is there just anything that I ought to do, Carter?" Guy does a great imitation of Carter, too. Disembodied voice from the grave. He says, "Yeah, brother Ralph," says, "if you can and will," says, "I've been down here seven years and haven't had a drink." Says, "Would you get me one?" So there may be an official legend, but some of the boys, you know—

Yeah, Ralph clearly decided to go a little further up the creek, you know. And he'd always been that way. I mean, those guys were really different kind of people. Carter was outgoing and verbal and always full of ideas, reaching for things outside his experience, and while you have to say he was a traditionalist too, he was never so much as Ralph was. I think Ralph just did what he'd always wanted to do. He took over direction of the band and he had to do whatever Ralph Stanley could do. Obviously. What else could he do?

Furthermore I think he'd been running it a long time. Does that John's Gospel Quartet stuff sound like Ralph Stanley or does it sound like the Stanley Brothers? Like Ralph Stanley. Yeah. It does to me, too. There's a difference. It's a subtle difference, but there's a difference. There was a looser quality with Carter. That's the only word I can come up with. And there was a tightness and a precision that came with Ralph. And you even hear it in that four-by-six studio in Baltimore. It was more Ralph Stanley than it was Carter. Carter wasn't in shape to boss a band or hardly to do anything. Got to remember also that it would have been tough even if Carter had been healthy. Those were hard times for traditional music.

But I don't think the festivals or any of those things were really affecting Ralph Stanley until about '70. I mean, it was little joints. Wherever you could do little jobs, you know. It was tough, too, really tough, too. That takes a dedication and almost a—dedication's not really the word—a single-mindedness, a singular vision, a focus.

There's one thing you could do if you want to learn where Ralph's religious music comes from, just for the hell of it. Have you ever come across the Chestnut Grove Quartet? You know, everybody from that part of the country—Ralph, me, I'm from there, too, of course—we all grew up in country churches, where we heard a

lot of singing. And that always comes in when people discuss country music, but it's left kind of nebulous as to what effect it had on
your movement into other forms of music.

But I think in Stanley's case—I wrote something about this in
one of our program books for a National Folk Festival when we were
presenting the Chestnut Grove, that literally all of this singing of a
cappella gospel by bluegrass bands came from Ralph. But Ralph
got it from Chestnut Grove. If you ever hear Chestnut Grove, any
doubt—They're neighbors of Ralph's. They're from Holston and Abingdon, Virginia. But Ralph not only got the style from them, God,
he got a lot of those songs, too. Not only did he do it, I notice this
brand-new gospel album by the Johnson Mountain Boys has a
Chestnut Grove thing on it, done as much like Chestnut Grove as
Dudley could pull off.

It's funny that bluegrass sources are sometimes amazingly obscure from the bluegrass audience. Even when it's a living group
that works as much as the Chestnut Grove Quartet does. Kind of
shows how all of these ships pass each other in the night. Chestnut Grove has probably traveled, well, at one time they were traveling as much as Stanley, and in roughly the same area. But never
did their paths meet on the stage. And the audiences for each of
them are utterly oblivious to each other.

And I'll tell you something even weirder. Those things that Ralph
Stanley recorded of Chestnut Grove's: who would you think sold
the most copies of them? Chestnut Grove. You'd think the other,
because Ralph's a household name. But around home, within listening range of that radio station that Chestnut Grove worked on
in Abingdon, they've got a bigger and better audience. Yeah, it's crazy, crazy, crazy. Makes no sense at all.

Have you got Chestnut Grove's *Church by the Road?* Bill Nunley
is the tenor that's singing the part that, the stuff that Ralph does.
Bill Nunley incidentally thinks very highly of what Ralph's done.
They barely know each other, though they come from the same
area. He's kind of bemused by Ralph doing that. His attitude about
it is that it's a great thing for him to do. "I'm glad he likes that stuff.
He's taken it to places where we could never take it to. More power
to him." They're some other folks of that type. Ever heard the Spencer Family? They live in Shiloh, Ohio, but they're from down around
there. Yeah, this is a generic form. This does have a home. That
sound is one that Ralph Stanley grew up with, as these people did.
You can't say that he invented it. But he sure has done a great job
with it.

The style—have you ever listened to the older recordings from that area in any depth? Ralph becomes a lot easier to understand as you get deeper into that musical background, that culture. He's a representative of it in a way. I remember from the first time I ever heard him that there was always this quality in him. I always found Carter a lot easier to talk to and Carter found me easy to talk to. And I always found Ralph a hell of a lot more musically interesting. I mean, if I were going to be a lead singer and a guitar player I would have to be the kind that Carter was—if I had the talent. I don't, you know. But I can't even contemplate being the kind of singer that Ralph is.

Did you know it was me that nominated Ralph for that Heritage Award last year? Usually people'll get a lot of people to nominate them, but there was one nomination for Ralph Stanley. That was me. But I wrote a good one, you know, and picked the musical samples nicely and it worked. I think they sent him some stuff in the mail and then they asked me to call him so I guess I was the first person to talk to him about it, though I don't think I ever told him that it was me that nominated him.

Ralph says to the committee, "Thank you very much," and I says, "Hey, you won the thing. I might have put your name out there but I didn't have anything to do with you winning. It was your music that did that. It's what you've been doing with your life that did that. I didn't have anything to do with it. I didn't teach you a thing on the banjo, did I, Ralph? Never taught you anything about singing, did I?" Which I think is the correct way to look at it. It's awfully easy for people that sit in the kind of positions that I've been in to get full of windstorms about how important they are to the careers of people they work with. The truth is that people either got it or they don't. And Ralph's got it. His "it" is different than anybody else's. He's got it. It's his. He owns it. He made it.

7

George Shuffler

"It was a good friendship"

For an extended period during the 1960s George Shuffler was such a vital part of the Clinch Mountain Boys that the act might well have been called a trio rather than a duo. Shuffler could sing when he wanted to, in a relaxed, pleasant baritone, but his greatest strength lay in the instrumental area. Even today, some twenty years after he left bluegrass, instrumental fans are fascinated by his unique and original cross-picking guitar style and his immediately recognizable four-four, or "walking," bass.

Shuffler was an innovator, as his invention of these musical techniques would suggest. Though his childhood musical beginnings were, as he himself says, so standard as almost to amount to a cliché, traditionalist conservatism was never a part of his makeup. His first professional work, for instance, wasn't even in bluegrass (to say nothing of the pre-bluegrass music the Stanley Brothers started out with), but in relatively modern country music.

Shuffler's personal relationship with the Stanley Brothers was complicated and hard to summarize. On the one hand, he was as close to both of them as any brother; he was very fond of and close to the boys' mother, and in particular we get the feeling that his personality and that of Carter Stanley were very similar. On the other hand, he was and is a proud and independent man. He resented his unequal billing, and was not afraid to say so. He quarreled continually with Carter Stanley about the appropriateness of his musical innovations to the Stanley Brothers' style, and in fact generally won those quarrels. Finally, though a loyal and hardworking employee, he was always ready, after giving proper notice, to pack up and leave whenever he felt like it.

Under these circumstances, it is not very surprising that Shuffler did not stay with the Clinch Mountain Boys very long after

Carter Stanley's death. In fact, what is surprising is that he stayed on as long as he did. His final parting with Ralph appears to have been a little rougher than the public version would have it. But blood—even adoptive blood—is thicker than water, and Shuffler was happy to come to the Home Place in 1986 to help Ralph celebrate his fortieth anniversary in music. And Ralph was happy to have him there.

It's an interesting measure of the great distance that separates the various forms of vernacular music in America that many bluegrass fans, even Stanley Brothers fans, are totally unaware that George Shuffler is still alive. In fact, as one observer recently remarked, he's probably more alive now than he ever was in the old days. He and his family have of course moved into the field of southern gospel music, which is a world of its own, with its own fans, circuit, festivals, record companies, and record charts. As performers and songwriters, the Shufflers are now near the very top of this world.

––––––––––––

My family's music background? Well, this'll sound like a broken record, I know you've heard it a thousand times, but our singing started in church. Then they was a lady over here that ordered a little old guitar from Spiegel or Montgomery Ward or some of these mail order companies. Never could play it and slid it under the bed. And my mother was awful good at crocheting, at needlework. We didn't have electricity, just a little old coal-oil lamp. So I would chuck the fire at night; it gave a better light than the lamp did, and my mother crocheted and knitted doilies at night for this lady, to go on her vanities and things of that nature, and worked it off that way and got me that guitar. That was my first one.

I didn't have anybody to teach me, I just kindly learned. A guy came by one day and tuned it for me and maybe showed me a G, C, and D. So I started from that. The rest of them were just homemade chords. I got to where I had pretty good time and rhythm and people was going to play with me but I was ashamed, I was afraid I was making the chords wrong, you know.

I got an opportunity to play with the local people around here and then the Bailey Brothers came through, Charles and Danny, and the Happy Valley Boys. They were on WSM at that time. And I went to see them. They were doing shows over here at a theater in Granite Falls. And Junior Husky and another boy they was carrying was traveling in another car and they didn't show up. So I went backstage, very shyly, and met them, and they got to asking about musicians. I said, "Well, I've never played a bass any. Maybe just a time or two. But I'll be willing to try to stand in." So I did and they hired me. I went back to Nashville with them and stayed till their job terminated there.

Then I came back home and I formed a band here and played around some of the little radio stations. You could build up in a few weeks on radio and we'd go out here and play these dates, things of that nature, and then I had a little work with another group or two. Finally after I got married I got with Jim and Jesse and worked with them a couple of years, something like that. Over a year, anyway. And then I came home.

I got home one day and Carter called me the next day. I had met him before. Curly King was working out of Bristol, and a boy from here was working with him some. He would go up to Bristol once in a while and visit friends. So I went with him a time or two and met Carter and Ralph. But I never did play with them any up there. In fact I hadn't played any bluegrass up to that point. Jim and Jesse was playing more country than they are now.

So I went with them. They were leaving Bristol and going to WVLK in Versailles. And they had Curly Sechler and Charlie Cline, Ralph and Carter and myself. And that's when it started. That was in '50, I believe, and I stayed with them off and on till '68.

Yeah, off and on. I'd get tired of the road. I'm kind of an outdoors person. I like to farm, and mess with livestock, and I'd get tired of just the grind of the road, and I'd come home to relax and rest and farm and buy and sell horses and cattle. That's one of my weaknesses, maybe, but it's something I like to do and it's always been a good livelihood for me. So I would come home and do that for a while and then I'd go back and work with them.

I never was hired but the first time. I never was fired. When I'd come home they'd call or something, want me to go and record with them. And I'd go and record and they'd say, "Well, we got a pretty heavy weekend coming up next week. What about just staying on through that?" And I'd stay on and work a couple of years and then I'd come home a while and then they'd call again. The first time, though, you can ask Ralph, that's the only time they ever hired me. We just took the rest of it kindly for granted. When they wanted to record and I felt like going I'd go and then just stay on a while, you know. Maybe the recording was the cue and I didn't pick it up. I don't know.

But anyhow, it was a good friendship. Ralph I guess now seems about as much like blood kin as anybody in the world got to be to me. I told him one time, about the time I quit the last time we came in, after Carter died, I told him I'd slept with Carter and Ralph more than I ever did my wife. But we were close.

Their mother was a very special person to me. Carter and Ralph always said if you wanted anything when we were there on the Ridge you had to go through George to get it from Ma. We were just that close, you know. I loved to go there and help her break her garden and help her plant and gather and things like that. I didn't have a vehicle there and when they'd come in for two or three days I couldn't get on home, so I'd just stay there around Smith Ridge. Learned a lot of the people in there, learned to appreciate and think a lot of them.

I played bass with Carter and Ralph for the first five, ten years I was with them, I guess, and then somehow King Records—the Delmore Brothers had dropped out and they wanted somebody else to do some guitar work. Bill Napier, he went in and did one session on guitar and then he dropped out, and then Curley Lambert I think played a little guitar, I don't know. Anyway, I went on guitar then.

And everybody was trying to pick a guitar like a mandolin. Either that or Maybelle Carter. Or Chet Atkins, and that didn't fit, you know, this stop time, stop picking. So I started using that cross picking on it. Cross picking, you do with a flat pick what most people do with a banjo roll. You get the three strings with the flat pick, you follow me? And you got to go down and then pick up. In other words, you're crossing backwards and forth on three strings. You're playing your own melody and harmony too. You got to make up your own little runs and things for it to come out. And you get your left hand in some of the awfullest positions. You look down and you think it's broke, sometimes. Like, you're not a-playing an open string, like if you're playing in G and you're not a-playing an open string in F or E flat or something like that.

So it's just a homemade thing. Jesse McReynolds and I, when we were together, Jesse was working it out and had it pretty well on the mandolin at that time. And I started creating some things on the guitar and I never did get a chance to use them until I started using that cross pick with Carter and Ralph.

And they didn't like it, Carter and Ralph didn't. Chuck Seitz was the engineer at King then and I guess Chuck gave me more encouragement than anybody did on it. Go ahead and put it on the record and let the chips fall where they would, you know. And it was guitar and it soothed old man Syd Nathan there a little bit, enough to, well, to keep the contract a-going. Then after I got to doing it, why, I liked it and I noticed the crowd liked it. It seemed like the overall thing fit them. Ninety percent of the time they was just Carter and Ralph and myself on the road. And I could fill in more with three or four strings going than I could the little single string.

So I would pick it and Carter, he would say, "Well, why don't you change? Get off that roll. Get off that lick you're doing there. Do something else. You want to play it like a mandolin." Well, in fact I never was a great mandolin buff to start with. I used to play a little bit but I never did care enough about it to pursue it. Everybody to their own thing, you know. So I would go ahead and do it irregardless because I thought that it fit better than anything I could put behind them.

And then after I quit it, why everybody started trying to do it. And I've never heard the first one do it right. I never have heard the first person that plays it do it to my notion, to my satisfaction. They'll get into it and then screw it up, you know, and have to break it, get off of it. And that's about it on the old guitar.

And on that bass fiddle thing I just—everybody was just playing a boom-boom or something and I saw where there was a note for every time you hit with your right hand, there was a position for your left hand. And I started that old—I don't know, they've named it everything in the world, called it Shuffler bass or four-four drive or something, I don't know what all.

And there was this poll business and they put out the statistics, the figures on it and I beat Bill Monroe on his instrument. I got more votes on the bass than Bill did on the mandolin. And I got more than Earl did on the banjo or Doc did on the flat-top. I really did. And I think I come in like maybe first or second two or three years after I'd come home. My friends had remembered, you know.

I recall them asking for a picture, they said you've won the bass fiddle deal and I said, "I've not got a picture." They said, "Well, would you get one made?" I said, "Who's paying for it?" They said, "You." And I said, "No ma'am, I won't." If it wasn't going to pay anything why should I go out and hire a photographer and make my picture? So they finally found a picture on an old album that I did with Reno and Harrell and took it off. I was standing on the end. They cut it off and put it in there for that.

I was in Europe with Carter and Ralph in 1966. We were over there and we'd done these things for Ray Davis, the disk jockey in Baltimore. And over there, why, Carter, I think he named it John's

Gospel Quartet. And Carter told them over there that that was my group. We had to predate the things. There's a lot of things went on that year.

Carter'd been in declining health for a year, really. You could tell he didn't feel good. He just wasn't himself, you know. He slept a lot and he didn't feel like driving. That was the mainstay with just the three of us most of the time, you know, was getting to the places. They was taking us farther and keeping us longer, you know.

So Carter, he just didn't feel up to even going on the stage part of that time. He was going downhill. We came back from Europe in the spring. Well, late winter, March or something like that. And we worked that summer, and Carter, he was sickly all summer, really. Then that fall we went to the Disk Jockey Convention and they was a lot of activity there such as special awards, you know. The fan club really put on a big gala for them and for us and they gave me a trophy even for being with them a lengthy time and all of that and we left there. We had to start back again up towards the week-end, Thursday or Friday.

And so we came on into some part of Kentucky that night. I think Melvin Goins was with us. He didn't go to the convention but he met us at the date that night. Anyhow Carter had to leave the stage after just a few numbers. So Ralph and Melvin and myself finished out the program. Carter was bleeding all the time and we left there and got up on the Mountain Parkway, Carter, Ralph, and myself. Melvin met us that night and then he went on back home. And we were coming back into that area the next night.

But we were going to Cincinnati, I believe, the three of us, to pick up some records the next day. Carter was in the back and he said, "Pull off. I'm sick." We pulled off. I believe Ralph was driving. We heard the awfullest sound. It was a four-door car and he opened the back door and we could hear something hitting the ground, and Ralph said, "My God, what's the matter?" And we turned on the light and saw it was blood, you know. And that was the first.

So we started on to Lexington with him, to the hospital, and it eased off a little bit and he said, "Just turn around and take me back to Ma's," he said. "I feel better now." And so we took him back over to Smith Ridge. And I believe we were supposed to play in Frenchburg, Kentucky, the next night, at the courthouse, I think. Ralph and I went and met Melvin over there and left Carter there on the Ridge.

We went on and played the courthouse and started back and a patrolman stopped us, over about Wayland, Kentucky. And I was driving. I didn't know what in the world I'd done wrong. He put the light on us and the sirens and pulled me over and he said, "You are, are one of you Ralph Stanley?" I said, "Yes." He said, "Well, you better get to Bristol quick as you can. You got a brother just at the point of death." So we knew that he'd had another hemorrhage.

We went on and they had him in intensive care. They'd tried to get the blood stopped and I believe the doctor said they'd run a hundred twenty pints of blood through Carter, trying to keep him alive, trying to keep his veins from collapsing. And they couldn't get it stopped there so they took him to Charlottesville and got it stopped. Ralph and I went up to see him and the doctor came in, and he just told Carter in front of us that there was no way out of an operation. And he said, "You stand about a fifty-fifty chance with that." He said, "Don't expect to—you're going to have to stay in here about six to eight weeks till we can build you up before you can start thinking about playing."

We left him in pretty good hopes; the bleeding stopped while we were there, no trace of blood whatsoever. And he was real pleased and he got up, set on the side of the bed and everything. And it was long just about Thanksgiving and he had two other brothers, Doc and Lance, half-brothers; they went up to see him during Thanksgiving and he talked them into bringing him back home. And Ralph and I, Ralph was living in Florida, but I'd moved back up here then. So Ralph brought me home and he went on to Florida for Thanksgiving. We came back on a Wednesday or Thursday after that and we was supposed to go out.

It was the last day of November, after Thanksgiving. We got in the Ridge there about ten o'clock that night. And all the people from down in Live Oak had sent Carter best wishes and said if they's any way they could help or anything that they could do, anything at all, just to let them know. Even the car dealer down there, I remember, sent Carter word, said whenever you're getting ready to trade for a new car, why we want to work with you. And all that kind of stuff. And Carter said, "Well, it's a funny thing that you have to get down just about on your deathbed before people will show sympathy and offer to lend a helping hand." I think he said words to that effect.

And so we were sitting there, and Ralph and I were tired. He'd drove from out of Florida, and then he came here, to Valdese, and then I drove on up there and so rested him. But we got in there just about ten o'clock and we wanted to go to bed because we had to leave out the next morning. But Carter, he was sitting on the couch, and he kept begging us not to go to bed. He said, "Let's set up and talk a while." He said, "Up here it's just me and Ma." He said, "I'm lonesome and I want to talk." And we sit there about an hour I guess and all of a sudden he started just upchucking and— Ma couldn't find a thing, just a box, like, and he's just, oh spewing just the awfullest—looked like a gallon of blood there, you know.

And they was just an old blue frozen snow on the ground and we called the ambulance over at Clintwood and Harold Stanley came in the ambulance and we carried him out of the house in the snow and put him in the ambulance. And Carter asked me would I ride with him in the ambulance to the hospital. And I said I'd be glad to. And Ralph followed us in the truck and we went on to the hospital and we got him checked in. When we got to the hospital I had on a white kind of coat and it was specked with blood all over and they opened the back door of the ambulance and the blood was running out of the back of it. And they got him back in the hospital and he had less than a pint of blood, they said. Veins collapsed. They went into his foot and finally found an artery there, a big vein or something, and they got the blood started and he kindly leveled off.

So this was getting up towards about eight o'clock in the morning, December first. We'd been up all night and traveled all that distance, too, and Ralph said, "George, I believe Carter has eased off some." I said, "He's a-resting. Let's go out and get us a little bite of breakfast and some coffee." So we walked down to a little diner there and we stayed I guess probably about thirty minutes.

We came back and we was sitting down out in the lobby there and I was smoking and Ralph said, "Go ahead and finish smoking. I believe I'll step in here and check on him and see how he's doing." And he went in there and he came back in just a few seconds and just ghostly looking and he said, "George, Carter's a-dying." And that just killed us both, you know. So we sit out there and the nurses, they's a-paging the doctor, doctor, doctor, and so finally he got up there and they went in there and stayed about ten minutes. They came out and just give us a real solemn look and went on in again and directly, oh, about five minutes, why one of the nurses came out and said, you know, he's gone.

So we had to go back to the Ridge and tell everybody. I called a neighbor there. I told her to step over and tell Ma that Carter had died and kindly get braced for us to come in there. Then we had to take care of all the funeral arrangements and call all the family. He had one half-sister, Ruby, lived up around Pontiac or Wyandotte, Michigan. I was a pallbearer.

I'd went with Carter to Norton and he'd bought him a new suit just about a month prior to that. Well, back in October, because he wore it to the convention in Nashville. And he thought that was the finest suit in the world. And it was. And it cost a ton of money back then even. And he said, "It's the best suit I ever owned." And he loved that suit, oh, just something out of this world, and Ralph said, when he come down, "George," he said, "let's pick him out a suit."

I said, "Ralph, as much as Carter liked the suit that he and I went to Norton and got," I said, "they's nothing that would please him more than to have that suit cleaned and put it on him." And so that's what we did. Ralph and I both thought that was the thing to do. We discussed it a little bit, you know. So that's what we did. Hard time, though, for the family that is. Two or three day wake.

Now Ralph, he didn't have any direction. He said, "I don't know, George, what to do. All I know is music." And he said, "I'm going to try to go on." And so he said we'd just have to do the best we can. He said, "Let's take off a few days." So he called and canceled some dates. I come on back to my house here and in about three or four days or a week Ralph called. He said, "George, are you ready to go?" I said, "Yessir, I'm ready, Ralph." And he said, "Well, I just can't stand a-sitting here no longer. The suspense of the thing's a-killing me. So let's just hit the road and see what happens."

So Melvin, he was still—and Curly Ray, he come in then and started fiddling. I don't believe Curly Ray fiddled any with them before Carter's death. Just a time or two, you know, a couple of weeks or something like that. And while Carter was in Charlottesville, up in the hospital a few days, why Curly Ray came in and helped us with some dates, too, I believe. I guess Ralph had called him or something but anyhow Curly Ray came in and Melvin and Ralph and myself. And we worked like that just a little bit.

Well, Ralph and I, we'd sing in the car or sing a duet on the stage even, but it just wasn't the blend, you know. And so we discussed it and Ralph said, "Well, I'll just get a lead singer." And I reckon, let's see, Larry Sparks was the first one that came in, right? And Larry stayed an awful long while, I think, with Ralph. And I didn't stay too long after that because seem like it was, it was on Ralph's mind and he and I were so close till we got distant, you know, and we just got to where we—I don't know—we didn't fall out or have no fights or no cussing battles or nothing but I could just tell that I was out of place. It wasn't the same, in other words. So I just excused myself and came to the house.

Then I went with Don Reno and stayed two years. I came back in February and Ralph was down at Camp Springs. Carlton Haney had called me in for a Stanley Brothers Memorial Day to do some things. I went down on Saturday and I worked with Ralph Saturday and Sunday and then we did this thing for Carlton Haney on Monday. And Ralph said, "Well, I've got a hard weekend a-coming up, George. What about driving up and meeting me and helping me?" They was going into Ohio, I think. I said okay.

So I went, and then we got back and I was about ready to get out of the bus and he said, "I've got another hard week coming up." I kindly know what it was leading to, so I said, "Okay, I'll be there." So I went back then and worked about ten months with him again and then I just lost interest, you know, in traveling.

By then I had a new baby and I had a lot of stock and other interests here in Valdese that demanded quite a bit of my attention and my time. And so I just came back to stay. I just really had gotten involved in church work and I didn't even know my girls could sing. They had a little music choir here at the church. I went there and they would kindly hide their faces from me when they were singing. They was eight or ten other children in it. And I came home and I asked Sue, my wife, I said, "Who was those two pretty voices there?" "Daddy, that was Debby and Jenny." I said, "You've got to be kidding me."

I pulled an old guitar out from behind the couch there, my old Gibson I carried for so long. I said, "Children, come here a minute." We was sitting right on the couch. And I said, "What about trying a verse of a song?" And they said, "Why daddy, we can't sing." They was ashamed to sing. Not that I was better than them but they was afraid of my experience, like thirty years on the road, they was just afraid to open up around me. So I kindly just pinpointed them a little bit and we sang a chorus of it. "How Tedious and Tasteless" was the name of the song. And man, it was just like electricity went up my back was all.

And so we started with that and then I called a brother of mine, brother Dude, he's a powerful bass singer. He's one of the best country bass singers I ever heard. He stayed with us about five years and now I've got my son-in-law singing the bass part. His name is Tony Brittain. I've got myself, and Debby, and Jenny Lynn, and Jenny's husband Tony as the voices.

And we've absolutely been accused by a lot of our peers that we've got the best band in gospel music. We got my son Steve plays the bass, and my nephew Jo Eddie Shuffler plays drums, Ronnie Brown plays electric guitar, and Jay Bowman plays steel, and I'm still trying to strum a little rhythm on the guitar.

We did some albums for Rebel and then we went with Trail, in

Kingsport, Tennessee. We did two albums for them. Then we went to Granite City with the Easter Brothers and did two albums for them. And I think we're maybe going to venture out and form our own publishing company and get our own label. That's very common in gospel music. So I'm not tied to a label now. But we are negotiating a deal. I did just about all the finalizing this morning.

And I've got a song, "When I Receive My Robe and Crown," that was in the top five the biggest part of 1984, on the national charts in gospel music. That's made us feel pretty good and that's opened a lot of doors for us. And we've got songs that I've written that's been recorded by the Kingsmen, the Florida Boys, the Rex Leland Singers, the Harvesters Quartet, and just on and on and on. Seem like they're using my work a lot. And they're selling records. That's what I like about it, you know.

We got a nice bus to travel in. We've ventured out to, well, going as far south as Georgia and then out in the Midwest as far as the western part of Ohio and Indiana, and on up north around Michigan and over into Maryland and Delaware and upstate Virginia, which is a pretty good pull from here. Right now we're having to turn down more dates than we can book. We try to keep it to weekends, but it's about got out of hand. Looks like we're going to have to make a decision.

The twenty-fifth of February, I was sitting around here that night and my wife said, "You know what it is?" I said, "Yeah." So and so, gave her some smart little answer. And she said, "It's Ralph's birthday." And I said, "Well, I have a notion to call up." And she said, "Why don't you?" So I did, and got him, and we had a nice chat. I hadn't talked to him in a couple of years.

Lester Woodie

"Ralph has always played that straight style"

"Now we've done well, considering the rehearsing we done. Each man ought to take them songs and study them about a month before we cut them. Get them worked out, you know, work out something on them that people'll notice. Not just get through it, just, you know, put in something that people'll notice. Just like old Woodie done on the 'Man of Constant Sorrow.' Look how many copies there was on that." Thus Ralph Stanley in April of 1986, mildly lecturing himself and his sidemen as they developed their arrangement of "Hot Night in August" in the Maggard Sound Studio in Big Stone Gap, Virginia.

"Old Woodie" was in fact a very young man in 1950, when he created the famous fiddle break that Ralph Stanley was still holding up as an example of instrumental work some thirty-six years later. He was born and raised in Valdese, North Carolina, and he is living proof that skill in old-time music is not necessarily something one is born with, but an art that can be studied and learned.

Describing the way he and his neighbors, John and George Shuffler, picked up their music as boys, Lester Woodie told Wayne Erbsen in a 1980 interview, "There weren't all that many musicians that played around Valdese then. Of course, there were old fiddlers here and there, and there were some homes that had a banjo hanging on the wall that was played for sheer enjoyment once in a while. But good musicians were really rare. There must have been more music played when my daddy was growing up than when I was. . . . Most of the music we heard was on record, though we did catch some stuff on the radio." And most of the material they did catch could scarcely be called traditional. "We heard records of the Sons of the Pioneers, and we copied their singing style. I used to sing lead, George the baritone, and John, he had a great tenor. We did stuff like 'Tumbling Tumbleweeds,' and 'Cool Water.' Occasionally, we'd try a Monroe Brothers song, me and John." Like George Shuffler, Lester Woodie moved from a country and western to an old-time style only on joining the Stanley Brothers.

He was a young man then, and he still looks like a young man now, perhaps because he had the good fortune or good sense to quit the road life before it had a chance to start taking its inevitable toll. After a four-year stint in the air force he worked his way through college, finally winding up with a job as an executive in a radio station in Altavista, just south of Lynchburg, Virginia, where he has remained ever since. But his work with Carter and Ralph Stanley produced some of his fondest memories, as he showed when he reminisced about the old days in a trailer on a Sunday morning, during his visit to Ralph Stanley's Fortieth Anniversary Homecoming in September, 1986.

————————

I was born in Valdese, North Carolina. I had one brother and one sister. And ironically this past Memorial Day I lost my brother in a boating accident, just this year. So, one of those tough things in life that you get through, you know? George Shuffler and I kind of grew up together. He had a bunch of brothers and sisters and we became like family, you know. In fact George I guess was responsible for getting me into music, period. I was about eight years old when we started and all through high school we organized some country music and one time we were doing western music, western trios, Coolwater and all that stuff, you know. We played pretty constantly all through high school.

We started from that and I graduated from high school about the time of the Korean War. I was undecided what to do and floundered around trying to decide to go to college and took a job at a bakery in Valdese. And the bakery had some pretty weird shifts there. You'd work morning one day and hoot-owl shift the next, you know. I'd been working there about a month or so and about ten o'clock at night the supervisor came around and said, "You've got a visitor." And I looked up and it was Ralph and Pee Wee.

They had been playing in the area and needed a fiddle player at the time, so they asked around and I guess they ran into somebody, maybe—we'd been playing some with Jim Shumate. And I think they had talked to him and Jim had told them I might be available. So the next day we went down to the hotel in Hickory and I played a few tunes with them. I don't think Ralph even played. Carter and Pee Wee and myself did a couple of fiddle tunes and I decided to go to Bristol with them. They were on "Farm and Fun Time" then and "Farm and Fun Time" was a very popular radio show at the time. So that was in late 1949 and that was my beginning with the Stanley Brothers.

I worked a little over two years with them. During that time we played Bristol twice, headquartered in Bristol twice. We did some of the first TV shows in the area. We moved up to Huntington, West Virginia. WSAZ-TV was one of the first stations in the East and we worked there for a while, did TV and had some pretty lucrative, comparatively, not as compared to today, but it was pretty good territory. We worked Kentucky, Ohio, and that area. West Virginia.

So from there we signed on with the Louisiana Hayride at Shreveport and worked down there a while. That was back in the days when the Wilburn Brothers, Red Sovine, Webb Pierce, and all that gang were still at the Hayride. We worked some territory down in Texas with Slim Whitman. Slim was down there in that area then. And we had an early morning radio show on KWKH. Everybody was doing about a thirty-minute show early in the morning in addition to working the Hayride. And I think we were on like 8:30 and the Wilburn Brothers were on, followed us, and Red Sovine did his stint.

But Ralph and his mother were really very close, and he didn't like Louisiana for that reason. So we moved from there back to Bristol and worked a second time in Bristol. And by this time the Korean War was really heating up and I was a prime target, on the verge of being drafted, so I just decided to beat them to the draw and I joined the air force for four years.

But during that time we—I feel like I was rather fortunate. Carter was really coming into his own as far as his writing ability and I worked with Carter on several songs. We were living in a hotel in Huntington, West Virginia, on the banks of the river there and you'd see the old tugboats come up the river, you know, and we did some work on some of the songs that have become standards now that Carter wrote. And I'd help him with a line or this and that. If I'm not mistaken now one song that comes to mind is "Would You Love Me One More Time." I believe that song was written there in Huntington, and several of those songs in that era were written there.

You know as a writer sometimes you need a little different idea or you need a thought or maybe a word to rhyme with what you got going and so on and so Carter and I would banter back and forth. Maybe I'd drop him a word or a note or something, you know. So I feel very fortunate in that because some of those songs have been recorded by a number of—even in the country field. That particular song especially was.

I did most of the Columbia sessions. They were recording for Columbia then and I think it was a little bit unusual as far as— you know, bluegrass music hadn't really come into its own. I guess it wasn't even called bluegrass at that particular time. But strangely enough Art Satherly, who was president of Columbia Records, and Don Law, who was vice president and kindly in charge of production and talent and so on—each time we would record in Nashville they would fly out of New York and come and sit in on the session. They kindly got hung up on Virginia hams. I remember one time we took Art a Virginia ham down, you know. But for somebody of that stature to take an interest in a country band from Mc-Clure, Virginia, I thought that was noteworthy.

I guess of all the work that I did with them, and I still get remarks on this, was a song that Ralph did—I think he has recorded that song more than one time—I'm sure he has, but—"Man of Constant Sorrow." I run into a lot of musicians now that say they liked the break and the kickoff on that particular song and so on.

Ralph and I and Carter had a very good association. We had some good times together and some rough times. Back in those days festivals were unknown and the big auditoriums were out of the question, so you played a lot of schoolhouses. And I remember playing in little rural schoolhouses, in Virginia and Kentucky especially. Some of them didn't have electricity at that time. So you work without a P.A. set and you light a lantern and you go to it, you know. Build your lungs a little bit.

I think Ralph is certainly to be commended in carrying on after the loss of Carter and I think he's shown good judgment and kept a good organization over the years, you know, and it speaks well for Ralph.

As far as singing is concerned, Ralph is doing what he was born with and reared with. And this was all new to me, coming out of North Carolina. I was the Southern Baptist type and I didn't know anything about the Primitive Baptists, which they were. I had the occasion one time to attend a funeral of one of Ralph's relatives. And it was one of the saddest things I ever attended and one of the most amusing things as well because everybody was sitting in the church and it was so quiet you could hear a pin drop and all of a sudden somebody in the back of the room started singing one of those old hymns. A cappella, no music of course. And somebody else joined in and the whole church was singing.

Well, Ralph used to do that. We'd be riding along two o'clock in the morning and everybody dead tired and half asleep. I guess Ralph was probably singing to stay awake or something. But it had a real lonesome, weird feeling to it, you know. It was completely different from what I had been used to. A lot of it's in kind of minor keys and gives it that weird sound. But he was singing what he knew. And still does.

I'm sure Ralph was exposed to it by maybe attending church and the people he associated with, but I think maybe his mother had a big influence on it, too. She was a great lady and she played the old clawhammer banjo and taught Ralph that and I'm sure, you know, when Ralph was a real young boy she probably sang some of that old stuff to him and it was ingrained in him.

And the Stanley Brothers' style, too—as I said I started playing myself at about eight years old and we had played different kinds of music and even played bluegrass, but there was still—it's kind of hard to describe but it's a little bit of different timing that set Stanley music apart from the other people who were playing what you might categorize as the same type of music, bluegrass or whatever. But they had just a little bit different—and it took a little bit of getting used to, you know, even playing fiddle with them. It's something that kind of stands out.

And I think that's the secret to Ralph's success. He has never gone off on a tangent or tried to—you know there's a lot of people that play fancier music and more notes and slick runs and all that but Ralph has always played that straight style and I think it's recognizable anywhere.

I think Pee Wee Lambert added a lot. I thought a lot of Pee Wee. He was talented, and I really feel if there's one song that established the Stanley Brothers it was probably the "White Dove." And I think part of the reason for the success of that was the arrangement and Pee Wee singing a high baritone part. While we were together they worked very hard on their trio numbers and Pee Wee sang in that arrangement and I think that got some recognition from people.

I believe the first session we cut for Columbia was one mike. And then I think maybe by the last session they had started getting a little bit better, but it's certainly a long way from what's being done in engineering today. It was altogether different. It's amazing to think now what it takes to put on a respectable festival, the work and the expense really of sound systems and like that. Back then you carried it all in the car and did it, you know? But I don't regret a minute of it. I think it's one of my fond memories. And like I say, sometimes it wasn't easy.

I came out of service—I'll tell you a little story along the way as we go with this. George Shuffler's younger brother, John, who was more my age than George was, he was in the army and saw some pretty heavy combat during the Korean War. I got out of the air force about the same time John got out of the army and we were at a crossroads and didn't know what we wanted to do. The little town I was in was a cotton mill town and not much opportunity so we decided we would go North and get a good job.

I happened to have a good friend who I'd met in service in Middletown, Ohio. And we went up and stayed with him a week and job-hunted which ended up, we didn't have any success with that but during that week we were downtown in Middletown one evening just walking along the street and I hear some bluegrass music.

John said, "What is that?" I said, "Probably somebody playing a record." He said, "No, I think that's live." So we followed our ears down to a little place in the wall. Red Allen and his group were playing live in there, so we spent the evening and most of the next day with Red and talking to him and so on but since we didn't find anything of consequence as far as a job we came back to Valdese.

I liked the military pretty well and I decided I was going back in the military. Of course John had a different view. His experiences dictated that. And I said, "Well, I think I'll go back in service." And George had been to Charlottesville to make an album with Bill Clifton. He got back home just before I'd finally decided to go back in service and he said, "We stopped in Lynchburg and there's a group up there that needs a fiddle player." And it turned out to be Bill and Mary Reid. So I said, "Well, you know, I really want to play music and I want to go to school some more."

So I came up and went to work with Bill and Mary Reid in Lynchburg. They were doing three television shows a week and radio every day and playing personal and they'd just got a Columbia contract too and were about to record. So I went to work with them and enrolled in college over there and combined the two and that was a hectic thing.

As it turned out the college was within walking distance of the radio station so I'd take a lunch hour, walk over to the radio station and do the radio show and come back that night and do the TV show and then play out and go to school. It was a full-time job, you know. So during that time I married a girl from near Lynchburg in a little place called Goode, Virginia, and I kept on playing till I finished school.

By this time my wife was pregnant and I decided maybe getting off the road would be good, you know. Everyone knows how that family life is for a musician, so we went back to North Carolina and I went to work in Hickory, North Carolina, with a dime store, McClellan Variety Store, as a manager trainee. And I worked there a year and a half or so. Built a house in Valdese. Lived in the house about three months and got transferred to Roanoke.

So I was running the store there in Roanoke and in the meantime one child was born. And I ran into some people who were musicians and Bill Jefferson was in the group. Bill was working for a radio station. I was used to doing a little MC work here and there so he kept saying, "You ought to get into radio." And I said, "No, it's a pretty good company. I think I'll stay with them."

But anyhow about a year, another transfer to Kingsport, Tennessee, and by this time I'd decided I didn't want to be moving every year. So I got into radio and worked there for about a year, I suppose. And a fellow who I'd worked with previously was building this new radio station in Altavista, Virginia, and he asked me to join him on that. So that was twenty-four years ago and I haven't got enough money to leave town yet.

I might mention just as a postscript here, we had a comedian one time who was a classic comedian, Smoky Davis, used to travel with us, Stanley Brothers. And another fellow that a lot of people will remember is Leslie Keith. Leslie played the old-time fiddle. We used to have fiddle contests between him and myself. Those things I guess would compare to a wrestling match. You know how they hype a wrestling match? We'd get on "Farm and Fun Time" and talk about who's going to beat who and he hadn't got a chance, you know, but we got a lot of interest stirred up and we'd go out and play a contest and sometimes he'd win, sometimes I'd win.

So I was playing fiddle, playing comedy, singing bass in the quartet. And Leslie was with us and he had a bullwhip act. I believe he was from Oklahoma and he really was adept at handling the bullwhips, long twenty-five-foot whips, you know. So we worked up an act. I would do my comedy routine and then Leslie was, I don't know, three-quarters Indian or something and he'd pull his hair down and put a headband on and he looked like Chief Wahoo, you know. He'd get his whips out and I was in my comedy rig and I would hold papers and he would cut them with a whip.

I was scared to death the first time I did it but Leslie said, "Les, I can cut your arm off or I can cut that paper and never touch you." You know, that gave me a little confidence. But for the grand finale he would be on one side of the stage and I was on the other. I would be bending over with my head between my legs, a paper in my mouth and he would come over and set it afire and then he would cut the fire out with that whip. A big, big show.

So I kind of feel fortunate to have worked with people like that. Smoky Davis and Leslie Keith. Another thing I'm kind of proud of and this is more recent. Curley Lambert called me one day and Charlie Moore was cutting an album. He was coming to Roanoke to do it and wanted to know if I'd play fiddle on it. I said, "Sure, I'll play fiddle." So we went to Roanoke and cut the album. It turned out to be the last one. In fact Charlie Moore died before that album was released. And of course since, Curley has gone on too so that's kind of a milestone to be on that album you know. I'm kind of proud of that.

Melvin Goins

"They laid the true foundation"

"I can take care of that, too," the punch line to an old comedy
skit that Melvin Goins used to perform with the Clinch Mountain
Boys, could well serve as a motto for this entertainer's entire life.
When the Stanley Brothers took Goins on as a sideman early in
1966, their career had just about hit rock bottom. "We couldn't get
any dates," Ralph Stanley recalled not long ago. The Live Oak, Florida, well had definitely run dry, and Carter Stanley's illness had
reached a point where even the band's staunchest friends and admirers could no longer ignore or deny it.

There was no miracle waiting around the corner for the Stanley
Brothers, but Melvin Goins turned out to be the next best thing.
Grateful for the chance of doing any musical work at all, and dou-
bly grateful for the chance of working for a group which, though
down and out, was still a legend in its own time, Goins put his in-
domitable energy and spirit to work in patching the Stanley Brothers' career back together again in the Appalachian area in which it
had first begun. Ostensibly the Brothers' rhythm guitar player and
comedian, he was in reality their personal manager, booking agent,
cheerleader, conscience, and whipping boy, as well as nurse and
general caretaker to the ailing Carter Stanley.

Melvin Goins isn't one to brag in public about his work for the
Stanleys, but even after a short conversation with him it is easy to
imagine the sort of bubbling enthusiasm and fast-talking sales-
manship he must have brought to the task of finding engagements
for the Clinch Mountain Boys in 1966. And we can only guess at
how much those little school dates and drive-in appearances, individually so tiny in their scale, went to providing a bedrock of lifetime fans on which Ralph Stanley was able to rely when times got
better. But it is hard to escape the conclusion that Melvin Goins's

quiet, behind-the-scenes work was vital to the continued career of the Stanley Brothers during their last year together.

After staying on—the loyalty this speaks of is typical—with Ralph Stanley for several years after Carter's death, Melvin Goins joined his brother Ray in forming the Goins Brothers band, in which he still serves as rhythm guitar player, lead singer, and master of ceremonies. He continues to be a bluegrass promoter in the best sense of the word, arranging shows, festivals, and television programs in the eastern Kentucky area, and tirelessly and selflessly boosting the cause of traditional mountain music wherever he appears.

Back in '66, Carter and Ralph was working out of Live Oak, Florida. They used to come through here about once a month, at the old home place, where Ralph has the festival. Their mother lived here, you know. So they would come up from Live Oak and they would work a few days here.

I wasn't doing a lot then. I was just kindly freelancing, and Ralph, he wrote me a letter, wanted to see if I could maybe set up a couple of weeks of dates for them. I said, "Well, you might not want to work what I could set up, Ralph." Ralph said, "Oh, we ain't doing much. We'll work about anything right now." So I got to booking, setting up schools, and we got to working four or five days a week. The first school we played was January the eighteenth, 1966, me and Ralph and Carter and George Shuffler. That was the crew then. I set up about two weeks of schools for Carter and Ralph and myself and we played those two weeks of schools.

I never will forget it, we was working in Pontiac, Michigan; it was on a Sunday, and me and Carter was at the backstage, tuning up, and he said, "Well, you've probably heard all kinds of tales about the Stanley Brothers," and I said, "Well, that's true, you hear all kinds of tales about everybody." And he said, "Hey, why don't you just stay on with us for a while?" My two weeks was up, you see. Old Chase said—you know, they called Carter "Chase" back then—he said, "Why don't you just stay on with us? We're old country boys, you are too. We're going to get along good. We've really had a ball the last two weeks. The Stanleys'll treat you right." I said, "Well, I ain't got no question about that. But Carter, I don't know if I could do the job or not." He said, "By God, you ain't done bad this last two." And I said, "Well, I'll try it. I don't care, you know."

So Carter talked me into staying on. Back then, that was before the bluegrass festivals ever started, and buddy, it was rough. If you got out and played one or two little gigs a week, why you was flying. And most of them was on percentage and everything, and it was just hard to keep a band together unless you had a lot of dates to work.

So that was the best thing about us, we got into the schools, and we got to working four or five days a week. We'd work matinees and double back and play night shows that night. I done a little comedy act back then. Carter, he called me Big Wilbur. I wore a polka-dot suit and a black derby hat. So we done comedy and it worked out real well, me and Carter and Ralph and George Shuffler.

We could play three schools a day. You see, I'd set them up on forty-five-minute shows and we'd work maybe a couple during the morning. Say we'd do our first show at 8:30, which meant you had to get up early and drive. So we'd do one at 8:30, and then maybe I'd have the schools set up where we'd have about a thirty-minute drive on to the next school. Well, we'd catch two in the morning before dinner and then we'd catch our last one in the evening around one o'clock, before school turned out at three. So we'd catch about three schools a day that way. And we usually played— like, we started on Tuesday and played through Friday. Well, then, Friday I'd always have a night show to go somewheres and then we'd have Saturday night to go. That give us schools about four days a week and then night shows on Fridays, Saturdays, which averaged out and made us a good week's work.

The schools, that was strictly for the children. We taught them the basics of bluegrass music, the old-time tunes, and me and Carter would tell little stories and I'd do comedy. We just kindly taught them the real roots of bluegrass music, how it got started, and then ideas, how people got songs wrote, and then Ralph would explain about the banjo, the old clawhammer style and then the other style, you know. It was more or less just like a class, you know, a music class to the children, because it was stuff that they had heard about from the old folks, like their grandpa and their grandmother, that they really didn't know the real facts about till we went and played the schools. So it was more or less teaching a class and music, too. We combined it together and it made a pretty good little show, and a good subject, too, to do about old-time bluegrass music. They used to call it old-time hillbilly music, you know, till later they hung bluegrass on it. It made a pretty good thing. People really enjoyed it.

So we stayed busy. We got into that thing and Carter and Ralph, they was lucky if they got to go back to Live Oak once a month then. And when summertime come on, then we would play the drive-in theaters. They would show the movie and then we would go on top of the concession stand, right on top, out in the air. Bugs'd eat you up, man, bugs, mosquitoes, but we'd always do a forty-five-minute show on top. Then the biggest flat rate that the drive-ins would ever pay was a hundred dollars a night. They'd pay you a guarantee of a hundred dollars a night.

We had a few we played like Hazard, Kentucky, and we would play Olive Hill, Kentucky, Tom T. Hall's hometown, we played the drive-in theater there, and then of course we'd work the other drive-in theaters through eastern Kentucky through the weekdays. On Saturday night, I'll never forget, on Saturday night they would pay you a hundred dollars flat, but through the weekdays you had to work them all on percentage. They would work it fifty-fifty. They'd take the price of the movie off the top and the posters and then we'd split fifty-fifty. And the admission back then was seventy-five cents. Finally got it up to a dollar. But, as the old fellow says, it kept us eating, and we all had work and it kept the band together. And that was the most important thing.

And I think back then, that's the reason so many people didn't keep the same groups together, cause they just didn't get enough work. You take back in the fifties, rock and roll, when Elvis Presley come out. Man, it was rough on bluegrass music. Course I've got nothing against rock and roll music. I like all kinds of music. But it sure made it rough on us old boys playing bluegrass. Because he was the king of rock and roll and man alive, every town you'd go in that's all you could hear, was Elvis Presley, rock and roll. Movies and stuff like that. I never will forget, I was always kindly glad sometimes when we played where they was showing an Elvis Presley movie. Boy, we'd always have a big crowd. If they'd get to see Elvis and the Stanley Brothers and the Clinch Mountain Boys, why we didn't have to worry about eating that night. Elvis was one of the greatest in rock and roll, and I thought a lot of the guy because he just had his style and of course we had our style which started many years before rock and roll ever come out. But the old saying goes, we couldn't quit eating just because rock and roll was big. We had to go on.

But I really wish that Carter would've lived to've seen the festivals to get as big as they have now, because the festivals had just begun to hit back in those days. Carlton Haney, I think he was the man that kindly first started the bluegrass festivals up in Fincastle, Virginia, near Roanoke, you know, back in '65. People, they didn't know what was going to happen. Carter told me they was Carter and Ralph and Bill Monroe and Don Reno and Red Smiley, and I think they only had maybe a couple, three hundred people for the first festival they had ever at that horse farm at Fincastle. And they just, they didn't know what to think.

And I think Carlton just kindly divided the money up, paid them all a little bit. I never will forget, Carter said, "Now, Shorty"—he called Carlton "Shorty"—"don't forget, we all got to eat." That's just the way Carter was. Carter was plainspoken but he was a great guy. And he was just Carter, that's what he was. But like I said, I would give anything if Carter would've lived to've seen how big the festival grew at the old home place. And I just wish Carter could've lived to've seen all the festivals. Cause back then you was lucky if you cleared seventy-five to a hundred dollars a week. It was just that rough, you know. But still, you had to eat and you was lucky to get that much work.

Carter would always let me send his wife money. See, they was living in Live Oak then, Carter and Ralph was, and Carter'd say, "Ah, you'd better wire a little grocery money home to my wife and kids." He said, "They'll think I've deserted them." And I know a lot of times Carter has given me twenty-five or thirty dollars to send home for his family to live off, eat, for a week. Course that was about all we could afford back in them days because, you know, we was traveling on the road.

And he always did respect—he liked his family. And that's one thing I'll give Carter credit for. If he had a dollar he wanted to make sure that his family got that part of it to live off of, you know. And he had a fine family. Yes, he had three boys and I believe two girls. And that's one thing I'll give Carter credit for. He was a family man. He liked his family. He missed them a lot, you know. Cause I know on the road he would talk about his boys and his girls and everybody like that and his wife. He was a good fellow. I really liked him.

You know, when Carter and Ralph first went to Live Oak, back then, they worked for Jim Walters. They had these TV shows for Jim Walters Homes there. And of course they probably made good money, big money when they first went there. But as the old saying goes, you know all areas and territories, they play out. And I think at the time Carter and Ralph got in touch with me they was getting ready for a move and a change.

I thought it was a good move myself, not only for my benefit but for Carter and Ralph too, because we got to work a lot and we traveled a lot. The last year Carter lived, 1966, we played a lot of schools and we had a lot of good times. Course after I went to work with Carter and Ralph they got that overseas trip, they went overseas. I didn't get to make that trip with them because they'd already had all their plans made, and their shots they had to take and all that stuff. While Carter and Ralph was gone overseas, I went and set up a lot of work for us here.

And then I got us a regular spot on the "World's Original Jamboree" in WWVA in Wheeling. We played that once a month. So I went to work on a lot of stuff like outdoor theaters. And we played a few Sunday jobs back then. You could play Oxford, Pennsylvania, Sunset Park there, and we could play Chatauqua Park there in Franklin, Ohio. When we went into Wheeling, that opened a lot of good dates for us up in the New England states. We could play parks and things. Allentown, Pennsylvania, parks there you know. And so, with the schools then about three to four days a week and then the drive-in theaters and then our park shows on Sunday, man we really thought we was doing great.

Course we *was*. I mean that's the best—I know I heard Carter make the statement one night to a man at Olive Hill, Kentucky, somebody'd walked around and asked him there at the drive-in theater, he said, "How's things going, Carter?" And he said, "I believe it's the best I've ever saw. We've worked more this year than we've worked in years." Course I was enjoying it, cause to be with a group, the Stanley Brothers, a big name, they learnt me a lot about show business, and I appreciate it.

I worked until Carter passed away, December the first of 1966. At that time we was booked for shows so me and George and Ralph went on and played the shows, worked the shows out, you know. Carter went into the hospital—his first time in the hospital was right after they come back from the Disk Jockey Convention in Nashville, October of 1966. They had been down there working and I met them in a little town called Hazel Green, Kentucky. That's down in Wolfe County, right out of Winchester.

I met them on a Friday night. We was playing a school there and they had been to the DJ Convention and I had a date booked for us to do on a Friday night and Carter went on the stage and he sung about three songs. Me and George and Carter and Ralph, and he started bleeding at the nose, Carter did. So he went off the stage and me and George and Ralph, we finished the show out.

Well, we was scheduled to be in Menefee County, in Frenchburg, Kentucky, the next night on Saturday at the courthouse there. And so I told them, I said, "Boys, I'll meet you there." So Carter said, "Well," he said—they was supposed to go to Cincinnati and pick up some records, King Records. And they was going to meet me back at the courthouse there on Saturday night. But on the way down there Carter started bleeding, I guess through his nose again. Carter told Ralph and George, he said, "I guess we better turn around and get on back into the farm, over at home," the hills here, where the festival's at, you know.

Then I asked Ralph that Saturday when I come out, I said, "Where's Carter, Ralph?" "Ah," he said, "I thought I'd let Carter set this one out. He wasn't feeling too good." So me and Ralph and George went on and done the show that night, at the courthouse there in Frenchburg, Kentucky. Well then, I guess before Ralph ever got back that night Carter took another spell. They had to rush Carter on to the hospital over at Bristol, by the time Ralph and them got back in that night.

And Carter, of course, never did play any more shows. The last show that Carter ever played was the three songs he sung that night in Hazel Green, Kentucky, at the school there, near Campton. So that was in October and of course he passed on in December. And I think it was a great loss to bluegrass music.

I stayed on three more years with Ralph because I didn't know what the situation would be. I knew Ralph wasn't going to quit but I knew it was going to be rough on him to go on after Carter's passing on because Ralph and Carter worked close together. They was close and of course Carter done all the MC work. He was more or less the leader, the front man. So I told Ralph, I said, "I know that Carter would want you to go on with the Stanley Brothers sound, you know." And I said, "If it'd been you, Carter would go on, because you boys have donated your life for it, you know." So I told Ralph, I said, "Whatever it takes, I'm with you."

With Ralph, it was still about the same platform. Ralph is a good guy to work with. Ralph is a business man and Carter was too, but they both was great guys to work with. To me they was both the bosses, you know. I admired one just about as much as I did the other. To me they both was just real good guys to work for. And I knew that I could go on and work for Ralph and fare with him just as good as I did when I was with both of them. Because I figured he needed the help and I was right there because I wanted to do everything I could to help Ralph go on.

So me and Curly Ray Cline and George Shuffler, we stayed on with Ralph and we worked. And then later on Larry Sparks, he come into the show and started singing lead with Ralph. I believe that was in—seem to me like it was in February or March, Larry come into the show. Well then George, he went with Don Reno and Bill Harrell. And Larry stayed just almost as long as I did. Larry came into the show, like I said, in February or March and he worked up through October of the same year that I left, in 1969.

The latter part of June of '69 I formed the Goins Brothers, me and Ray did. But me and Ralph are still the best of friends and I still consider Ralph Stanley's one of the best old-time mountain singers and banjo players in the business. Because Ralph is still doing it the way he learned it, back when he was a young boy, him and Carter. And it really makes me feel good that Ralph carried the name, went on with the same sound that the Stanley Brothers, him and Carter started with. And I'd say Ralph is one of the biggest and one of the biggest-drawing acts today in old-time mountain blue-grass music, Ralph Stanley and the Clinch Mountain Boys. And I guess he's been one of the most requested guys on all of the major bluegrass festivals. I know he has on mine. I know every one that I have, he plays mine.

He's got a good group, and what I like about Ralph, he's kept the same outfit together. You know, Curly Ray's been with him ever since Carter passed away and of course he's got a fine young lead singer now, Charlie Sizemore. Charlie worked with me and Ray when he was sixteen years old and he went with Ralph back about '78, I believe. He was playing lead guitar and singing with us, me and Ray. He was only about sixteen, seventeen years old. And at that time you know Keith Whitley had left Ralph. He went with J. D. Crowe. And Ralph needed a lead singer.

They's a lot of people say, "Well, did you get mad?" I said, "No, I didn't get mad." Cause that was always Charlie Sizemore's dream. He wanted to be with the Stanley Brothers, sing with Ralph Stanley. So I never get mad at nobody if they can better theirself. You know, you can't fall out with a man that's—so many groups, that's the first thing they do, they get out and they start cutting people down, bad-mouthing, talking about them. But I think that's the wrong way. I think that hurts bluegrass music instead of helping it. So I think a man should just really be friends. The world's big enough and there's enough money out there for everybody to make a living if you want to get out there and get it.

We was in Indiana, working a Saturday night show, and Charlie auditioned some two songs with Ralph. And he told Ralph he had to play out his notice. Made a man's decision. You have to respect a man for that. If he's a kid, you got to think that much of a kid that will do what a man would normally do.

Charlie, he still says that you're the guy that gave me my start. And I appreciate Charlie Sizemore. Charlie Sizemore is a real close friend of mine and just about a kid to me, same as my brother or my kid, because I think a lot of the boy. He never forgets me when he comes around. He ain't like a lot of guys, you know, get a job working with somebody with a big name, next time he sees you he don't know you. Charlie'll always come, he's got a joke or something or other or he's always got a good word to say. You have to respect people like that, you know.

Charlie was a good boy. Charlie stayed with me about a year there and it was just a good opportunity. I'm not saying that he wouldn't've got the job with Ralph but maybe that was his break in his life. By Ralph hearing him with me, you know, working and singing. So you never know.

Just like me and Ray, you know. We got our break starting with the Lonesome Pine Fiddlers and had it not been for Ray working with the Lonesome Pine Fiddlers back in the early years, 1952, why probably me and him neither one would never have been working as a brother act with the Lonesome Pine Fiddlers, with Ezra Cline. But the way it worked out, Ray worked with Ezra back in the early fifties and then had quit and come home. Well then, Ezra was working up in Michigan in 1953, working the Big Barn Frolic, WJR, there in Detroit. And he was getting ready to make a move and come back to Pikeville, Kentucky, going to work on a new station, WLSI, and so he needed a couple of fellows.

He needed a guitar player and a lead singer and a banjo picker and so he called me and Ray there one night from Logan, West Virginia, in November, 1953, and he offered us the job. Well, things was kindly slow. We was working out of a radio station, WHIS there, and winter time was beginning to set in and we didn't have a lot to look forward to. Mountain section in there and it's rough, picking and singing, getting out of them mountains in the wintertime. So this was a good chance for us to go with a big, well-established group, you know, a name, so me and Ray, we debated on it a night or two and we decided we'd take it.

So me and Ray left Bluefield in 1953, November, and went to work with the Lonesome Pine Fiddlers. Now I think that was the smartest and wisest move we ever made cause we got a lot of publicity. We learned a lot of things. We got a lot of exposure and it's been a lot of help to us since we formed the Goins Brothers show.

Because with a big group—people remembered the Lonesome Pine Fiddlers and we recorded a lot of records with them and so it's really been a lot of help to us.

It all helps, you know. It's like the old saying, rolling a snowball with snow, the longer you roll it the bigger it gets. If it's good things it all helps. I like everybody in bluegrass music. I don't dislike nobody. I like everybody and I think everybody should be that way. If you can help a man, help him, don't try to knock him. I think that's what makes bluegrass good and I think that's what adds a good flavor to it, if you can get out and say something good about a man. Then you don't have to worry when you see him, well, I talked about that fellow. You dodge, you worry, trying not to meet him, you know. So it's kindly like a book. You can write a good book, you can write a bad book. If you write a good book, you're proud for everybody to read it. And if it's a bad book, you kindly dread people reading it.

But Carter and Ralph to me, they are legends in this business, and of course Carter's gone on and his song writing will never be forgotten. He wrote a lot of songs that Ricky Skaggs recorded, you know. And to me their music will never die. Carter and Ralph will go down in history as one of the greatest brother acts that ever was. Just like Flatt and Scruggs. Acts like that, it's like a fire, you don't put it out overnight. It's something that lasts just right on from generation to generation.

If it hadn't been for people like Bill Monroe and the Blue Grass Boys, the Stanley Brothers, Flatt and Scruggs, Don Reno and Red Smiley, I just wonder what would have happened to this kind of music. They laid the true foundation, the good pattern for old-time bluegrass music. And we're kindly like the pups, you know. We're following the old dog and it's been a lot of help to have a good leader. Just like a leader in anything. You got to have a leader and you have to go along with it and it really helps if you've got a good leader that will lead you the right way to go, you know, and teach the old-time music.

Larry Sparks

"I guess Ralph liked what I had to offer"

One of the more mysterious events in the early solo career of Ralph Stanley occurred at Tom's Tavern, a well-known bluegrass venue in Dayton, Ohio, on February 7, 1967. The house band at that time featured Roy Lee Centers, generally regarded as a musical, and in some ways a personal, reincarnation of the late Carter Stanley, whose work was already well known to Ralph Stanley. Ralph was also there and had already decided he needed a new lead singer. But the apparently inevitable did not happen. Instead of hiring Centers, as the result of an audition that took place that evening Stanley took on a very young musician from Ohio named Larry Sparks, who had performed off and on with the Stanley Brothers as a lead guitar player but who had done almost no singing with them.

Stanley would later explain this odd decision by saying that he was reluctant to face such a vivid reminder of his recently dead brother at this time. And there may be some truth to that. But it is hard to escape the conclusion that Sparks got the job at least in part because in a quiet, self-effacing, but completely determined way, he took the initiative and asked for it.

Sparks proved to be an excellent singer and performer, both in his three-year stint with the Clinch Mountain Boys and in his subsequent solo career, which continues to flourish to this day. His success is in an important way a measure of one unique quality of bluegrass music and the bluegrass community: while other forms of commercial vernacular music—rock, country, pop, folk—tend to concentrate very strongly, for better or for worse, on the performer as a personality, the bluegrass style and the bluegrass audience are much more prone to let the art stand by itself. Even more than any of the other top-ranked bluegrass stars, Larry Sparks has no public persona. He does not demand that you love him (or hate him) as an individual: he simply gets up on the stage and does the job. On stage and off, he is quiet, self-disciplined, and sane, a complete professional—qualities that have served him very well for the past twenty years and promise to continue to do so for a long time to come.

I was born in Lebanon, Ohio. Nineteen forty-seven was when I was born. If I make it till September I'll be thirty-eight. Thirty-eight years of almost nothing but bluegrass music. My daddy and my mother, they moved to that area back years ago, I guess back in the twenties or thirties. From Jackson County, Kentucky. They were from McKee, Kentucky. One of my sisters and one of my brothers was born down there and the rest of us were born in Ohio.

All the people back then, when they moved up to Indiana, Ohio, Michigan, or wherever, it was for work, you know. It seem like most people—well, maybe not most, but a lot of the people settled in the Dayton, Cincinnati, Miami Valley area. That's where a lot of people settled from Kentucky. My dad did just different kinds of jobs. He was a farmer, and then he went into factory work for several years. Worked in a factory right there in Lebanon for a long time.

I think my music must have been sort of a thing where it just happens. It was just a natural thing, meant for me to be into, I think sometimes. Wasn't any persuasion, like "You go and play" and "You got to do that." Sort of took it on my own to do it. But I can remember listening to all the different music when I was a kid. A lot of the old-time stuff. I remember listening to the Opry on one of those big old-time radios. I was only about four or five years old. And I can remember back when we didn't have electricity. Had lamps. That's a good memory. And stuff like that, you know.

Let's see, my first guitar. There was always a guitar around the house. It was an old Harmony guitar, one of the S-hole Harmonies. And I'm trying to trace that down today, if it's still around. My brothers played a little bit. They would play just at home, and I had a couple of brothers would go out and play some of the clubs and stuff around. So there was always a guitar around the house. And they'd bring people over to play at times.

And my sister, Bernice, we grew up pretty much together. She's a little bit older than me, but we grew up sort of together, and she sang and played. Back then we sang in church and stuff. And she showed me some chords on the guitar. She was a big help. She's pretty responsible for me learning the chords, starting out. Then we sang. We made some of these little old record things, that little home outfit, what do you call it? I got those at home, that we sung together on. I got them put away. Maybe down the road sometime, someone might be interested in something like that. You never know.

I was good enough to play in a band when I was fourteen or fifteen, playing lead guitar. And back then, rock was real heavy, real popular, and I played some rock in different clubs and stuff, Dayton area and Franklin area.

But bluegrass is what I liked. My sister, Bernice, she married a guy that played bluegrass, and I think that influenced me even more. And I always liked the Stanley Brothers, too. We used to listen to their stuff on the radio. WCKY was a very popular station. You can ask anybody about the Stanley Brother records on WCKY. They were probably more popular than anyone on that station.

That station I think did a lot for me. I'm sure it did a lot for other people, too. You know, just being able to have that to listen to. Such a big, powerful station, reaches out so far and everything. Shame it's not that way today. There was Wayne Raney. Then they had another guy there in Middletown, I remember, used to come on with a Scruggs tune, where he turns the keys down on that thing. I think it was "Flint Hill Special." Tommy Sutton. I remember him very well, listening to him every day. Well, that was just the thing, you know. Everybody'd turn their radio on every day when he was on in the afternoon. Just like Moon Mullins. Seem like that show just was a must right there in that area. Like Moon's show he had in the afternoon. People look forward to that, you know.

So I was playing with a bluegrass band there. I played some mandolin and dobro and lead guitar and was learning to sing. I worked with my brother-in-law, and I worked with Taylor Gilbert. He was a banjo player in that area. And different ones. Irvin Mackintosh and his band. We'd play about two or three nights a week, in clubs and everything. I guess I was about sixteen when Moon Mullins came to Middletown. And a friend of mine, a banjo player, Wilbur Hall, he liked my guitar playing and him and Moon were friends and he told him about my playing and everything.

And Moon knew the Stanleys. So they came through one time and worked a club in Hamilton. They were short a lead guitar player. So that's how really I got started with the Stanley Brothers right there. They had called him to see if there was someone in that area and he put them on me. I think Ralph called me that day and Carter liked my guitar playing real well.

So we played that club and the next week we went and played the University of Chicago. I got a tape of that show at home. I'd like to see Ralph or someone put that out some day. Be something good. I remember we went over that song, "Sharecropper's Son," up at the university in a hotel room, the room we stayed in. Carter and Ralph had a tape recorder, and they were fixing to record it later. And on that tape that I have from that show Carter is singing that. Because we practiced it that day, went over it. He was showing us how the song went and everything. We worked it out and Carter and Ralph did it that night on their show.

We traveled by car. A lot of the interstates, they were just—there wasn't a lot of them finished. So we did a lot more driving. There was more two-lane roads a-traveling. One time we were coming out of Ohio going someplace. And they let me drive. I guess I was probably eighteen. I must've took over about twelve o'clock at night. Ralph got in the back of the car, the back seat, and went to sleep. Carter was watching me close but he must've got pretty tired and dozed off for a couple of hours. He dozed off for a good three hours, I guess. And I got on this big interstate and man, I must have gone two hundred miles out of the way. And we had to be somewhere next day for a show.

Well, Carter woke up. I remember him waking up long about break of day. He said, "Well"—he called me "Laro"—"Where're we at here, Laro?" I said, "Ah, I guess we're getting close." But it didn't look right to him. You can feel it, boy, when you're traveling the road. If you're going the wrong route, you know, you got that feeling? Something's wrong. Something's wrong. He squirmed around and woke Ralph up. Hollered at Ralph, "Ralph, where're we at?" And Ralph—you know how he clears his throat? "Ahem. I don't know, Carter."

They checked their map. We went on down the road and saw a big sign there. And the sign said—now we were to be way down in the southern part of Ohio, or Kentucky somewhere. At daylight that morning we should have been there, you see. And when we thought this out it must've been six or seven o'clock in the morning. And I think I was twenty-three miles out of Cleveland.

Oh boy. Ralph, he said, "Pull it over." He took the car and took it on in. I think back now, that was pretty funny. After it was over. Twenty-three miles out of Cleveland! We were supposed to have been about two hundred fifty, three hundred miles south from there. Well, they didn't—you know. They understood. It just was real lucky that we had enough time to get on in. If we hadn't, they might have got on my case a little bit more.

And another time we were in Detroit. Carter and Ralph, you know that they always dressed alike, same coats and stuff. Wore nice stage uniforms. Nothing real fancy, just simple, but real nice. They had these things hanging up in the car and we went in to play this date. Fay McGinnis was with us. It was Carter and Ralph, Fay McGinnis, me, and Roy McGinnis. And we had Red Stanley with us, played fiddle. That was the party right there.

But we went in this place, and somebody, I never have been able to find out who, but one of us left the car door unlocked when we went in. And we came back out and the first thing they noticed— the coats had been hanging up in the car, okay? They didn't wear them that night. And the coats were gone. The jackets were gone. The stage uniforms were gone. And they had some other stuff in the car that someone had got, you know.

They were real nice jackets, too, boy. Real pretty. They had them on some album. I think they wore those on the *Folk Concert* album, maybe. They didn't wear them no more after that date. Somebody got them.

So I worked part time with them off and on for a year and a half or whatever, different shows and stuff. Carter died in December of '66, and I worked with them up till about two months before he died. Did some shows with them and I heard that he died in December there.

Back when I was working with them I'd done a little record, recorded one of their songs, a single record, for Jack Lynch of Jalyn Records. And I guess Ralph had heard me sing somewhere too, you know. But maybe it was off that record, or sometime. I didn't do any lead singing with him and Carter. I just sung a little baritone, I think.

And Ralph came back to Dayton in February, after Carter died, and worked a couple of nights there in Dayton. And I went up to see him. He was looking for a lead singer, somebody to sing with him. He played a place there, Tom's Tavern, used to have a lot of bluegrass there, out on Fifth Street. And I got up to sing with the other band, Roy Lee Centers's band. He was playing as a house band. I'd played some with Roy Lee. We worked a lot of clubs around Dayton, off and on. When I wasn't playing with the Stanleys I'd work some with him.

So I went up there and set in with him, did a couple, three

tunes. And Ralph liked my singing good enough to where he, you know, wanted to talk to me. That's where I took the job with him that night. I think Roy Lee had sung some with Ralph that night and I had sung one with him too, on stage, with Ralph, and sung some with Roy Lee's band. And I guess Ralph liked what I had to offer and thought I'd work in with what he had. So I took the job.

I moved down to Clintwood, Virginia, and stayed there a while. And I got married about that time, real young. I lived there I guess a year, year and a half. Then I went back to Ohio and worked with him probably another six months after I moved back.

Ralph had a station wagon. We'd travel in that, four of us: Ralph, myself, Curly Ray, and Melvin Goins. That was it. Played more clubs then. Played a lot of drive-ins, drive-in theater type shows. That was an experience, too. We'd play on top of the drive-in roof. They were popular up till I guess about '69 or so, '69 or '70, and then they started fading out. But you could play those drive-ins on Monday nights, Tuesdays, Wednesdays, Sundays, you know. They were good things to have. Really was a good base cause if you was going somewhere and you needed a date going and a date coming back you could always book a drive-in theater, usually. Especially in Kentucky and Virginia, Tennessee, places like that. I guess they're gone out now. There's no more of them.

Well, after a while I got to where I really wasn't satisfied. I felt I could do more for myself on my own. Working with Ralph was fine. I learned a lot, and it was a good experience and he's a fine man. Couldn't beat him to work for. But I just felt I was limited a lot, in my talent, what I could do. Ralph wanted to play it a certain way and that was it. And I couldn't really go any farther with anything. Which, you know, I respect him for that and that's his thing, so that's what I tried to do when I was with him.

But I felt I could do good on my own and maybe come up with a different style. And I did. Took me probably about three years to get started back, you know. I did an album for Pinetree Records, a couple of albums for them. I moved into Michigan with an album up there with Old Homestead Records. Then I went to Starday, King Records, Nashville, and did an album. That gave me a good boost right there. That started me where I needed to be. That put me on the road quite a bit. Then, you know, it's been good ever since. There's a lot of work that's had to go into it but it's been good. Raised two kids with it. You can make it in bluegrass. You have to manage yourself good, have something different to offer the people.

Curly Ray Cline

"I've lived a lot in my time"

Curly Ray Cline is not called "the old Kentucky fox hunter" for nothing. Fox hunting as practiced in eastern Kentucky has very little in common with the aristocratic sport of riding to hounds that we associate with England and tidewater Virginia. It is a working man's pastime, done on foot. It requires cunning, perseverance, and the ability to stay up all night after a hard day's work. Above all it requires a very sharp ear, accurate enough not only to distinguish the voices of one's own hounds from anyone else's at a distance of several miles but also to determine whether those hounds have found a scent, lost one, or holed their quarry. And if a man is to enjoy it, he needs an excellent sense of humor, since Kentucky-style fox hunting is a sport that is unsuccessful far more often than not. It also helps to be a good storyteller, since a good part of fox hunting consists in simply sitting by a fire in the middle of the night waiting for something to happen, and a good story always helps to pass the time.

Ralph Stanley had known for years that Ray Cline was a first-rate old-time fiddler. It was perhaps more his fox hunter's qualities that led him to take him on full-time shortly after the death of Carter Stanley. At any rate, it was one of the best moves he ever made. "Now Ralph would always have someone on *his side*," a close associate remarked some years later.

Cline had, and still has, an inexhaustible fund of loyalty. He is grateful to Ralph Stanley—as well he might be: he was earning only a marginal living for himself and his family, and that by backbreakingly hard work, when Stanley hired him. And the ties are mutual: Stanley bankrolled Cline's first venture into solo recording by offering to buy up any albums that Cline failed to sell, thus taking the loss himself (more than a casual gesture considering the band's financial state at the time). And Stanley insisted that Cline make his albums all his own, rather than share the billing with some other artist.

The Clinch Mountain Boys generally don't play the bus radio while on the road. "Curly Ray has the floor most of the time," Stanley says. "He keeps us well entertained." It may have been for his talents as a private entertainer that Cline was first hired, but he soon developed into a very effective public entertainer as well. By now his comic stage personality is so familiar, and seems so much a part of himself, that it comes as something of a shock to realize (through listening to taped performances) that in the early days of the band Cline scarcely said a word on stage, limiting himself strictly to fiddling.

Cline's singing career, like his recording career, was his boss's idea, and since then Stanley publicly effects to regret ever having made the suggestion. But in fact—and Stanley surely realized this—it was just what the act needed. In the old days Carter Stanley could crack jokes and banter with the audience and his fellow artists with no effort whatsoever. Ralph Stanley could not, and given the terrible intensity of his art a bit of comic relief was very much in order. Curly Ray Cline provided it and continues to provide it.

There are some (a minority, to judge from crowd reaction) in the audience who object very strenuously to Cline's singing and the rest of his antics. These people like to call themselves "purists," but if purity consists in sticking to the traditions of old-time music then the real purists are Cline and the people who appreciate what he does. His model as a fiddler was the austere Arthur Smith (who lived with the Cline family for a while when Ray was a boy and who is the source for many of the numbers on Cline's albums). But as an entertainer Cline is following, deliberately or otherwise, in the footsteps of such great crowd-pleasers as J. E. Mainer and Uncle Dave Macon. Even in the old days there were no doubt those who objected to the boisterous clowning of entertainers of this sort, and in fact Smith himself told young Ray (who is himself the source of the story) that he "ought to be shot" for winning a fiddle contest through showmanship rather than artistry. But no one can deny that cornball comedy is an integral part of the tradition of old-time music.

Ralph Stanley would have to be the last to deny it, despite his public stance of disdain and embarrassment over Cline's foolishness. For in fact he himself is the source of just about all the most notably outrageous excesses on Cline's albums, from "Pop Goes the Weasel" played on a turkey call or the genuine recorded hee-haws that interrupt the playing of "Braying Mule" to the "improved" lyrics of "Blue-Eyed Verdie" and "Boar Hog." It is hard to escape the conclusion that Cline is really a public expression of Stanley's hidden alter ego, of the Ralph Stanley who, as those close to him know, likes nothing better than a practical joke, even, or especially, one that takes six months to come to fruition, or who can happily sing, given the right company, the unprintable lyrics of "Hook and Line."

Curly Ray Cline's saving grace is that he never, in public or in private, takes his comedy seriously. His albums reflect this: cut in as short a time as possible, they are full of ad libs and unrehearsed slipups. Ever the salesman, Cline takes time and trouble only with the design and production of the jackets, since, for an artist doing point-of-contact work, covers are what sell albums. Again, the "purists" recoil. But those who can appreciate being allowed, so to speak, to eavesdrop while a group of great musicians let their hair down and have a good time are far more fortunate.

My daddy, he didn't have much time to fiddle. He had too many mouths to feed. He worked in the mines some and on the farm and played a little music on the weekends, sometimes. When I first started playing, my arms wasn't long enough to even reach the fiddle neck. Had a full-sized fiddle. I'd sit on my daddy's knee and play on the floor. I can remember playing on one string, cause I couldn't reach no more.

Our first group was just a family band: me, and my brother Ned that got killed in the army, and there was Dillard Cline in it to start with, and Ezra Cline. We just mostly had a family group there. We'd play on the weekends, when we could get to it.

During the war, there was about four years there they didn't make any cars, from '42 I believe to about '46. And course we didn't travel much then. We'd play maybe on a radio station, go out and play a pie supper or a dance. Some little organization would sponsor a show and we'd make a little for spending money. They had to have stamps then to get gas and most of the people that got them was the people that was in business. Used them with the coal trucks and the school buses. You just about had to play local then. I mean, there wasn't any way of getting around.

I guess I worked in the mines there about four or five years, coal mines. I was telling the boys coming up here that I once worked fourteen straight days, nine hours a day, loading coal, and on the fourteenth day I can remember coming out and Dad had a churn of home brew. Man, I never tasted anything so good in my life. I got on my horse and got me about a quart of that and I felt like a man ought to feel. I'd worked myself to death, buddy.

In fact then you had to work or somebody had to work. They'd took all the local boys in the army just about. I guess they'd've took me, if I hadn't got deferred on account of that. They had to leave somebody to work, take the rest of them into the army. You see, Dad, he got his foot poisoned in the mines; he had a toe cut off. He worked like that about three years, till it started up his leg and they cut one of his legs off and he used a wooden leg for a while. Then after that, about three more years, he took it in the other foot.

When he died he was only fifty-seven. He'd had both legs cut straight across, eight inches up from his ankle. And I've seen him take an old jenny down there when he was almost blind, ploughing them gardens, with a plough stalk, one of them bull's tongue plough stalks. People would stop along the road and wonder what was going on, seeing him going through that cornfield ploughing. That jenny, it just showed him what to do, I guess.

I guess that's what they call the good old days. They wasn't too much money but they had a lot of fun. Didn't take too much then. Everything was cheap, you know. They had something called rations, it was something like commodities. Bring it on the train, you know, every month. People go and take sleds and horses and load their sleds up and haul it in, enough to do a month at a time. Beans, corn, flour—they'd get flour in big barrels back then. They'd allow so much to each family, you know, and then they'd put it in bags after they got it home.

But I just wonder about people like that today. I don't think they could raise—I believe there was fifteen in our family, and Dad died young and left the older ones to take care of the younger ones. Be pretty hard to do that today.

After the war we got the Lonesome Pine Fiddlers back together. Course, the brother that got killed, Charlie replaced him. I believe Charlie was sixteen years old when he started. We had several record contracts. The best one was for Victor. I believe we cut twenty-six numbers for RCA Victor. And then we cut several on other labels. I cut four numbers on King. Then we had a Cozy record we cut some on, with Bob and Larry—Bobby Osborne and Larry Richardson—Ezra, and myself.

We was playing up in Michigan in the fifties. We had a pretty good thing going there. We worked in the factory, the Hudson plant, and then we'd cut shows for this Tennessee Blackwell Sausage and then we'd do the Big Barn Frolic, WJR, on Saturdays. That was where we helped the Davis Sisters get on Victor. We played the Big Barn Frolic together. We helped them make the audition record, "I Forgot More Than You'll Ever Know," the hit record that they made, we helped them on that. And I believe they got that on Victor. Then B. J., she got killed before it, I mean when it was going good, she got killed in a car wreck.

Then me and my brother Charlie, we cut a session done in the style of the Delmore Brothers but I don't think they ever did release it. For Jack Clark, used to have Fortune Records. With a different style, you know, something like the one me and Keith did on *The Pikeville Jail*, the "Brown's Ferry Blues," we cut four numbers something like that.

That was in the fifties. So we stayed around about I guess about eighteen months. The records got to playing pretty good, so we'd go home for vacation, and when we got down in Pikeville, Kentucky, we found a sponsor and just moved in to there.

I was in the coal business, and I had a truck driver called Doc Blankenship, and he didn't know what a house trailer was. We was hauling coal and I said, "Buddy, we're figuring on moving to Pikeville." We still had our trailers in Michigan. And I said, "You know anything about pulling a house trailer?" He said, "No." "Well," I said, "could you rig up something to go and get one? We got two up there." Me and Ezra.

So we fixed up a trailer hitch and got protection with the chain, got the license and insurance and everything and we got through working over there and we took out and left and got into Michigan about two o'clock in the morning. He got in a poker game and lost what he had and we had just enough to get gas to get out of there. So we left out of there. We pulled Ezra's trailer first in there, into Pikeville, and we missed the turn-off. It's so dark up there. They went to bed with the chickens.

We got that trailer up there in Pikeville, with those little old narrow one-way streets and we never did like to get out of there. We met one of the announcers coming to work down there, Stewart Odell. He was walking to the radio station, and I said, "Where in the world is that place, that Van Hoos trailer lot?" He said, "You done passed it." There we was, all tied up in town, couldn't get out.

Well, we finally did get out. We got this one trailer down to where we could cut loose and we hadn't slept any. We took the tags off it and went back to get the other one. So we ended up, there was two tired boys. We took about a week and moved both of them trailers down there. And he'd lost more than he'd made playing poker so we had to borrow some money to get the second one down. That's how I moved to Pikeville. So I'll tell you this—we was just talking a-coming up—I said, I've lived a lot in my time.

When we moved down to Pikeville the original band, they split up. Charlie went with Bill Monroe and Paul Williams, he went with Jimmy Martin. So that's where the Goins Brothers came in. I had an old '46 model Plymouth and I was up around Bluefield and they wasn't doing anything. They were working part-time and playing part-time. Ray Goins had already cut some records with us but Melvin had never started. I knew Melvin was a pretty good cook and I had a trailer down there, nobody in it, so I just drove up and got them. Brought them down to Pikeville. All three of us married up the same hollow. We been down in that county ever since. Melvin I reckon's moved out now. He's down round Catlettsburg. Ray's still on the Rockhouse. He's about a mile below me, maybe half a mile.

Verdie, I met her at the Baby Ritz Drive-In, right at the edge of the outskirts of town there. This Sergeant Cornett, with the state police, he was a good friend of mine and Ray's. He'd come down to the trailer and he'd bring us something to drink. When we wasn't playing we'd have a good time, you know, together. He told me they's some good-looking lady up there at the Baby Ritz wanted to meet me. So we went up there one morning for breakfast and he introduced her to me and that's where it all started. Then she got Ray a date with Helen, his wife. Then Eddie, the sarge, he got a date with the lady's daughter that run the Baby Ritz so we had it right in the family there, for as long as it lasted.

Man, we'd have bands coming through there. That was the Grand Old Opry there at that trailer lot. They wasn't about two or three trailers and when it got dark why that bottom'd get full of people. We had parties and everything there.

What we made was clear, I mean, we knew enough people to get by, you know. But we never traveled like we do now. We just traveled where the radio station reached out, you know. We didn't travel nationwide, like we do now. The Fiddlers I don't guess was in four or five states in all their fifteen years. Just traveled to where they played the radio, listening audience, you know. We was on a big record company but it didn't benefit us none; we didn't get out.

I remember one time Eddie, he really liked the Stanley Brothers and they was playing down in there and Eddie said, "Why don't you get the Stanley Brothers to stop as they come back?" They was playing out of Prestonsburg. Well, they's a little restaurant over there called Kelly's Restaurant, over from the trailer lot, and me and Ray walked over and they was having coffee. And Carter said they'd stop as they come back up.

Eddie, if he didn't have something he'd go and pick up something. So we had half a gallon of good moonshine liquor, anything they wanted to eat there in the barracks, so they stopped. Ralph didn't—why, he'd take a drink but he didn't do much drinking. And I think we set there and talked about three or four o'clock the next morning. We had a show on every day down there from 11:30 to 12 for Home Furniture Company so we didn't have anything to lose. So we stayed out there till almost daylight. Ralph said they got in— well, they had a show, "Farm and Fun Time," was up in the middle of the day so they wasn't in no hurry. So they really enjoyed that. And Eddie did, too. He really liked the Stanley Brothers.

I knew them, you know, on the radio stations but they had never been down in there since I'd moved there with my trailer. That's the first time they got acquainted down there. And they'd play the records there where we'd eat about all the time, they'd play the Stanley Brother records. And I knew that'd be a good time, you know, for them to stop. Oh, Carter really enjoyed that.

The '57 flood, we still had the trailer when the '57 flood covered us. It got the trailers and everything. The rest that'd come in there, they didn't have any insurance. I had the insurance from Michigan and this guy, he came in there and my brother-in-law was going to work. And this guy wanted to know where in the world was Curly Ray Cline. My brother-in-law said his trailer'd got covered up and he'd moved up to Rockhouse with his father-in-law and he turned around and brought him up there around eleven o'clock in the night. Got me out of bed. We got on some arctics and some old boots and went down there.

We couldn't get in the trailer, it was so bad and muddy, we just got the serial number off of it and went over there to where we could see and he wrote out the papers and everything. He asked me, "You want that trailer back?" He said, "I can't do nothing with it." I said, "Well, I might pull it out of there." He said, "You give me a hundred and fifty dollars and you can have it."

And I had just renewed the insurance. I just got it paid for and I believe for every dollar I paid I collected a hundred. And I come a hair of not getting insurance. I believe I got twenty-five hundred dollars. But I was the only one that collected any insurance because they didn't have any flood insurance down there. And I'd got this in Michigan. And I was the only one.

We took that trailer and pulled it out of there. My brother-in-law had a wreck truck. All what few clothes we had we washed them out in the creek up there in the hollow and we pulled that thing out of there and I went up there and made a place to park it. Took a coal truck and a scoop and made a place to park it. And I stayed in that thing about—I believe before I got the house built I stayed about seventeen years.

And I still sold that trailer, after I'd stayed and it went through that flood, I think I sold it for about as much as I had in it and I lived in it seventeen years. And it had been through all that flood and this give us something to do, I mean we just got up there where we had water and everybody in the family helped me. Got it fixed up and somebody come along and wanted to buy it. And I was getting my house about done and we sold it for almost as much as I had in it. Course they was cheap then. Everybody laughed, they said they started out of that trailer down in the hollow. Some guy bought that trailer. He said they was rats and everything run out of there, where they'd got up in, you know, and couldn't get out. He just about tore it all to pieces getting it out of there. Some lady was wanting it just to keep for a souvenir or something. I don't know whether it's still down there or not. Man, I'll tell you, this music racket is something.

That flood, that water, they never had had anything like that in a hundred years, they said. But I swear after that went down them yards and them places where all that rich settling was was prettier than ever. You couldn't even tell they'd been a flood there. They's some old chickens stayed there; they almost starved to death on top of a pump. They'd come out of there and got as high as they could go and they wouldn't move. Some people finally come in there and got them in a truck and picked them up after that water went down. They was riding them boats up and down the road there.

This old gentleman we stayed with, Ernest Skeens, when he thought we was washed off he just about went wild. He got down there and found out that trailer was there and he come walking through the woods and found us. "Daggone," he said, "get out of there," he said. "You can go up to my house and stay." I said, "You reckon it's safe to go up through there?" He said, "I got down here. You all can go back with me."

So we stayed up there and we got straightened out, up in the hollow there, where we're at now. He lived on one side of the creek, so I married on one side of the creek and built on the other. And every one of us that met there except Melvin, and Eddie's dead, we all just in about thirty miles there, we lived together about ten or fifteen years.

Well, the music business got pretty rough and then the coal business was pretty good, but you had to work hard. I got in the mines there and stayed. I guess I put ten or eleven years in. I first just worked for my brother-in-law and then I finally bought a part out of him one. We used buggies and ponies and drag cable motors. Just the old-time way I guess of getting the coal out. You used a lot of men then and got a little bit of coal. Where they use less men now and get a whole lot of coal. The production was different.

I think about as high as we got for coal then was about four, four-fifty a ton, down low as three-fifty. I'd take this boy and maybe two trucks there on the weekend if I wasn't playing and maybe contract a couple of loads of house coal, get fifty or sixty dollars out of it. That was a lot of money then, enough to get groceries with or pay the rent or something.

Well, I had this coal mine and the Stanley Brothers, they was going overseas. They was needing a fiddle player and they wanted me to go with them, but I couldn't get the word through. I wasn't playing, I was running the mine. So Melvin, they couldn't take Melvin, so he comes up—we were at a funeral—he said, "Curly, if I'd knowed I'd've got you a trip over in Germany with the Stanley Brothers." And I said, "Where they at?" He said, "They're gone now." So I got knocked out of that. I think that was about a month's work. And I wasn't making much. I could've got somebody to take my place. Later on Ralph told me about it, said, "We really needed you on that trip." After they came back I started working with them. I'd play with them on the weekend and work in the mines—two jobs, I couldn't hardly make it.

It was getting on my nerves so I had to quit one. I couldn't handle them both. So after Carter died we was playing over there in Virginia one night. I rode with Ralph, and some of the band had another car. And Ralph said, "Well, I don't know how well I'm going to do. But I would like to have you regular, you know, just so we'd take a chance at it."

I said, "Well, I've tried, I've took chances before. I ain't making too much now." He told me what he would do. He'd try to give me enough to make a living. So I sold the mine; I started with him. I didn't know how long it would last but it's been eighteen years and

I'm still with him, probably will be as long as I play. I guess it must've got a little better or, Melvin says, the gravy got a little thicker, or something.

You know, the public, they eat that up. They's so many leaders can't keep the same band. Somebody in a band fifteen or eighteen years they know there's something good somewhere. They don't look to see Ralph without seeing me or seeing me without Ralph. Anywhere we go, that's what they look for. Even truck stops, restaurants, anywhere we stop. It's like him and Carter, you know.

I've been up on the stage with Ralph so much that he's just like a father to me. I may be a little bit older than him but he's taught me a lot of what I know. You know, when I first started playing with him I never did stay at a motel. I didn't know what they looked like. And one time me and Larry Sparks and Melvin ordered up some hotcakes and they brought the butter out and we ate the hotcakes. We didn't know what the butter was. We thought it was ice cream. So we went out and jumped on the manager and we told him we couldn't get any butter. And he said, "Why, the waitress brought you some butter." "No," I said, "that was ice cream." He said, "Go back and taste of it." It sure enough was butter. I didn't know the difference.

Why Ralph hired me? Ah, buddy, I don't know. Well, just to hear me talk, I guess. Traveling they'd have somebody they called a shotgun, you know. I'd do a lot of talking then, when I could stay awake. I can't stay awake now. Man, we rode for hundreds of miles. Ralph's one of the best drivers then that was. He'd drive, man, he could just keep driving. I wondered how he was holding up. We'd have a long weekend, he'd do most of the driving and the playing. George, he'd drive, but he'd take them stubborn spells, like a mule. Yeah, they wanted somebody to talk to the driver. They called it shotgun. I never did travel much, that's the first time I ever heard that, call it the shotgun.

I don't think I could've done any better. I'm well satisfied. If I had it to do over I'd do the same thing. Cause you try so many jobs that people promise, you can't live on a promise. But Ralph's not going to promise you something he can't pay you. He'll pay you every penny he promises or more.

And that means a whole lot. Cause a little bit's worth more than nothing, when you're paying bills and eating. And I had kids in school, too, and I had to make—if you didn't make forty-five, fifty dollars a week you couldn't hardly make it. A top band, lot of times, they'd get a hundred, maybe a hundred and fifty, seventy-five some nights for little clubs and things. Them little schools, they didn't pay much, cause the kids, they didn't have much money to spend.

I don't believe they's anybody else in the business as could've ever done what Ralph's done and not be on the Opry or a regular television show. Just do it from the house and make records. I don't know of any top band as had ever done that. He's sure been lucky. And then doing his own business and paperwork, booking and all that stuff. And he's done good, too. He's built that festival and he's got a nice home there and a nice family. I don't think he'd bettered himself. I think we both done well by staying like that. I'm well satisfied and I think he is too.

12

Jack Cooke

"Keep it mountainous"

A most revealing interchange, as far as Jack Cooke's personality is concerned, took place at the Clinch Mountain Boys' record table at a small festival in Ohio in the summer of 1986. Cooke was handling the record sales as usual, and a fan came up to introduce a visitor from Japan who had somehow managed to make his way to this remote country spot. The young Japanese could speak almost no English at all, but Cooke greeted him in Japanese, listened with endless patience to his broken sentences, exchanged names of mutual acquaintances and places in Japan with which he was familiar thanks to the band's tours in that country, signed the inevitable autographs, and bid the visitor farewell with a cheerful "sayonara." Anyone watching would know for certain that this was one stranger who would go back home with a memory he would treasure forever. And Charlie Sizemore, who was at a nearby table selling souvenirs, remarked that there was nothing unusual in this performance of Cooke's.

Vernon Crawford Cooke, as his constantly used nickname would suggest, remains a country boy to the soles of his boots. This is his real identity, and it should not be called a mask, but behind it there is something more—something that, rightly or wrongly, is not usually associated with the typical country boy. Sophistication is perhaps not quite the word for it; rather, it is a deep understanding for and sympathy for the wide world beyond the hills in which he was born and raised and still lives. The endless years of touring, which began when Cooke was hardly more than a child, have not been wasted on him. He knows people and likes them. He can feel for them, listen to them, and make them feel important. It is hard to imagine that Ralph Stanley had any conscious knowledge when he offered to let Cooke handle the record sales—which means, in reality, to handle all the fans on a day-to-day basis—on the day he hired him. Jack Cooke is the ideal ambassador for the Clinch Mountain Boys.

He is also an excellent bass player, an exciting singer, a quick and astonishingly sharp-eared learner of new material, and a powerful stage personality. He is invariably patient and good-humored with his inevitable bass player's role as the butt of jokes. As often as not he will pull the whole act up by its bootstraps with his shouted "Here we are!" as the band, for the countless thousandth time, takes the stage, or with the well-known but always appreciated "Thank you, music lovers" with which he ironically acknowledges applause after taking his solo. Finally, as a cousin and sometime driver for Dock Boggs, the great traditional singer and banjo player whose original career dated back over half a century ago, he forms a valuable link with the old-time music of the past. Here he is, ladies and gentlemen, the ex-mayor of Norton, Virginia—the title is a genuine one, by the way—Mr. Jack Cooke!

I was born in Wise County, Virginia. I growed up in a family of nine. My father, he played the old clawhammer style banjo picking. Drop thumb, you know. He could pick that just as clean as a bell. A lot of people, when they play they make a lot of noise. He could sing on—he had a finger for every string. And his coordination was just perfect. He was just like steel, you know, hitting steel together. Just clean, clear. And my mom's side of the family, they played, too. So I guess that's where all of us got it from. But every one of us, five brothers and four sisters, all of us plays and sings. And we was all raised in church, raised up in a Christian home. Started out singing in church.

And then me and my brothers, we had a band and we worked local, you know, mostly local. We'd go down to Knoxville, Tennessee, maybe once in a while and be on the Knoxville Barn Dance. We had Kenny Baker playing the fiddle with us some back then. He hadn't left home and was still working in the mines. I went with the Stanley Brothers after me and my brothers broke up. That's the first professional job I ever had, was with Carter and Ralph, over in Bristol, WCYB. "Farm and Fun Time" was what they called that show.

Carter and Ralph had a contest going. The best band was going to get a record contract. So me and my brothers, we entered that contest and we won first place. Then my brothers, they started going in the coal mines, working, and they got married and started having families. And I run into Carter one time and I asked him about a job. So I went to work with them playing the bass fiddle. That was back in around '55 to '57, somewhere along in there. I worked with Carter and Ralph about two and a half years.

I was playing guitar with my brothers' band and of course I started playing the bass with Carter and Ralph. And I went with Bill Monroe for about four and a half years, played the guitar and sung lead for Bill, recorded a lot of stuff for Bill. And then I had a band of my own for a while up in Baltimore, Maryland.

Ralph calls it the Haysi Ha'nts, but that's joking, Ralph's joking about that. It was Jack Cooke and the Virginia Mountain Boys. We worked around Baltimore there for a while and played some television shows and radio, had sponsors, played all the outdoor parks. Like they'd have a show every Sunday, like Sunset Park, West Grove, Pennsylvania, and New River Ranch, Rising Sun, Maryland.

While I was in Baltimore, Carter and Ralph, I'd always do shows with them. They'd come through and they'd always call me. We recorded some stuff for John's Gospel Quartet. It's a used car lot there in Baltimore, Johnny's Used Car Lot, 4801 Harford Road. I never will forget that. Johnny was sponsoring the show and Ray Davis, he was the announcer, the MC on the radio station. And we recorded those albums up over top of the car lot, in a building up over top of the sales department. We had a little studio up there. And we done, I guess it was about four albums of that, John's Gospel Quartet. And Carter and Ralph, they was tied up with a record company, you know, and so that's the reason they called it John's Gospel Quartet.

And we recorded some for Alex Campbell, was on Cabin Creek, I believe. That album was kindly mixed, we wanted to mix it up. Probably some of us didn't know all of the songs, maybe a couple of verses of each one. That's a collector now, you know. Cabin Creek, you can't get that any more. And I recorded some with these Greenbriar Boys, out of New York. With Ralph Rinzler. He's a fine guy. And I recorded an album with them. I've been on several recordings.

After about four years of that my mom, she took sick and I disbanded, came home to stay with her. I got to stay with her about six months out of her last years, you know, that she lived. And after that—they's a flea market down right out of my hometown, Norton, Virginia, called Ramsey, a little settlement down there. And I was down there one day looking around and run into Ralph.

George Shuffler had just quit or Ralph had let George go or something.

Ralph asked me, he said, "Jack, would you like to work some?" I says, "Yeah. I'd sure love to." I said, "After Mom passed away, it's really boresome around here. It's hurting." So I took a job with Ralph. That was on a Wednesday, and he told me to meet him Friday. I met him up there at Norton. He came through and I got with him. I guess that was 1969, the latter part of 1969. I believe that's right. And I've been with Ralph ever since.

The first day I took the job Ralph said, "You can have the record sales." That works good. I enjoy talking to people and sitting around the table and selling a few records and tapes. It's a commission, yeah. I get a good commission on them. Sometimes I make real good and sometimes, you know, you have to take the bitter with the sweet. Good weather, you can sell good, but fighting the rain and everything, it's a job. You have to be there to make the sales, because once you miss a sale, you'll never get that sale back. It's done gone. If you're not there to handle the business, you know. Yeah, we've sold records in snow, rain, and everything else.

Now Carter and Ralph—I thought Carter was one of the best MCs that was in the business. He was very smooth. He could sell the sponsor. He was just relaxed with it, you know. And he was a happy-go-lucky guy. Nothing didn't get to him. You know, he really had the bull. Back years ago, Ralph and Carter, well, their dad told me when I was with them the first time that if it hadn't been for Carter, you know, the bull in Carter, just to keep striving, he said that they would've been out of business. Lee told me this, you know. That's Carter and Ralph's daddy.

He told me that and now Ralph does a good job on MCing. They's a little difference there, but not that much. Ralph, he's getting where he's more relaxed. He was tense there after Carter died. Which, naturally, you know. He didn't do any of the MC work. Carter, he done it all. But I guess he might get just a little tense, doing something like that.

Ralph, he's strictly business, Ralph is. When he tells you something you know you can depend on it. And he's real easy to get along with. That's the whole thing. If you're working with somebody you can get along with good, I mean, that takes a load off everybody. And that's the reason Ralph has carried his Clinch Mountain Boys, you know, he's not changed that personnel too much. He's just as good as his word is. If he tells you something you can depend on that one hundred percent.

Ralph, he's born and bred in this music. He can pick that banjo straight three-finger style, and then he can turn right around and pick it clawhammer style. The city people calls it "frailing," see, but Ralph explains it right on the stage. "Now this ain't frailing. This here is clawhammer." He's about lived this stuff. He's just about lived what he sings about. I mean most of the time it's true stories, you know, the songs. That's about all I know to tell you about that. He's lived them times one time or another. He sings a cappella, you know, that lonesome sound.

He was the first one that started that. We was listening to these—well, they's a quartet down at home called the Chestnut Grove Quartet. And they sung them songs like that without any music. Well Ralph, he was raised in a church like that, Old Regular Baptist, that wouldn't even allow a piece of music in the church house. And Ralph says, "Well," he says, "you think that would sell, to put that on a record like that?" And I says, "Yeah. I like it." And all of us agreed to do it. And we done, I believe it was "Old Village Church Yard" that was the first one we done. And Ralph, on those a cappellas he sings the lead and I do the tenor. But those are hard songs to sing. Their timing, you know. Two words'll be fast and one word'll be slow. It takes a while to get on that. But that was the first song we ever done like that, and people loved it in New York, they loved it everywhere.

Ralph would explain it, about the church. They'd maybe have one songbook or two or three songbooks or not enough to go around to everybody, the congregation, and the man would line it out, and then they'd come right in behind him to sing it that way. So we started doing that and people just loved it. And every album we've ever cut yet, they've been two or three a cappellas on it. And they's people asking for a whole album, you know, with nothing but that a cappella singing.

I sing all parts really. I sing the baritone on the trios when Ralph is singing tenor. But on the gospel songs I do all the tenor singing on those a cappellas that Ralph leads like that. Range, I guess you'd call it probably, pretty good range. Learning harmony, I guess it probably just come automatic. Just having an ear for it, just tell how it goes. It's hard to explain. Just come right in there, you know. Ralph, he'd just start off on something like that when we would be like rehearsing and then I'd catch it right in there. Blend it all in, all three of us or four of us.

That timing on "Act Naturally," well Ralph, he says delaying a word is singing like Mac Wiseman. I knowed what he was talking about so we got that straightened out. I was delaying a couple of words, you know. It was in time but it sounded like it wasn't in time. Sometimes the public couldn't hardly figure that out. I mean, musicians could tell that it was in time, the people that plays the music. Ralph, he don't want you to sing like Mac Wiseman, hold them words too long. That's what it was, I was just holding them too long. So you see he called it delayed timing.

But we got it worked out. We generally know what each other's going to do. It falls in place pretty good. Sometimes you have a bad feeling day or something and it seem like it ain't right, but people comes and tells you it's the best they ever heard you do. You have your days like that, you know. Sometimes you're doing a good job and other times it don't seem right. I guess everybody has days like that.

I remember one time back when I was with Carter and Ralph the first time, we went up north, up in Pennsylvania I believe, and Carter was telling me, he says the only thing that you could get to eat up there on Sunday was like spaghetti. And all them cheeses on it and everything, you know. And I didn't like that. Carter, he's joking me. I didn't know any difference when I first left home like that. Man, I like to starved myself to death on that trip. So we stop in a place where they had real good food, a place down in Maryland somewhere, and I got two big dinners. I got a cold plate and a hot plate too. You know, I like to eat till I can bust.

And we played this New River Ranch and Carter said, "Come out there and see what they got to eat, Jack." So I went out there to this other place where they had pizza pie. I didn't know what pizza pie was back then, back in the mountains like that. So I come back and I said—I called Carter "Chase," you know, everybody called Carter "Chase," and I says, "Chase, they got some of that good peachy pie out here." That tickled Carter to death. I hadn't been away from home, you know. Hadn't been out of the county too much.

When you write this stuff up, you should leave it the way people talk. That's the way it should be. I mean it should be just like anybody says. It should be. Like that mountain music, or bluegrass, however what you call it. Ralph, he calls it mountain music a lot of times, and then he calls it bluegrass sometimes. But that should be based just right down deep, you know. Right to the roots. It should talk country, cause that's where you are, in the country.

And it should be just like that, you know. If they say "ain't," that "ain't" ought to be in there. I mean, you should keep it down, you know, not take it uptown. All this fancy stuff, people can't understand that. A lot of people is ashamed to tell how they was raised and everything, I believe. But a man ought to tell it like it is. Got to keep it country. Keep it mountainous.

Ralph Stanley at the Appreciation Days ceremonies at McClure, Virginia, April 22, 1988. Photo by Miles Ward.

Jack Lynch, Ralph Stanley, George Shuffler, Carter Stanley, and Bobby Osborne, Dayton, Ohio, early sixties. From the collection of Jack Lynch.

Publicity photograph from 1968. From the collection of Jack Lynch.

Ralph Stanley, Melvin Goins, and Larry Sparks, Norwalk, Ohio, July 6, 1968. Photo by Frank and Marty Godbey.

Curly Ray Cline, Melvin Goins (hidden), Ralph Stanley, Larry Sparks, and unidentified bass player, Culpeper, Virginia, 1968. Photo by Mike Seeger.

The "old-time" car at
Culpeper, Virginia, 1968.
Photo by Mike Seeger.

Ralph Stanley and un-identified fan, Culpeper, Virginia, 1968. Photo by
Mike Seeger.

Publicity photograph of Fay McGinnis, early seventies. From the collection of Jack Lynch.

Bill Monroe, Ralph Stanley, Roy Lee Centers, and Jack Cooke, Bean Blossom, Indiana, 1970. Photo by Mike Seeger.

Ralph Stanley and Roy Lee Centers, Lavonia, Georgia, July 26, 1970. Photo by Frank and Marty Godbey.

Ron Thomason, Lavonia, Georgia, July 25, 1970. Photo by Frank and Marty Godbey.

Ricky Lee, Roy Lee Centers, Ricky Skaggs, Curly Ray Cline, and Ralph Stanley in Floyd Bunch's motor home, Okeechobee, Florida, ca. 1973. Photo by Tom Henderson.

Curly Ray Cline, Renfro Profitt, Jack Cooke (hidden), Ralph Stanley, and Keith Whitley taping "Bluegrass Bluegrass" for Kentucky Educational Television, Lexington, Kentucky, June, 1977. Photo by Frank and Marty Godbey.

Junior Blankenship and Charlie Sizemore, Old Town School of Folk Music, Chicago, Illinois, March 9, 1984. Photo by John Wright.

Ralph Stanley, Maggard Sound Studio, Big Stone Gap, Virginia, April 2, 1986. Photo by John Wright.

Frank Neat in his shop at Dunnville, Kentucky, June, 1986. Photo by Jack Mansfield.

Ralph Stanley with the Anniversary Stanleytone banjo, Smith Ridge, Virginia, September 27, 1986. Photo by Jack Mansfield.

Anniversary Stanleytone: detail of Tree of Life neck. Banjo by Frank Neat, inlay by Bryan England. Photo by Bruce Williams.

The Clinch Mountain Boys

Presents the

Ralph Stanley Homecoming

to Celebrate His 40 Years in Music at the Old Home Place on Smith Ridge
12 miles from Coeburn, Virginia

FRIDAY – SATURDAY – SUNDAY
☆ September 26, 27, and 28 ☆

☆☆☆ FEATURING ☆☆☆

Ralph Stanley and The Clinch Mountain Boys
Ricky Skaggs
Keith Whitley
George Shuffler
Lester Woodie
Original Marshall Family
Larry Sparks
Dave Evans
Goins Brothers
Kentucky Sage Grass
Kentucky Ramblers
Redwing
Brickey Brothers
Darrell Adkins and Silver Wind
Sammy Adkins and The Sandyhook Mountain Boys
Clyde Bolling
Landon Messer and Riverside Grass
and others

Reunion of The Clinch Mountain Boys on Sunday
with
Ricky Skaggs
Keith Whitley
George Shuffler
Lester Woodie
Larry Sparks
and others

☆☆☆

Out of Coeburn
take Route 80
approximately
1½ miles, turn
on 652 go ap-
proximately 7
miles, then take
643 to the Old
Homeplace.

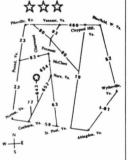

☆☆☆

Limited Number of Electric Hookups
Concessions on Grounds
Sound by: REDWING

— MOTELS AVAILABLE—
Three-Way Motel, Western Hills Motel — Coeburn
Buck's Motel, Lamberts Motel — Clintwood
Hill Top Motel — Haysi
Other Motels in Norton, Castlewood and Pound

Flyer for the fortieth anniversary Homecoming. From the author's personal collection.

Souvenir program for the Ralph Stanley Appreciation Days, McClure,
Virginia. From the author's personal collection.

Curly Ray Cline, Ralph Stanley, and Jack Cooke in front of a newly unveiled sign recognizing McClure, Virginia, as Stanley's hometown, April 22, 1988. Photo by Miles Ward.

13

Ron Thomason

"The greatest road experience I ever had"

"Come on in," Ron Thomason says in response to the visitor's knock on the door of his restored farmhouse in western Ohio. "Want some Coor's beer? Somebody left it here and I'm trying to get rid of it because it's made by scab labor out there in Colorado." Hospitality, wry humor, and social conscience all wrapped in three sentences: a perfect introduction to one of the most interesting sidemen ever to serve with Ralph Stanley.

Ron Thomason is in origin a hillbilly—the word is his own—from Honaker, just across the county line from the Stanley Brothers' home in Dickenson County, Virginia. (Honaker Harness and Saddlery, by the way, was one of the Brothers' very first sponsors.) As a boy Thomason knew and loved commercial mountain music before it came to be known as bluegrass, especially the music of the Stanley Brothers. And while still a boy he migrated from Honaker to central Ohio, where he attended and graduated from college toward the end of the sixties. He joined Ralph Stanley and the Clinch Mountain Boys in the spring of 1970 and worked full-time for the band for about a year.

As a college-educated sideman Thomason was able to view his experience from a unique perspective: he was both an insider and an outsider at the same time. As an insider he was able to produce thoroughly authentic music; he fitted in at once without any training, joining the group after the briefest of informal auditions. As an outsider he could appreciate, better than anyone else connected with the enterprise, just what the music of the Stanley Brothers and Ralph Stanley meant in the larger world of history and culture—and he came to the correct conclusion that it meant something very important indeed. All of Ralph Stanley's fans believe that he is the greatest singer around, but for most of them this opinion is based on faith. When Ron Thomason says that Stanley is "one of the five best singers in the world," his opinion is based on *knowledge*.

In fairness to the truth it should be pointed out that while Thomason's position is privileged it is not necessarily infallible. For instance, in the eyes of many modern critics the kind of explanation Thomason gives of the emotional depths of mountain music, the way he connects it to and explains it by the poverty and wretchedness of mountain life, would smack of a fallacious romanticism. Such critics would remind us that most people from this sort of background have no creative or artistic ability whatever, and that, on the other hand, many artists who have produced immortal works have lived comfortable and uneventful lives. Real art, such critics would argue, is the product of talent, hard work, and thoughtful choices; and an imaginative sympathy for the human condition is really more important for producing masterpieces than pain and deprivation personally experienced. But it is hardly likely that Thomason would deny all this; his position is, after all, a matter of emphasis, and it is certainly true that his sort of explanation is the one most congenial to the great majority of fans and practitioners of traditional mountain music.

The ironic detachment that Thomason can assume toward his own art and background makes him a great storyteller as well as an excellent analyst, not only in these pages but also on the stage, where he continues to appear with great success as the star (though his sixties attitudes would lead him to avoid the term), mandolinist, lead singer, and master of ceremonies of his band, the Dry Branch Fire Squad—in between bouts of hard work as a schoolteacher. Not surprisingly, his show has had its greatest success among the city people of the Northeast, for whom Ron Thomason serves as a good-humored and sympathetic ambassador of mountain people and their culture.

Singing, country singing, like Ralph does, is probably as high an art form as opera. And even to begin to understand what Ralph's singing, it's like T. S. Eliot. You have to bring knowledge to the poem. You can't just start off reading T. S. Eliot, and you can't start off liking Ralph Stanley's singing. Oh, you can like it the same way you can like Pavarotti, I suppose: white guy, fat, sings the opera; black woman, fat, sings the blues kind of thing, you know. Hillbilly, redneck, sings bluegrass. But, more than the prototype, Ralph's the culmination of several centuries of a very high art form. And it's all vocal.

The banjo, of course, was a frustration to him to start with. And the banjo has gotten in the way of his singing a lot through the years, especially with the Stanley Brothers, although he still did the great tenor, but it was when he laid off the banjo—Which doesn't mean to say he's not a great banjo player. I think he's probably the best banjo player there is. But what's become defined as banjo playing is not what he's doing. And in recent years he's gotten to where he almost sets the banjo aside. It's a prop, you know, and he knows it's expected of him, but the very best music he does of course is when he holds it to a minimum. Or just plays essentially—Ralph will say, "I play what I sing." It's not true. Because he sings more notes than you can count.

What Ralph's doing vocally, to even begin to appreciate it requires so much knowledge of what's gone before. And it's a fantastic gift, you know, this tremendous music, which—which screws you up. Artists, creative people have to be screwed up somewhat because anybody with their head on straight can't really deal with, you know, dying mothers and drunken sons and dead sons with drunken mothers. And this terribly painful culture that it comes from, that most people don't even know about.

We do a lot of our playing up around Harvard and Dartmouth and places, and part of our gig is "the wry sense of humor with which Ron Thomason presents his show." Well, I suppose that's the way people interpret it. That's garbage. People think it's funny: why does Grandma got her appliances out on the porch? Oh, stereotype, everybody in Appalachia has a washing machine on the porch. And so I try to present it in a humorous way: a Maytag repairman is an outdoor job down in the country and what not.

But the plain truth is, yeah, we bought Grandma a stove and she put it on the porch. Why would she want to put it inside, nobody'd know she had it? But Grandma also took a hatchet down and chopped coal out of the hill for eighty years, you know, and hauled it up and cooked on it and everything.

Grandpa meanwhile was strung out on heroin in the mines. He was a white slave. All those people that live back in those counties come from that culture, literally a slave culture. They did it to the blacks, they did it to the orientals, and eventually they did it to the white people because the blacks and orientals were kind of shunted out of the country or it was kind of stolen from them.

And not wanting to expose that pain, and consequently the kind of messed up people that come from it—you know, my sister's a criminal. My sister comes out of the same family life. Love my mother and father, but I must accept the terrible things that they did. My father and I are in business today but I have to accept the fact that as a young man he taught me bigotry. And it took me a lifetime to overcome it. I'll probably never overcome it. And it was taught to me by that hillbilly family.

And they can write all they want to about the Dry Branch Fire Squad, they can write anything they want to about that music, but they're never going to understand it unless they understand that oppressive poverty, that was combined with an incredible amount of independence, almost like one eye in the middle of your head to succeed and rise above it. Tremendous encouragement, incredibly tight-knit family unit.

The people that have sung the blues have really had it made as far as having their music understood because, since they were black, nobody worried about saying bad things about them. And they made reputations on how bad they could be. "Oh, I can take more dope, I can get drunker—" You know, Jones has done it in country music. There's a book out about Jones called *George Jones* which deals with the demons that sit beside this man's head, you know, and sing into it, I suppose. And through knowing that people can know this music.

I've sort of looked at country living from two perspectives in my life. And I remember going through one particular part of my life when I thought I'd never romanticize it. Now I'm in a part of my life where I guess I'm kind of in a process of making a romantic return to it. And if I process that too much I almost want to go live in a condominium again.

Remember, it's all right to live in the country if you can afford to live in the city. But it's really bad to be trapped in the country. You know, my wife's working on a book right now. She's doing the writing with this veterinarian. I'm really not diverging, I think this will be relevant. It's on dairy farming. And one of the things that keeps getting driven home to her as she's going around traveling and working with him is how these people are—there's never any break. If you're a dairy farmer those cows are coming at you twice a day, seven days a week, all year around. That's their whole life. It's four in the morning and four in the afternoon. It's regular and it never changes. And to a person that has variety in their life or lives what we would call a normal life, it's so oppressive as to be unbelievable. That's what country life is, you know. It's habit beyond belief.

Ralph is quiet, Ralph is shy, Ralph is hard to understand. Bill is quiet, Bill is shy, Bill is hard to understand. All of them are. To cover up these hidden secrets, this thing, and—so consequently all the words that get written don't carry the agony. Closest anybody's come to it in *Bluegrass Unlimited* I guess would be the Goins Brothers article I saw. And Melvin got into it a little bit: the motel rooms, letting the one-eyed hot plate stare up at you, parking the bus down on the hill there in Prestonsburg, you know. It was so close. And I thought, of all people Melvin is finally going to get down to the exploitation and the embarrassment of playing bluegrass music, the real agony, the pain of being pushed around. But he didn't. Which is okay. I thought he made a pretty healthy step.

I'm probably not telling you anything you don't already know. But I'm simply saying that for what it's worth I know a little bit about this and I've thought about it some. It's my business now and I love it. I want it to be understood and accepted because I love the people in the hills. I wish I could afford to live there. You know, when I got out of college I went to New Lexington and I taught kids that lived in mining towns and I found my whole paycheck was going for toothbrushes and shoestrings and crap and I said, you know, I can't do this. I've already been poor long enough. I'm too self-centered to do anything good. And I'm not making any excuse for that. I'm just saying that that culture lives there. And there is a need to realize that these people are real, that the more you know about the folks the better you can understand the music.

Take *I Can Tell You the Time,* Ralph's new record. I just got it a couple of weeks ago. "Jerusalem My Happy Home," that's good. It is long. It had a movement, you know. But it's painfully long for people that don't understand what's going on. "Je, ru, sa, lem," you know? "Little Old Church by the Road" I think is real good. But even my band, which does this professionally, and had, you know, like Dave Edmundson's got six years nominated best old-time fiddler in the country and everything, and you get down there and Ralph'll sing, "There, my, mo, ther," and their first reaction is to make fun of it a little bit. And then finally it starts to sink in. Wow. We didn't think of that. Doyle Lawson didn't think of that. I mean, that's Stanley thinking of that. After all these years. Now where's the well that comes from?

He'll say he just always sang that way, and he always has, you know. It's nice that he's about the age now where he can actually sound as old as he's always wanted to sound. Because when he was sixteen or seventeen he wanted to sound like an old man. And it doesn't take much, but there had to be an old man, there had to be that old voice somewhere.

He probably doesn't know where—it took me years to remember

where *I* heard it. And I've analyzed, trying to remember it, and for me it was a street preacher that used to come off Big A Mountain and sit around Sid's General Store mostly preaching. That's all I'd ever remembered and now I realize, yeah, but he used to stand on the street corner and holler out these songs. And it has an impact, you know. It was a sound. You carry it. And I think that a seed was planted somewhere in Ralph's youth that made him do the work he had to do in his adult years.

But in the late sixties Ralph was religiously collecting entire taped transcripts of conventions of old-time Baptist ministers and hard-shell Baptist ministers and mountain Methodist preachers and going through hours of these tapes on the bus listening to them and occasionally he'd get one. "Guys, I want you to get in here." And he had the old Wollensak, you know, and it'd be just one song, or one sermon, or one thing in the voice.

Now if he were a professor or something everybody'd say, "Oh, that's where he's coming from." But he was doing a type of scholarship that's just as disciplined and just as committed as anybody's. And tirelessly. I mean, for no payoff. Other than you got the product you've got today and you've had for about the last ten years, starting about '74, '75. An incredible thing.

When I first went to play with Ralph I met him in a scuzzy bar in Columbus called the Astro Inn. At that time the house band was John Hickman and some other people. And Ralph was playing there. And I was playing in the house band and I don't think Ralph was a man short or anything. He just asked me to come out and play with him or something. I don't remember that part exactly. I ended up on stage with him.

He said, "Oh, you seem to know the Stanley Brothers songs." I said, "Yeah, I know them all. It's my favorite music." The irony being that I'm from Russell County, he's from Dickenson County, and we probably lived twenty-five miles apart down there, and we wouldn't run into each other in Virginia. And he said, "Well, what are you doing? Why don't you just come on and play with us?" "Well, you know, I'm teaching school now." "Good," he said. "When are you done?" I said, "June."

So, June he came up and played a bar in Springfield. He said, "Why don't you go get your stuff?" So I did. I didn't have much stuff. Got it and put it on the bus. And that was it. Just went on and played with him. His version, which I think is much better than mine, is, "This guy came up and said, 'I got to play the mandolin,' and I said, 'Well, if you got to, come on and do it.'" Which is pretty much the way it was, you know.

Great honor. Great honor. And the greatest road experience I've ever had. What can I say about it other than, you know, he's one of probably the five best singers in the world. And he knew I really appreciated his singing, and so like at night I'd be driving or something, getting sleepy, and he'd come up and just sing a few bars of music a cappella, and wake me right up. And I could drive further. Heck, I could drive all night. Maybe every two or three hours I'd have to holler at him to sing a little bit, sing "Two Coats" or something like that. And it worked.

I can tell you about the first time we encountered Skaggs and Whitley. We were down there in Kentucky. Seem like it was around Paintsville or one of those places. We were going to dinner at somebody's house, and these people informed us that there was music at a bar that was right around there and we went on down. And, I'm trying to remember, seem like they were in a little band. They weren't just by themselves. And when the Clinch Mountain Boys and all came in they just started doing all Stanley songs.

And Ricky's parents and Keith's parents were also there. We were playing this outdoor thing, kind of like a barbecue or something the next day, and they were going to be there and they invited us over for dinner. And I think right off the bat Ralph sort of dubbed them the Little Stanley Brothers. If it wasn't him it was Ray. And then for a long time, maybe three or four months, whenever we were down there in that southwest corner of Virginia or eastern Kentucky, their parents would bring them around.

And we had played some numbers with them that night in the bar. I forget whether we backed them up or something. I don't believe Ralph ever did any actual singing with them. And whenever they'd come around then, he'd just kind of pick and sing with them, or just get them on stage and just have them do one or two numbers, you know. It just sort of started real slowly.

The whole time they were with him it was somewhere between uncomfortable and unhealthy. They were sleeping in one bed on the bus. And those bus beds were about—I think you got your choice of thirty-six or forty inches wide. I think Ralph's were the more narrow ones. And I just couldn't believe they were getting along at all. Essentially buying their own meals and things whenever they went out. Course it was quite a thrill. I mean, I think they really wanted to do it.

That Skaggs and Whitley record, I was on that, yeah. They actually hired the Clinch Mountain Boys to play that record. Or their parents did, you know. We were playing up in Dayton and we were sitting around Jack Lynch's apartment over there and Ralph said,

"Oh, let's go on over there and help these boys. They gave us this money." Or something. We'd done another record back then with Lee Allen, the same way, on the Jalyn label.

That was actually the first time I ever recorded with Ralph. And I'd say that was probably four hours' business for us. I remember we just shot right through it. As I recall I don't believe Ralph sang at all on that record and played just a little bit of banjo. Hardly any at all. Roy Lee mostly played the banjo. All Ralph actually did was just sort of lend his band out. He might have sung on "Lonesome River" if it's on that record. I think Ricky sung the real high part. I think Ralph did tenor one song there and I can't remember which one it was.

Roy Lee Centers was one of the nicest men I ever met. He played around the Dayton area for years and years and was pretty well known back then for sounding like Carter Stanley. And I had played a lot of music with him in those years, before I think he'd ever met Ralph. I think he finally met Ralph as a result of people just telling Ralph he sounded like Carter. And then when Larry Sparks quit he needed somebody that could do that.

You could meet Roy Lee in a bar or something, you know. He played up and down Fifth Avenue there in Dayton for years and years as part of what they called the Lee Brothers. It was Fred Spencer and Roy Lee. And they called themselves the Lee Brothers. Then he played with those multitudinous bands Jack Lynch had, called the Miami Valley Boys or whatever they were. And he played banjo and guitar and could sing all the parts.

I remember one night I had met him. He was playing in a band Frank Wakefield was in, and I was talking to Frank and we had sung a couple of numbers. Roy said, "Come on down to the house next week and I'll show you how to sing that baritone part." You know, just real accessible, real fine fellow. Then when he got with Ralph he moved down to Jackson, Kentucky, there, which was probably his undoing. He was so jovial and nice, it'd be hard to think of anything critical to say about him. I think he smoked cigarettes. He never drank too much. He was just a real nice guy. Real talented musician. If anything, probably the reason he's hard to flesh out is because he was a little bland, you know, from just being so nice.

How he died, the guy that killed him figured out that Roy Lee'd been running around with his wife. And I've heard that that wasn't so, from people that I would assume would tell me whether it was so or not. I can't remember anymore who told me. I just remember that having conversed about it I was satisfied that it wasn't so. Knowing Roy Lee I can't believe it. I mean, it would have just been so out of character for him.

The guy picked Roy Lee and his son Lennie up in a car, supposedly fairly harmlessly, going to give him a ride somewhere and took him out in the country and pulled a gun, told him to get out. And he got out and said he was going to draw down and shoot on him. And Lennie ran away and hid in the bushes—it was night, you know—in the dark, and listened to his daddy get shot. You know, he just got shot to death. I've played in the same bands with Lennie several times since then, and had his account of it. He said his dad cried out and told him to run and he ran. And that was that.

I assume it was a shock for Ralph. Of course, I wasn't in the band at that time. It probably was lessened by the fact that at the time Keith was available and so obviously the person to take Roy's place was right there, you know, so that he probably never skipped a beat professionally. Personally, I imagine he had as much respect for Roy Lee as any man that's ever played with him. I'm sure he thought a lot of him. You know, he was a trouper. He was just a good man to work with. Their voices matched perfectly. And it's doubtful that he's ever had that good a duet with the exception of some things he's sung with Charlie.

Unfortunately it never got the best treatment in recordings, but it got pretty good. I think those classics like "Cry from the Cross" and "Brand New Tennessee Waltz" and things like that are probably among the strongest stuff he ever recorded, and he did that with Roy Lee. *Cry from the Cross* is the first really great gospel album. It's probably the first modern bluegrass album ever recorded that's really got the a cappella singing and the things that have become standards in bluegrass gospel. Roy Lee was there for all that, and I'm certain he had a big influence on it because he sang all the parts so well. That was one of the first ones, probably the only one where they ever dubbed anything in. He dubbed in some baritone parts there.

And he's a person that's just been lost in the wash, in the same way that an engineer for Bell Labs would get lost, you know. Probably a lot of things that he did now have been credited to Ralph. And I'm not saying that that's not the way it ought to be. It should be. I mean, because he was in Ralph's employ. But were he still living, I think as these things have come to pass and as many people have followed some of those things that that particular band invented—

And I think they really did invent them. I mean, if you look around, and it's very difficult to do in retrospect, if you look around at the recordings which were available. I'm guessing, but I'll say it was early '71 at the latest when the *Cry from the Cross* album came out. And man, it was so far apart from anything that had ever been done before. Even though probably half the cuts were things that they'd done before. "Cry from the Cross" was.

But things like "Bright Morning Star" and "Sinner Man." There was nothing, nothing like it in bluegrass or country music had ever been recorded. There were people *doing* it. The Livesey Family Singers were doing it. You know, it sounded like a church meeting. I mean, the Baptist singers had been doing it for years. The Negro singers had. But it just had never been recorded and never been performed on stage that way. And there was a whole host of groups—a good example would be the Marshall Family—that came along and got invented and prospered as a result of that kind of singing. But that group with Roy and Ralph and Jack and Curly and Keith and Ricky were just the first people to do that.

Jack Cooke joined a few weeks after I did. George Shuffler had quit. You know, I still got a pair of George's pajama tops he left in my bunk up there. Just because I thought a lot of the man. George was very quiet, very stately, old southern gentleman type person. I always thought of him as a real man's man, you know. He's a pretty tough guy. Ralph is more introspective.

Anyway, George quit and we went out, we played as I recall either two or three jobs without a bass player. We picked one up a couple of places. I remember one of them was Paul Mullins and he threatened to shoot me. He was mad over something. I had written him a letter a couple of years before about something he had said at Bean Blossom which had irritated me and he's pretty headstrong. He just didn't know who I was until Ralph had introduced me and he'd been standing back there playing bass. He just pulled a gun and threatened to shoot me. And Ralph got in the middle of that.

And we went to Bean Blossom, I recall, that year, and that was probably the second or third Bean Blossom festival. Probably the second. And we didn't have a bass player and, you know, we were all bellyaching around. Mostly I was, cause George had been a good bus driver. And Ralph didn't like to drive and man, that left a real burden. So next week we got on the bus and Ralph said, "Oh, Jack Cooke will be over. I found him in Norton." He said he'd gone over to Norton and found Jack and asked him if he wanted to play some bass.

And Jack never had a bass. We were playing in Washington, D.C., that week. Fourth of July, the Smithsonian Folk Festival. And we were lucky. We got that bus up there to Washington and right on the outskirts some motorcycle cop came up and said, "I'm from—" Let's see. He wasn't from Dickenson County. He was from Council. He was from Buchanan County. Said, "I'm from over the hill from you fellows. Follow me." And we had a siren escort right down to the Mall.

Parked there on the Mall, and Mike Seeger and his wife come up and they were talking to us and Mike said that he had a bass up in the attic. Didn't know how many strings it had on it, but they'd sell it for, I forget, it was fifteen or twenty dollars. And as far as I know that's the bass Jack's got to this day. And for years he had only the three strings on it, that he got it with. I don't know whether he's put a fourth on it yet or not. He has? Well, that's good. I do know wherever they go around to a festival if there's any way he can borrow one that's already up on the stage he'll do it.

I remember one time we'd been out at the, again, it was either the first or the second, I believe it was the first Bill Grant and Delia Bell festival out there at Hugo, Oklahoma. And it'd been a long ride. We'd been out for a long time and we stopped somewhere in Tennessee, I believe, and got in this restaurant. And I guess I'd have to say that I was the first one in that band that ever—Ralph had always been pretty close with money, by necessity I'm certain. This was just when he was starting to make some pretty big money. And of course everybody in the band was. And I just didn't have no reason to be close with money. I was single and I had just graduated from college and, you know, from having been fairly poor all my life I was kind of I guess what they would have considered a spendthrift.

And you know, I was hungry and tired. I'd been driving all that way and I got in there and I saw down at the bottom of the menu this big New York steak dinner, and sticks in my mind it was like twelve ninety-five. It was high. It'd be fairly high by today's prices but it was ungodly high by those prices back then. And up at the top of the menu they had the chopped sirloin steak special, you know, for like a dollar eighty-nine or two forty-nine or something like that. I can't remember what it was, but that was something entirely different.

So we'd made pretty good money that week, you know. We'd been out quite a while and we'd played some big shows and everybody's feeling pretty good and I just ordered that big New York steak thing down there. And kind of, you know, man to man, well, Ralph had to have the same thing. So it kind of went around the table and Roy ordered it and Jack ordered it. Got to Ray and he ordered it. And it seemed right away, I can't remember why, but it was obvious for some reason he thought he'd ordered that special, up at the top, that chopped sirloin steak.

Well, you know, the meal came, and all through the meal all he was doing was raving about what a wonderful meal that was for a dollar ninety-nine or whatever it was. And we was just chuckling and giggling. We got into the spirit of it, you know. "Man, can you believe they can give you a piece of meat like this here in Tennessee for a dollar ninety-nine?" And, "I wonder if you got to pay extra for your coffee here?" And, "Yeah, I thought they said all that was thrown in for a dollar ninety-nine." Ray, "Oh yeah. And I think you can get the free coffee refills and everything." Well, one thing led to another and he had some dessert and everything and come his check and it was about fifteen or sixteen dollars. He's still giggling. "Boys, look what a mistake they've made on mine. Why, they've got the decimal point in the wrong place." Or something, you know. We got up there and paid and everything. Everybody kind of snuck up there and paid, you know, kind of leave him behind, see what's going to happen. He got up there and I thought he was going to cry. I mean, he was close with money.

To this day he's close with money. One of our favorite games was to run up behind him and throw down a quarter and act like we found it, like it had dropped out of his pocket. For a long time, you know, if you could be just sneaky enough about it, it'd just almost drive him to distraction. And I've more than once found money of my own right around him. I'd plant it on his seat on the bus. You know, I'd plant a dollar there and wait till he got up, knowing I was running the risk of losing the dollar, just to pull it out of the seat and drive him to death.

Well, we probably had another hundred, two hundred mile to go, I can't remember, and all that distance Ray was perfectly quiet. I couldn't figure it out. But we got up there to Rockhouse, close to Rockhouse where his truck had been parked. And he never got his fiddle or his luggage or anything. He just jumped off the front of that bus and run in the store there. We'd never seen nothing like it. Thought he had to go to the bathroom. And, you know, we was sitting there and killing time. Everybody's kind of laid back, kind of dozing except me and I was driving the bus. But everybody was aware we was letting him out.

Directly, out he come, you know. He had a big sack, had some steaks in it. Said, "Boys, what'd you think about me down there eating that big old steak and Verdie and them kids up there on the mountain just eating a hamburger? Why I'm so ashamed of that."

And he *was*. That was the most important thing to him, was to get in there and equal it out. He had to get in there and buy those steaks. I'm certain that once they were purchased in his mind he felt okay. I mean, you know, he had gotten some steaks for his family. But he had to get in there and make sure he could get some good steaks. That was more important to him than getting his fiddle off the bus or anything. And that changed my opinion about him a lot. Now I'd always respected him, but I had to admire that quite a bit.

You know, I remember being in college and hearing that one of the Stanley Brothers had died and sort of in my own mind hoping that it wasn't Ralph. It sounds kind of gross with the exception that they were professional personalities to me, doing a type of music I'd loved since I was four or five years old. And I knew intuitively that the tenor was the great part of it. He could hire a million banjo players to do what he does. You just can't hire that tenor singer.

He's the only, the *only* tenor singer that sings lead and does both equally well. Most of them, even the great ones like Dave Evans and Bill Monroe and John Duffey, only shine, only truly shine on one of the parts, you know. I wouldn't walk across the street to hear Bill Monroe sing all the lead in the world, and yet I think he's one of the greatest harmonizers ever. He even sings flat and sharp and he's better than most of them. Oh, he's better than all of them, you know. *With the exception of Ralph.*

And Ralph's the one voice that stands out head and shoulders above all the other singers. Not only in bluegrass today, but of all the country singers who have ever lived. When you put it in the true context he's got almost as much vocal power as somebody like Uncle Dave Macon, whose idea of a good singer was somebody that can go into an auditorium with no sound system and holler out to people in the back row. He's got as much soul as somebody like Fiddling John Carson, and only a few musical scholars will ever know how great he really was because it takes so much patience to listen to things like "That Little Old Log Cabin in the Lane" and stuff that he did. And, and Ralph's got it *all.*

You know, if you could imagine getting Ralph in a session with an old-time fiddler, somebody just can fiddle like John Carson, and having him sing those songs. You just can't imagine how great it would be for the schooled ear. Or put Ralph in a setting where he's just going to use the guitar and the overhand banjo. Where the medium of the music that he'd be operating in would be actually truly fitted for what he does.

The unfortunate thing for Ralph is that he's had to make his living in bluegrass music, and he's not a bluegrass musician. *He's so much more.* You know, Bill Monroe's a good, the very best bluegrass musician. And bluegrass really is a modern music. The best bluegrass band in the world is the Seldom Scene, and the reason is, because they can play all types of bluegrass. People say, "Well, now, they're progressive." Yeah, but you listen to them sing old-fashioned, very traditional bluegrass and they'll be better than anybody else doing it. *Except for Ralph.*

And when Ralph sings with John Duffey, look how good it is. You know, you got "Lonesome River" and "The Fields Have Turned Brown" there that Duffey recorded with him. But the bluegrass idiom has never been the ideal idiom for him. And take away the bluegrass part of it, you'd have two things. You wouldn't have had him able to make the living he's made, but you'd have the perfect medium for his genius, which'd be something very similar to what the New Lost City Ramblers do.

Well, it's natural, you know. People are going to make a living where they can. He's made his in bluegrass. So it's an academic question. But if anything, the most successful music he's done and the most successful stage performances that he's done is when he's got away from bluegrass.

Much as I regret it, I think it's probably helped him that he hasn't carried the mandolin, because that's one step away from bluegrass. It's helped him that he personally has always hated dobro music, so that's been another good step away from bluegrass. Curly Ray does not fiddle like, say, somebody like Kenny Baker, although he does fiddle considerably like Paul Warren, so that's kind of a plus and a minus. His bluegrass guitar players have always played the bluegrass lick ever since Carter. You know, Carter had a kind of a thumb lick, almost a Maybelle Carter lick, but that never got to balance out because Carter was the one that was in the bands that carried the mandolins and all that stuff.

I've been most interested in the mandolin and I think there's only been two mandolin players he's ever had that's understood his music. And one of them was Pee Wee Lambert. And Pee Wee got a good bluegrass lick in it, but he also had a real sensitivity for playing the minor and modal notes that nobody played before or since, really. And of course, it's classic stuff. I mean, it's just the way it went.

You know, Ralph ran for treasurer of Dickenson County. He was running for County Treasurer and he had come up here to Dayton. This was actually a year or two after I'd been out of the band. He'd had these bumper stickers printed up and was passing them out to everybody, had them all over his bus and everything. And it said "County *Teasurer*." Didn't have no *r* in it. Nobody'd noticed.

I guess most of my stories that I really enjoy, that I think—you see, I think Ralph's two different men. The Stanley I've known. There's one of them I don't like, so I just kind of make it my business to try and associate with the other one. And that's the one that I actually knew best before I ever joined the band, and I have to say while I was in the band. The other one's the one that took over after he got an idea of his place in the history of bluegrass music or something. Which came fairly late. Probably came after Ricky and Keith had left, or at least after Ricky'd left and everything. It's the promoter Ralph. And he's distant.

But there's a Ralph Stanley the man there, that I knew back when they used to drive—we used to call it the Old Time Car. Had that station wagon, had a big box up on the top which Ralph had built, had "Old Time Music" on it. They never called it bluegrass music, and didn't really like to have it called bluegrass. And I can remember times when he'd specifically say, "Well, you know, they've called this bluegrass or whatever but I never called our music that. I believe we play old-time music."

And they'd play all these bars around Dayton and Middletown and Cincinnati and things. I'd go out and listen to them four or five hours a night sometimes. And even play a little mandolin with them and things. And he was a fine fellow, you know. He'd come over to your house and socialize and have dinner and he could talk about horses and guns and things.

Now Ralph Stanley the promoter can't do that. He's either reticent or he's a little bit distant. Bill's the same way. I was a little kid and ran into Bill Monroe right in Sid Whiter's restaurant down there in Virginia having a cheeseburger. I guess I was probably seven or eight. Would've been about '52. He was playing Honaker High School. This was back before he'd invented bluegrass music, by the way. Because he didn't actually invent bluegrass music until Ralph Rinzler told him he had. And, you know, sitting down at the table, a couple of us snotty-nosed hillbilly kids in there talking about this and that and I didn't even know it was Bill until my dad came in and everything. Then you go back several years later, first I ever played twin mandolins with him, and I realized there was a big change in the presence. You know, the business did better, Bill did better. But hell, even in '52 he was a big star. He was just a bigger man. He was still 1925 Rosine, Kentucky, ethics.

I think Ralph's picked some of that off people like Bill Monroe. Ralph really likes to drive, for instance. I don't know if he does it any more or not. I sort of get the impression he doesn't. He likes to do it, and it's a mindless activity and for a real creative man like him I'm certain it's a real joy. You got to be riding anyhow. But somewhere along the line he's got the idea that that's not what bandleaders do.

We were playing a show in Roanoke several months ago and staying in a motel down there, Colony House or something. And they were having Kenny Rogers and Dolly Parton in Roanoke that night and there was this other big civic center that was having Foreigner, a rock group. Things were really happening that weekend. And we walked out and happened to notice a bus. I hadn't paid much attention to it and then I realized it was Ralph's. And there it was, about eight o'clock at night. It was dark, and they were sitting there in the bus, in the dark, in the rain. They'd pulled off the road. They were on their way up to Dalwinter and didn't have to be there until the next day and they were going to stay there the night in the motel parking lot. There's nothing wrong with that, save a little money, you know, on the bus. But sitting in the dark, in the rain, in the bus, is—talk about your cave men, who haven't invented fire yet so its raining and it's night so we'll sit in the dark in the bus.

You know, there's another interesting thing. I think Ralph's kind of mad at me right now and I'm trying to figure out why. I think I've happened upon it. We hired him for our festival and I called him up and I said, "Ralph, what'd you need to come up to this festival one day?" I had Sunday open. He said, "Oh, I'd need—" you know, such-and-such an amount. I said, "Okay, send me a contract." Now this is a big money festival. I mean it's not like what they have in the South, you know, and I was prepared to pay that amount of money and I think he's worth it and I'm certain at most places he's not getting that also. And politically I'm glad to give it to him. But what I figured out is, the bad blood came down in that I didn't feed into the ethic. I didn't try to gyp him. "Oh, Ralph, boy, I don't, I only got—" such-and-such hundred, you know. I could've had him for, say, two-thirds of what he asked and he'd be happier about it. But now he's feeling, "God, blah, I should've asked for twice as much," you know? But I decided going in what I was going to do was either give him his price or not hire him. And realizing how easy it was almost took the fun out of it this time. So next time I'll probably play the game because it's not an even match anymore.

So that's kind of a fun thing, you know. They appreciate the type of contest, fencing, that you don't necessarily need to get immediate feedback from, but it's the preparation that counts. It's like getting ready for the game. You know, "God dog, went in the game and I didn't have all my equipment with me. Well, I'll never let that happen again." I don't know how that gets processed in Ralph's mind but that's what happens. "I'll be ready next time."

All that's hard to break through. Now it can be done. Like I felt at our festival, at Winterhawk, we got along real well. I thought, out of the times I'd seen him in the last two or three years, he had, for being up all night, and worn out, it appeared he had one of the best times he ever had. And I can't figure out what it was. I do know that knowing the kinds of things that worry him I just went out of my way to put his mind at ease on those. You know, just right off. Here's where you eat. Here's where you go to the bathroom. Here's where I'm going to pay you. We got all that covered. And, Why don't you sit over here in the bus in your running suit and we'll holler at you when we need you. And consequently, man, he lightened up, or appeared to.

And we talked about a million things. I wish I could remember what they were. None of which was music. Which I like and I think he likes. I think I've never known anybody that talked to him about music that they don't get the other Ralph. One of the things I remember telling him, I said, "Ralph, Mary wanted me to be sure and tell you that we just loved your contract. We get these contracts in here, eight or ten pages long, this and that. Thank you for sending us a contract said when you're going to play and how much we're going to pay you." And that kind of tickled him, I think. I don't know, I'm projecting, but it's something like, "Ah, yes, that's good. I did it my way." Or something.

And the other thing is that he is so insecure musically. On the one hand he will project the fact that he believes he has done the great tenor lines and he's the great banjo player and he's done these great things. And they are true. But he doesn't really believe that. Down inside there's a part of him that thinks everybody can play the banjo better and there's a million people that can sing better.

I heard it come out when we did a gospel workshop up at Winterhawk. And they had about eight or ten good gospel groups there, I mean, we had Doyle Lawson and we had the Nashville Bluegrass Band and we were all standing down there. We were answering questions and somebody finally asked Ralph a question and he killed the workshop with the answer. And it was, "Well, I don't know nothing about this music. I just sing it from the heart." So I came in and I used that line to wind up the workshop. I said something like, "Yes, Ralph does it better than anybody and the way he does it is by singing from the heart."

And I could tell he felt good about that because later on he was sitting around in the food tent just shaking and howdying with everybody. Which was entirely different from before he went down there and felt a little bit standoffish and everything.

Now, the way I perceive that is it gets the message through to him somehow that that's true. You do sing it from the heart, Ralph. And that *is* better than everybody else does it. And therefore that's okay. And I think he's received a big message from somewhere, it ain't okay. I don't know where that comes from, but I do know when I was with him, he was real—it's a combination of insecurity and cockiness that's almost extreme in both directions.

The plain fact is, there's a whole mess of people that really do believe Ralph Stanley can't sing and pick, and they're the people that are out there doing bluegrass that don't have no soul in it. And people that really understand what he's done believe that he's one of the best singers that ever lived. And the very, very good singers acknowledge it. I know Doyle Lawson's really quick to acknowledge the great depth of Ralph Stanley.

I introduced him with a true story at Winterhawk that I've saved all these years. I guess I can tell it now cause I've used it on the stage. One of our favorite arguments in college—we'd get in these intellectual arguments about who the greatest singers were, you know, just for fun. We'd sit around and we'd list them, and it'd be people like Ray Charles and Janis Joplin, Frank Sinatra, Caruso, and Ralph Stanley, and I told the audience that a lot of times the list would change but in almost every list there'd be Caruso and Ralph Stanley. Then one night we made up a list and Caruso didn't make it. And I'm certain that Ralph probably didn't listen. But in a lot of respects it's very true.

He used to introduce me, "Here's a fellow that went to the third grade down in Honaker, Virginia, and went up to Ohio and started teaching high school." My favorite thing that I ever heard him say—

this is a classic in the Dry Branch camp—we played a festival in New Jersey and we played first and we got a real good reception. It's a pretty hot area for us out there. And Ralph came on afterwards and it's not a very hot Stanley area. In fact, I kind of had to force Stanley down the throat of the New York promoters. So Ralph came on and said the same thing I'd said. He was selling some records and he said, "Now we're going to sell our records. We really don't need the money but the people we owe do." It's an old joke and I had already said it.

And there was dead silence in the crowd. "Hm. I guess Ron already told that joke. Guess I'll have to find a new joke." And he went back and sat down backstage and looked like he was pouting and didn't sing for three or four numbers. And I got introduced the next four or five shows: "THE MAN THAT MADE RALPH STANLEY FIND A NEW JOKE." I still can't live that down. It was classic. It was the old Stanley. "Hm. Guess I'll have to find a new joke." It was like real problem solving, you know. There wasn't no image to it. It was being a little annoyed, you know. "Hell, that was my joke. I've been telling it fifteen years. It's not fair that it doesn't go over here because somebody beat me to it out of nastiness or something." It was good stuff. It was the real old man. It was kind of a humanistic touch.

I'm just talking to hear myself talk. You come to ideas, you know, as you verbalize them. Well, you want to take a little walk down and see the horses?

14

Jack Lynch

"We just didn't have the money"

Dramatic success stories are always gratifying to hear and read. And stories of spectacular failure are fascinating in their own grim way as well. It's the middle-of-the-road sort of story, involving neither success nor failure, that seldom gets told.

Jack Lynch, formerly of Dayton, Ohio, and of Nashville, was an energetic promoter of bluegrass music from some of its earliest days. He worked with many legendary performers. He was closely linked with Ralph Stanley from the beginning of his solo career. He played bass with him, featured him on his radio program, and produced several of his most interesting early recordings on his Jalyn label. He was also involved with Roy Lee Centers, being, unofficially at any rate, something like Centers's personal manager.

All this, if the usual pattern we expect from stories had prevailed, should have led to fame and fortune in later years. But it did not. Stanley moved on to other record producers, and Centers was murdered before he had a chance to start an individual career. And Jack Lynch continued plugging along with what was and still is essentially a one-man operation. A new release every now and then. A van full of albums driven from festival to festival. And a host of good memories for one of the foot soldiers in the trenches of bluegrass music.

———

I'm originally from Richmond, Kentucky. It's over in Madison County, twenty-five miles south of Lexington, right down 75. There's some of my relatives played banjos, friends and so on, fiddles and guitars and so on. That started when I was a teenager. I believe I traded a gallon of moonshine for the first old banjo I got hold of. My dad gave me the first instrument I had. It was a fiddle he'd bought in Ohio when he was away on a furniture buying trip. Later I got a guitar.

I moved to Dayton when I was in my early twenties and got into the music business there. I'd been up there and back as a teenager a few times. I moved there about 1953. I got a job with the National Cash Register Company. And I'd been fooling with music over the years so, you know, I got into the music business.

I didn't start on the bass until I was in the air force, starting in 1957. I was on Okinawa. I ran a road show and we were always having trouble keeping a bass player. Finally the guys in the band said, "Why don't you start playing the bass?" I says, "Okay." So I checked one out of the service club and started on the bass. And I think that very weekend or that very night, I can't remember, but right away I started playing. I had big blisters all over my fingers. I'd have several acts. I'd play the guitar, banjo a little, do MCing, management and all that you know, comedy, ever what, and then it gave me a pretty steady job on the bass, besides doing all the other things.

Then I got out and came back to Dayton, started playing the bass around a little with this person and that person. I guess it would've been about '61 or something like that. I started playing a whole lot of bass for the Stanley Brothers and played some with the Osborne Brothers. Over the years played a bit with Charlie Moore, special occasions, never full-time. Larry Sparks, when he was young he sort of started out with me and some other fellows around Dayton and after he got a band I played for him. Lee Allen, he played some with me, then he got a band, and I played some with him. Frank Wakefield, he used to play with us. Roy Lee Centers, I'd say he started his professional career with me.

I was doing a DJ show on WPFB, Middletown, Ohio, and I used to have bands in from time to time. We had the Stanley Brothers, Charlie Moore, Bill Napier, Osborne Brothers, oh, just many of the leading bands, plus local bands. Roy Lee came in one day to play with one of the local bands and I got acquainted with him. I'd had some fellows with me by the name of the Burns Brothers. And I kind of split with them and I got Roy Lee and his brother-in-law started with me then to replace them. And about the same time I was still playing shows with the Stanley Brothers and then after Carter died I played shows off and on with Ralph for about a year. Then I went pretty much full-time back to my own band and producing, publishing, and working my record job, DJ show and so on and so forth.

I started the Jalyn Recording Company in 1963. I had some equipment over the years but I've usually always had a partner who was an engineer and we'd work together. I've worked with several studios. In 1970, I believe it was around April 1, I moved to Nashville. I tried to keep a band after moving to Nashville—it was Jack Lynch and the Nashville Travelers—but Nashville's a tough place to keep a band unless you're really big and working out of there. After a year or so I just dropped the band and now I just jam a little and play a little here and there on occasion. Play a few shows with Ralph Stanley and other people from time to time.

I believe the first time I ever met the Stanley Brothers was when they were performing at the old Labor Temple over on Wayne Avenue in Dayton, Ohio. We got the Stanley Brothers to perform there that one weekend, probably a Saturday night, best I remember. That's the first time I ever met them, I do believe. I'd called them. Got in touch with them some way or another, somebody'd told me about them, booked them with us. Ever since then why I've been associated with the Stanley Brothers and/or Ralph Stanley one way or another, producing them and doing some performances with them. And you know Ralph recorded some of our songs—a few, not too many.

I remember when Carter died. See, they had done a show in Indiana in October, before the DJ Convention they used to have in Nashville every year. And after they finished that show Carter Stanley and George Shuffler came by to see me. I had been performing in Cincinnati that night with my band. Frank Wakefield and I, I think, were there. We'd returned from Cincinnati, doing a show there, and they were waiting on us. We had a big steak dinner that night and Carter, he was feeling better and we had good hopes he was going to get better and I promised him I'd meet him down in Nashville there.

But I didn't get to go to the DJ Convention. So that's where Carter got sick then and then he came back to Bristol and then of course he came home and you know the story from there on out. And I went down for the funeral and was a pallbearer at the funeral. I called and talked to Carter one time while he was in Bristol after he got sick.

Well, you know, we were shocked by Carter's death. Him and I— you know, he was my best friend and it was a big shock to me and of course Ralph, too. And I think Ralph was hesitant and didn't feel too confident about it. But I think anybody with the exposure and the fame that they had can go on, you know. Carter could've gone on without Ralph and Ralph without Carter. However, either one to go on without the other is a big loss. Once you, you know, reach the peak that they did together it's hard to capture that again, I'd say.

Although Ralph's done very well. Larry Sparks was the first full-time singer he had after Carter's death. I believe a few people did sing a little in the stage of transformation and so on but Larry was the first steady lead singer that Ralph really had after Carter.

Then I believe it was Roy Lee Centers, wasn't it? Roy Lee was a great guy. He was associated with me for about six years one way and another, performing and this and that. And he was a real nice fellow. A good singer, good musician, good personality, just a great fellow and I think if he'd've lived probably he'd've been one of the outstanding vocalists, performers in bluegrass music.

He was already making a big name. We'd recorded a lot while he was with us, Jack Lynch and the Lee Brothers, plus he recorded a few here and there with other people and then of course many recordings with Ralph. He was a fine fellow and a great entertainer. That was another big loss. It was. He'd become about my best friend by then because he had stayed on with me more or less. And then if he'd ever gone on his own, you know, he'd talk to me about going back with him and being the manager and playing in the band, produce the records and so on and so forth. I think he hoped that one day like anybody else, most anybody, he'd go on his own, you know.

And of course before he ever did anything like that he got killed there over in eastern Kentucky, Breathitt County, Jackson. I think on Route 30 there I guess or 15. Which is it, 15? Both of them goes up through there, I think. I think they'd started up in Jackson to Hazard, up that way. They'd started up that road, main road.

I don't why he got shot. It would strictly be speculation and I really don't know the particulars of it. Perhaps not too many people ever will. His son was with him, Lennie, you know. He was I think about twelve at the time. And he doesn't know everything because he wasn't right with him all the time. They had been inside of a building and they'd come back out for a little bit of air or whatever it was and then it happened.

As for the records I made with Ralph, like I say, I'd been associated, friends to him and performed a lot with him and so on and we decided to record. There were really no major labels at that time, or at least in bluegrass. They'd just dropped it all for Elvis and other rock and roll acts and ever what they—you know, Elvis pretty much dominated the entertainment or the vocal scene, you know, style and so on and a lot of people were all trained to get the Elvis kind of product.

And a lot of people who were big singers and entertainers in bluegrass, they had really no place to record. If they had a contract they was just letting it ride. And about that time, why I started recording people with Jalyn. Recorded quite a number of bluegrass acts as well as some others and could've recorded many more and I wish I had. But the real big problem was we just didn't have the money. If I'd've had the money we would've done many more. We had Don Reno and Red Smiley scheduled for three albums. We had the Stanley Brothers scheduled. And basically all the major bluegrass acts I could've recorded if I'd had the money. But we just didn't have enough money to record as many as we could, not near as many as we could.

Now for Jalyn 118, we picked out that material, all old public domain type thing so on and so forth. We called it *Old Time Music.* And of course I always liked the clawhammer banjo and Ralph does a fine job on that and he likes it too so we recorded some of that. I believe I played the bass with him. I was going to play the banjo on one there but Ralph's strap was too short for me and Ralph's better than I was and maybe we have a better recording for it.

And Ralph played the mandolin on one of those. Played with three picks. "East Virginia Blues." That's the only song that he's ever recorded with a mandolin, he told me. He said he used to when he was on Bristol on—I guess it's "Farm and Fun Time." He used to on occasion pick up the mandolin and play the "East Virginia Blues" when they were on Bristol. I thought it might be a good idea to do that so we did it. Very unique, yeah.

"Bonnie and Clyde's Hop," that's one that Ralph and I came up with. I guess about the time that we were recording that we decided to put that one on because it was kind of like the old "Hook and Line" that I used to try to do or the one that he does called "Shout Little Luly." And kind of similar to that. Anyway we put that on there.

Then the other album was Jalyn 120, *The Bluegrass Sound of Ralph Stanley.* We did that at another studio, another engineer. I believe the *Old Time Music* we did with Leon Turner engineering. He later was an engineer down at radio station WPFB. And on the LP 120, I believe Howard Davis was the engineer. And we had Frank Wakefield on the mandolin and I think on the guitar on a few cuts.

Ralph wanted to use a full bluegrass band. Originally, you know, in the old days, they had had Pee Wee Lambert, Big Jim Williams, Bobby Osborne, other people had played the mandolin. Ralph liked that sound, but while they recorded most of their things with King it was in the rock and roll era where mandolins and fiddles was kind of out.

That's when they introduced the flat top lead guitar that you hear so many people do it today. I believe kind of as a fill-in and to bridge between bluegrass and rock—well, it wasn't to sound like rock, but anyway, the owner and producer down there wanted something like that and that's what they came up with which was a real good sound. The owner down there and president of the company didn't much want fiddles and mandolins and things like that in those days.

Another thing—along about that time it might be more into the folk era. You remember that? They were trying to get the sound like that, too. Everybody was. You know, the Stanley Brothers had *Folk Spotlight* and the Country Gentlemen had *Folk* this and *Folk* that and so on. I mean, it was just—it was a folk era. Pete Seeger was big and a lot of other people. Peter, Paul and Mary and the Lime-lighters and Burl Ives. Many people were big in folk music in those days. You know how trends of music go.

That song, "In Memory of Carter Stanley," I'll tell you exactly how that started. A fellow by the name of Red Duty, he was an inspector for General Motors, I believe, in Detroit. He inspected I believe Cadillacs. Before they sent them out I guess to the distributors he'd inspect them. And he worked on instruments some. He was the one that redid Carter's D-28—looked like a 45?—Red was the guy who did that. And he used to perform quite a bit with the Stanley Brothers. He'd guest with them, sing a few songs. Real nice fellow. He used to come and visit me in Dayton when we'd all get together there at my place.

He had written some other songs and Ralph later recorded I don't know how many of them. I know one was "Who Was That Beautiful Woman," was one of the ones he recorded of Red's. Red had started this song after Carter's death. And he was like me. He was a great friend of Carter Stanley, course a big fan of the Stanley Brothers. Anyway he had started this song and he said that Bill Monroe said he'd record it but he never did and Red got rather disenchanted with it. I said, "Red, what are you going to do with that song?" He said, "Jack, I'll tell you what," he said. "You want it, you can have it."

So I took the song and rewrote it. I changed it somewhat and I put different music to it. The music that we have now is not the music that Red had. And I published it and then later we recorded it—Roy Lee Centers, Fred Spencer, and our band—and then little later I got Don Reno and Bill Harrell, they recorded it. And then when we recorded *The Bluegrass Sound* Ralph said, "Well, everybody else has recorded it. I guess I might as well too, if you don't mind." I said, "No, not at all."

So we put that on Ralph's album and I believe it was the best cut that we had of all of them. Our cut that Roy Lee sung the lead on was real good but the engineer got a lot of distortion in it and we just had to drop it. After the original pressing we just dropped it because it was distorted real bad. I believe Bill's cut the thing too. But I think probably for a good recording and everything we did the best one with Ralph.

Ozzie Thorpe helped me to produce that album. He put some money into it. And he was to get so many albums and some distribution rights and so on and he did. He wrote several of the songs and I had them published with Jaclyn Music BMI. Later we fulfilled our obligation to Ozzie on giving him the records that he wanted and he was to get so many originally and distribute them, ever what he did with them, and then he came back and got more and we finished that obligation up.

And I don't know where Ozzie is. I haven't heard of him for a long time. He was a deputy sheriff there in Montgomery County, Dayton, Ohio. And he got out of that and somebody said he was in Indiana. I heard he was dead and then later I hear he's a-living somewhere around Indianapolis. But a lot of those songs that Ozzie brought us there are real good. You remember "Carter's Songs." I thought that was real unique. Actually I liked all those songs that he brought us. I think Ralph did too. Kind of sad that Ralph never did learn many of those songs, including "The Memory of Carter Stanley," so he hasn't been able to perform them out on his personal appearances. Cause he did most of them off of the paper, never did really learn them. But I wish he'd learn some of them. Maybe he will one of these days. He's talked about it, you know, learning some of them.

He did one for King a week later. That was the second one he did on King, I believe, after Carter's death. Well, Ralph was kind of in between contracts. He'd had the contract, but it was a duo with Carter, you know, so he didn't know hardly how he stood. Anyway he went back and they had him to record a few more more and then he left King. I don't really know if he negotiated a new con- tract with King. I'm not sure but I don't believe he did. Later King went out of business. But anyway that was in that era where blue- grass was kind of hard to get recorded. And King was one of the few places that did record some of it. At least they started back ear- lier than a lot of the others.

Jalyn 126 was Curly Ray's second album. He did one with Melo- dy and then he come and did that one with me. That was his sec- ond one on his own. Of course he'd recorded a lot with other peo- ple. Lonesome Pine Fiddlers and I don't know who else. But that was his first, or his second album for himself, you know. Since then I guess he's what done fifteen or twenty or more. That LP 126 had the "Braying Mule" on it. Those were live mules braying in Hugo, Oklahoma, I believe. They got that down at Bill Grant's, that has the big festival out there.

And then we did that LP 127. It featured Lee Allen. Lee Allen had written most of those songs and did the lead vocal and played rhythm guitar. Then Ralph and the Clinch Mountain Boys backed him up. And Roy Lee Centers, he played on that, played banjo on some of it and sung tenor I think with Lee. And I guess Ralph must have played—yeah, Ralph played banjo on part of it too.

Lee and Ralph had become friends over the years there and Lee had gone out and done quite a few special appearances with Ralph here and there and had visited with him and so on and so forth and Lee wanted to record an album. He got Ralph and George Shuf- fler and Roy Lee Centers and Curly Ray I believe and Ron Thoma- son. The Old Professor, yeah, Dry Branch Fire Squad. He played mandolin on that album. And they did that album and it turned out rather well. I think probably it's the best release Lee's ever had, in my opinion.

And then we did 129. I was over in Grayson, Kentucky, distrib- uting records and tapes over there at that DJ Record Shop, and John, the owner there, he said, "I want you to hear these two fel- lows." I said, "Okay." So he had them on a tape recorder, Keith Whitley and Ricky Skaggs. Course they sounded a lot like young Stanley Brothers and he says, "Aren't they good?" I said, "Yeah, they're fine." He says, "I'd like for you to record them." I said, "Well, I'd like to do that." I said, "Could you help some financially?" He said, "Yeah, I'll try to do that." But we never did get that done.

And then Ralph I understand was making a personal appearance at a high school gym or something of that nature. He was a little late getting there and Keith and Ricky were performing when he got there. And of course he was impressed by them and then they got acquainted. From then on out if I remember right they'd tour with him during the summer while they was on school vacation, high school.

And then, when they—well, I guess I'd better get this first. Ralph made the arrangement with me to record them. I believe he called me up. We got right into it, took them into the studio and recorded them. And Ron Thomason also played mandolin on that one. Ricky Skaggs played fiddle. When Ricky played the mandolin Ron I don't believe played but when Ricky played the fiddle Ron took the mandolin. Ron was appearing a whole lot with Ralph here and there at that time, guesting with him. Maybe traveled full time with him. Seem like he did, but anyway he traveled a lot with him. You know, he's from Honaker there, close to where Ralph's from. He liked the Stanleys' music like many of us do.

Course we have the one now featuring Curly Ray Cline we're releasing now. *The Deputy.* Real good job. I just heard it for the first time today. Hope we all get rich, don't you? Curly, he doesn't need any more money, but we do. I really don't need it myself, but my creditors do. Yeah, that's an old one. I believe I've heard Ron Thomason say that, too. Carter used to tell it. Carter had some real nice clean jokes he'd tell on the stage. I believe that was one of them. I remember he used to say that—I believe it was his uncle or somebody said, "I got all the money I need." He said, "I got enough to do me a lifetime—provided I die before breakfast tomorrow morning."

15

Dick Freeland

"Ralph was real easy to work with"

In the popular music industry, and in most kinds of country music as well, producers have a great deal to do with the success or failure of record albums. As often as not they choose most of the material, pick sidemen, dictate arrangements, and, not to put too fine a point on it, manipulate the artists like a group of puppets. When this process is working well, musicians (and their reviewers and fans) are full of praises for their producers. But sometimes we hear artists complaining that they've always wanted to record such-and-such a song, or try such-and-such an approach, but couldn't because their producers wouldn't allow it.

Most admirers of Ralph Stanley's music would agree that it was with his first Rebel album, *Cry from the Cross,* that he really hit his stride as a solo artist. All of the cuts on this record are splendid, but the a cappella numbers in particular were revolutionary at the time. And when we see "Producer: Charles R. Freeland" on the back of the album jacket, we naturally wonder how much Freeland and his company had to do with all this.

Approaching the pages that follow with this question in mind, we can see that what they don't say is as important as what they do. Freeland had the greatest possible respect for Ralph Stanley's art. He and his engineer, Roy Homer, produced an excellent sound for the band, and that they did it by means of live mixing—that is, by making all their technical adjustments while the band was actually performing—remains an awesome achievement. They exercised only the most minimal of veto power over Stanley's choice of material. They used almost no mechanical or musical gimmicks, and those they did use were so understated as to be almost inaudible. (Were any fans ever aware that there were drums on one or two of Stanley's Rebel recordings?)

They created chaste, plainspoken album covers, usually decorated only with a couple of photographs, color on the front, black and white on the back, and a typewritten list of personnel and recording data—a serious fan's dream. ("We saved a lot of postage that way," Freeland recalls.) They ran a well-organized, energetic distribution system, getting the records to the people who wanted them and not wasting their time trying to peddle them under false auspices to people who did not understand the music (as was often the fate of the Stanley Brothers' records during the early sixties).

But most of all, Dick Freeland and his company were content to stand back and let Ralph Stanley make his music in his own way. Freeland's successors, happily, have followed him in this, and the result is a monument, a permanent legacy of American musical art.

———

I'm primarily a music fan, not a musician. I can play a little on several stringed instruments, but not to amount to anything. I lived in Newport, Pennsylvania. I was a land surveyor by trade until I went into the music business.

The way Rebel got going, there was three of us that jointly started the business. One fellow also played some, matter of fact he was halfway decent. He also managed a band, Buzz Busby and the Bayou Boys. And he did some booking for Reno and Smiley. Bill Carroll was his name. So there was Bill Carroll, myself, and a boy named Mickey Loveless.

Well, we'd put out two records on Buzz on Carol Records and when we decided we were going to involve other artists, why we sort of changed things around a little bit. Initially it was just a lark and then when we decided we were really going to do something why Rebel sort of came into being. That was November 1959 if I remember right. It was three of us for about a year. Then the other two fellows decided it was taking up a little too much time and I bought their interest and sort of went on from there.

Initially it was just something I enjoyed. The record business was just part-time for the first eight years and I guess in 1967 I quit my job and went full-time with it. It was a quiet time for bluegrass. The only person that was going fairly well professionally that I knew real close was Charlie Waller, of the Country Gentlemen. I knew the Stanley Brothers, but just as a fan. I didn't know them that well personally.

We did some mail order early in the business. I had done some selling on WWVA. Matter of fact that's actually the first contact I ever had with Ralph. We sold an offer on Wheeling and then it went around to other stations in the country. Ralph was living in Live Oak, Florida, then and a check showed up in the mail from him for one of those offers we were selling on radio. It was the *Bringing Mary Home* album on the Country Gentlemen.

I guess that really sort of got things started. I got to thinking about him and then some tapes on him and Carter became available and I thought, Oh what the hell? I got his address. Why waste it? Those were show tapes on the Stanley Brothers, and I had to get together with Ralph and Carter's widow to put those out. That's how we got started.

Ralph's records were all made in Clinton, Maryland. It was a basement studio. The equipment really for the time was very good. It was all Ampex recorders and the top of the line Neumann microphones of the time. It just happened to be that it was in a person's basement. Roy Homer's. It was two-track recording. Everybody was miked individually but it was two-track. They didn't have to move in and out. They just stood there and we did the mixing on the board live.

Did I give him any material? No, I wasn't really that pushy. Course at that time I didn't particularly want to do "Roll in My Sweet Baby's Arms" over again. You know, I thought a lot of the standards had already been done. We were always looking for something new. Ralph would come in and we'd need twelve numbers and he'd have fourteen. And we'd go in and throw a couple out.

Some of the arrangements got changed in the studio. I guess we did some things that, you know, at the time the purists got a little upset about, but we never went too far with Ralph. You know, we used a drummer every now and then or something like that. And maybe a twelve-string guitar on particular songs. I think he did a thing called "Shotgun Slade" we maybe used a twelve on. I know we used drums a couple of times on a number that we thought maybe, you know, had a chance.

I don't know if we ever fessed up to the drums on the backs of the albums or not, to be honest with you now. I'd have to go back and check. But I know we did use them. Not loud, just something to fill. Course Ralph—he and Carter were working with Syd Nathan up at King, you know, and they weren't adverse to taking a shot in left field every now and then. I think "Katy Daley" might have been one we threw a little extra rhythm in behind.

The a cappella numbers weren't really a surprise to me. Al-

though I guess maybe we started doing those. They hadn't recorded any to my knowledge up to that time. But there was, oh, two or
three groups from down in Ralph's part of the country that did a
lot of music that way. The Chestnut Grove Quartet. And Jack
Cooke's in-laws, the Cooke Duet or the Cooke Family, whatever
they're calling themselves now. And Ralph did some of that on
stage, too. But it was just sort of an extension of what was happening around there then. We always tried to pretty much stick one
of those on an album.

Ralph was real easy to work with. The system that we liked to
use was to write out what we were going to do on paper. Like, you
know, if the fiddle was going to kick the darn thing off, we'd write
down, "Fiddle kick-off." Then when it was solo, we'd write down
who, and if the chorus was a trio, and then what instrument took
the breaks in the middle. And of course we needed to know what
instrument was going to be backing on the first half of the verse or
second half and all that.

Ordinarily with most groups we did all that when they came into
the studio, but Ralph was real good. He'd worked most of that out
before he ever got there and when he got there he'd just give us a
sheet of paper for each one. You know, he had it all figured out,
the band knew what they were going to do, so all we had to do was
twist the damn knobs right. If it was, you know, written out for you
why—pretty hard to screw up consistently. After the *Cry from the
Cross* he saw the way we were working and just fell right in. No
problem. He was great to work with.

I'm positive that we cut one or two albums in under five hours.
Generally if they didn't make a mistake and the machine was running and we got our part of it right on the other side of the glass,
why there wasn't no damn sense doing it again. That's the easy
part of it. You only have to do that sucker right one time. Doesn't
matter from then on what you do with it.

Curly Ray's records, one of those we did in an hour and a half.
A lot of that stuff was sort of impromptu but if it worked we'd just
go ahead and sail with it. Now particularly with Curly, the bulk of
his sales were point of contact with him and generally what the
person saw and heard on stage, when he got home and played the
record that's what he was going to get, right straight back again.
We sort of purposely never tried to create something that wasn't
going to exist on the stage.

I went on that Japan trip with them in '71. It's funny. We were
looking at some slides last night, and one of them was a picture
taken at our old house in Maryland. Had a bunch of boxes and

stuff underneath the tree and Ralph and Curly with the souvenirs they'd brought back from that first trip.

We did the live album there, and then we did a studio album that was for a—I don't remember what the company did now. It was sort of like—remember Firestone used to sell records here for a dollar to get you to come into the store? Well, we did one over there. I can't remember what the company was that we did it for, though. It's the album that had the naked woman on the front. I understand they sold about a hundred thousand of those darn things. They just sold it for the equivalent of either a dollar or a dollar ninety-nine. They were just leaders for the company.

How they were paid depends on the artist. Some of them did it for records. Curly did. Course, you know, we paid the engineer, studio, all that nonsense and then the artists had a choice of payment in money or in records. Most of them took it in records. Course we gave them a pretty darn good price on records and usually they could take them out and sell them and make about four times as much. Quite a few of them took records in lieu of cash payment. Which worked out, you know, better for everybody all around.

For distribution, like I said, we did some mail order then. We also had a rack dealership in the Washington area. So we had the ability to sell, you know, in grocery stores and that type of thing in the D.C., Maryland, Virginia area. Then we tried the normal distribution route with a small company. It was tough then. So we thought, well, that's not working too good, so we went to the Library of Congress and one by one went through all the phone books in the country and wrote record stores direct and we did finally start selling to some stores directly then.

And we pretty much maintained that as about 60, 70 percent of our sales right on through, even though the latter years, right before I sold the business, we were back working through a fair amount of distributors then. But we still maintained those key stores that we'd serviced for ten, twelve years. There were of course a number of other people that were mail ordering that we sold to, Alex Campbell in Pennsylvania, Jimmie Skinner in Cincinnati, those type people.

I sold out to Dave Freeman. I sold the business just twenty years to the day from when it was started. Started November of '59, sold it November of '79. I was living down here in Asbury when I sold. Why? It just wasn't fun any more, to be honest with you. I guess it's just like any other—I haven't done anything noteworthy since, other than farm. Although I may.

16

Fay McGinnis

"And who were they, compared with the Stanley Brothers?"

Fay McGinnis, at the time a completely anonymous housewife from Wyandotte, Michigan, began doing promotional work for the Stanley Brothers in the mid-sixties. One measure of what she was up against is the fact that the news of the death of Carter Stanley on December 1, 1966, which was surely one of the biggest events in the forty-five-year history of bluegrass music, literally took months to reach the ears of the worldwide bluegrass audience.

The information explosion that by now is such a cliché was still in its infancy, at least as far as this music was concerned. Professional folklorists, on the whole, were ignoring it; Mayne Smith's "An Introduction to Bluegrass," the first and for a time the only scholarly article on the subject, did not appear until 1965. *Bluegrass Unlimited*, now an international journal of record, started publication in the same year, but only as a mimeographed newsletter distributed to one or two hundred of the faithful. Discographical information was nonexistent, and the distribution of the records themselves was a very haphazard business. Many of the older artists who had laid the groundwork for the music were languishing in obscurity. The lack of a festival circuit and the fact that letters, rather than long-distance telephone calls, were still the preferred means of communication, made the spreading of even the most basic information difficult and time-consuming.

Operating purely by instinct, with no precedent or training to guide her, Fay McGinnis (along with some talented followers such as Norman Carlson of Indiana) set about attacking these problems on every front. She boldly canvassed her neighborhood, setting up show dates for the Stanley Brothers, and cheerfully turned her house into a dormitory for the Clinch Mountain Boys during their frequent visits to eastern Michigan. Her fan club newsletter featured not only the usual personal notes and appearance announcements but also serious, pathbreaking discographical studies of the Stanley Brothers' recorded work. The tape club she initiated took the place for subscribers of a national bluegrass radio program. She and Michigan record producer John Morris were responsible for the revival of the career of string-band pioneer Wade Mainer, who, together with his wife Julia, now once again has a nationwide audience for his music. All this work, needless to say, involved endless hours of unpaid labor and the cooperation of an unusually understanding and supportive husband and family.

And the story continues, as Fay McGinnis, now with the help of a music fan named Ron Smolka who is a Detroit police officer in his day job, is running a regularly scheduled cable television program called "Mountain Echoes" out of Wyandotte. Her studio is now an almost mandatory drop-in spot for visiting bluegrass and other traditional musicians. The show is becoming increasingly widely syndicated, and, like its producer, it just keeps getting better as the years go by.

I followed the big bands in high school. You know, Harry James and that kind of thing. I wasn't a total stranger to country music, of course. I had heard the Grand Ole Opry some in my early childhood. My dad loved the music. My mother detested it, but we heard as much as possible when I was little without irritating and upsetting my mother. And Daddy played the fiddle a little bit. Never knew I liked it. I guess maybe I think now I did. Apparently it stuck in my mind.

Anyhow, I think it started for me when I heard Carter and Ralph on WRVA, just by accident, on the radio. I just turned that on and I thought, "That's got to be the prettiest music I ever heard in my life." Then shortly after that they came to Detroit. I saw it advertised: there was a place, 101 Mack Avenue in Detroit. It was a union hall, still there, I guess. But Casey Clark for many, many years had a regular Saturday night jamboree there, and broadcast eventually.

And the Stanley Brothers were one of the acts. I couldn't believe it. So Roy and I went to see these people that we'd never even heard of before in our life. And of course, we didn't speak to them. Gosh. You know, that was like, oooo. You know? And after that we went to see Lester Flatt. They followed shortly after, and several other name acts.

And we had a stereo—maybe it wasn't even a stereo, at that time, but it was a tall wooden cabinet affair, a record player. It played 78 records, I think. Well, I had nagged Roy into letting me take out all the 78s. We went out in a field and threw them. We took them by his mother's big field in the back to see how far we could throw them. You talk about the height of stupidity.

Anyhow, after that I bought a record player that would accommodate long-play albums. And the first album I ever owned was the Stanley Brothers, King 615. I bought it from Sears. So I said, "I'll take everything that you have in that type of music." Because "bluegrass" didn't mean a thing to me, you know? And here I am. Oh my.

But from there on it was quite a devotion. It almost obsessed my life for a long time. I didn't know anything other than the fan club. How did it begin? Let's see. Some lady offered me a group of slips for fan clubs. And I didn't know anything about a fan club. I visualized Hollywood stars having fan clubs. All glossy and shiny, you know, that kind of thing. And I pulled out the one name that I recognized in that folder. It was the Stanley Brothers. It just kind of all fell together at the same time.

So I joined that and the lady that ran it asked if anyone would write about anything happening in their area. I took it literally. So I wrote in about everything that I knew in bluegrass. Roy and I were becoming, maybe not totally involved, but at least involved to the extent that we were going to see what we knew about, you know. And we had a lot of people from this area that went on to become a real Who's Who. Frank Wakefield and the Osbornes were here at that time. A lot of people that were not that well known then, but they were just in bars around about. That type of thing.

And so I would write in about all these things. And one time a phone call came and it was from Carter Stanley. Like the king of England called me, you know? And he said, "Would you take our fan club?" And I said, "Oh Lord, no." I mean, I was just flabbergasted. I couldn't talk to him in the first place. To think I was talking to Car—I couldn't believe it. It was just all unbelievable.

And I guess we saw them somewhere later. I can't remember just how it happened, but we went up and introduced ourselves, told them who we were. Then they called me a few times. I said, "Ralph, you're supposed to keep in touch with this lady that's running the club and keep her happy, because she might really quit." And they speculated that she might quit. And Ralph kind of indicated later they might have let her quit, you know, because—So they asked me and I said, "Okay. Sure. I'll do it."

I had no idea in the world what I was doing. Nothing. I just knew it should be something worthwhile. Carter told me one thing I never forgot. He said, "Write anything you want to as long as it's the truth, because you might have to face it or we might have to face it. Make it truthful." And I always stuck to that. For instance, suppose somebody wrote to me, saying, "We *heard* . . . ," well, I just disregarded that, because, you know, it's not the way I felt that it should be done.

So I got busy digging up as much as my time would allow with my three children. Lisa was tiny. Carter used to pick up Lisa. I have pictures at home of him holding her when she was a baby. He'd get her up out of the crib and hold her.

Anyhow, it just grew. I'm not educated at all in writing. I never was. I did very poorly in English at school. I did a lot better in arithmetic and algebra, or boys, you know. But I just struggled. Everything I did was really hard for me in that respect. And then time-wise, too. I'd work after I'd got the kids in bed. You've got to have some kind of home life for the kids, you know. Anyhow, eleven o'clock or so I'd go to the dining room table. Eventually Roy built me an office in the basement that I hated because I was so alone down there. But I'd go and write till sometimes the break of day. And I answered every piece of mail I got.

I never felt adequate. I never had enough help. I had lots of *encouragement:* "Oh, you're doing fine." But it was, you do, you do, never—you know. And a lot of people would say, "We'll help. I'll do this. I'll do that." But they never—it was verbal, you know? And I always felt inadequate because I could see me and the whole world that should know about Carter and Ralph.

And I think that I made a lot of inroads in that type of fan club. I'm proud of that, because I started it off in a different direction. We did the Mainer series, John Morris from Old Homestead and I, we did that when Wade and Julia Mainer were here. Nobody'd even heard of them. Nobody paid much attention. But I got to digging and digging, and between the two of us we did a lot on the Mainers. They were so willing to cooperate.

I couldn't devote the whole club to the Stanley Brothers. But Carter and Ralph were not resentful of the devotion I gave to others, because it was promoting the same type of music, you see. There're some that would say, "In my fan club you put my name only." So their fan clubs would never stay in business too long. They'd come and go.

But mine was always so big. And it became international. I had representatives all over the world, far more intelligent in—education-wise than I. But maybe they just didn't—maybe I had the leadership. I don't know. But I had people all over. It was unbelievable. We had them behind the Iron Curtain. That's the truth. They wrote and they would send me minerals and rocks and different things. They couldn't send money, you know.

I put hours and hours in there. I put so much of my life into that club. Basically to promote the Stanley Brothers first. I never lost sight of that fact. But also the music in general. You couldn't ignore the other things that were going on, and they never asked me to. That's what set them apart, I felt.

Roy and I spent lots and lots of time with Carter and Ralph. I have to start by saying that Roy was totally in favor of everything I did. He's done lots of dishes and lots of diapers, to make my time available for these things, to answer those letters. My postman, I had the same one for years. He eventually became a drunk. He fell off my stairs a couple of times. I swear I drove him to drink. He hated me. You could see it in his face, he hated me. I always had so much mail, he never could get it in the letterbox. Never. So he'd have to ring the bell and wait for me. Once I told Roy I could go stark naked to the door and he wouldn't know it because he'd just thrust that mail at me. I told Roy once, "I'm going to ask our postman if he wants to join our fan club." Roy said, "He'll get drunk and never finish up the route. Don't do it." He was just beside himself with mail. I had mail that came to me that was just addressed to Wyandotte, Michigan, with my name on it. And it'd always get to me. I think the postal people all knew because I got so much.

But anyhow, we got to know Carter and Ralph. I didn't hover, but they invited us a lot. They'd call a lot. I did a lot of booking for them. I did things I didn't know I could do, I never dreamed in my life I'd do. Carter called up one time and he said, "We have all this week right now and we'd like to come up and see you. Why don't you book us for a week?" I said okay. So a friend of mine—she's dead now, but she was my closest friend. I said, "You've got to come with me, Pat, because I've never been in a bar alone in my life and we're going to go to some bars." So we must have been the two most timid souls ever walked in Detroit bars. Of course it wasn't that tough a situation in those days.

We went to different bars and I booked them. And I'd say, "I want—" I don't know what I was saying then. Four hundred? And they were real poker-faced. So anyhow, when they'd start smiling I knew I had them and I'd say, "Okay. That's good." I didn't know what was good, really. Carter didn't say. And Carter did all the business in those days. I booked them for—Lord, I don't know, probably two fifty or two hundred. But I got money for every day, you know. And if you ever did see a grown man close to tears—I can still see the look that came over his face when I told him. "Well," he says, "what kind of money a night?" "Well, you're getting two hundred here, two fifty here." Or whatever, you know. He never said anything, didn't complain, but you could see all the disappointment washing over his face.

I remember one night we were all in this bar where they played, and Roy and Larry Sparks and Ralph and I went out to the car. And we took the clothes—they had matching jackets—we took the clothes to the car and hung them up on a hanger. So we were waiting in the car and we were waiting and we were waiting and we were waiting for Carter. Finally Ralph went back to see what was keeping Carter and get him going. It was directly across the street.

After a while Roy said, "Well, I'm going to get Ralph. Come on now, this is getting ridiculous. Soon morning's going to be here." So Roy went to get Ralph. And in about another ten minutes Larry went to get the whole bunch and I went after Larry. One by one by one. And somebody stole the clothes. Somebody stole all their clothes out of the car and they didn't realize it. They came and jumped in the car. Roy and I got in our car, and they left. Some friend of ours was at the show the next day, down in Ohio, and they said Carter and Ralph came in with such awful clothes on. They never saw Carter with such big baggy clothes. They'd borrowed somebody's pants or something because they didn't realize their clothes were not hanging there until they'd gotten there. They called back and they said, "Go find our clothes." Well, a likely story. Somebody'd watched us all go trailing in, you know, and that was the end of the clothes. That was an unbelievable thing. I'd forgotten about that. Just came back to me.

We had lots of good times with them. Times were not always hard. They didn't always get their clothes stolen or get poor money. Things did pick up all the time. They had constant promotion help, some I'd like to think from us, and, well, things just picked up a little bit.

They were at our house after they had worked their first bluegrass festival for Carlton Haney in 1965, the very first festival as such. So old Carlton definitely gets credit for that, though they were not all that happy with him then. He'd given them a bum check and they were calling on the phone. But eventually it all worked out. Carlton lost his shirt. But it brought people from everywhere and so I think all of this, the way things are now, directly leads back to Carlton and his foresightedness.

In the first place they had to get those people to cooperate, you know. They had to get all the bands to speak to each other first. There was not that great a relationship between them. You'd not see bands associating the way you do today. So the first step was to get them all to cooperate with each other, or at least be civil to each other. So I really think that Carlton deserves so much credit. I really do. People don't always see that, but I do.

But anyhow, things picked up for them. They went overseas. They came back to our house from New York after they did that tour. Carter sat on the couch and talked to us about the—"Wonderful World Outside," is that the name of the song? He had this thought in his head when he was over there in one of the countries with the high mountains and he looked out and how beautiful it was and all. And that's how that song started. Didn't mean a lot to me then, until he passed away, and then it meant a lot. And we heard him singing the Sharecropper song at our house. He never got a chance to record that either, before he died.

Anyway, he would stay at our house, he stayed a lot. He and Larry Sparks stayed at our house a lot. Boy, that kid really stayed a lot at our house. Carter stayed with us. Ralph would go stay with Ruby and Bill. They lived in Detroit, and he usually would stay with them. Ralph has stayed at our house but not a lot. And Carter would drive with Roy and me. We'd go with them wherever they were booked and we'd take Carter to the shows and bring him home, bring him back to our house.

And he would talk and we would listen. And he was such an insecure person, just so insecure. And I just couldn't imagine him feeling that way with this beautiful voice. To me, there's never been better. And he loved his children beyond any—it was unreal. He'd come in the house and go get mine, get Lisa out of bed and pick her up and hold her in his arms. He was always with them, because they were kids and made him think of home, you know. He said that when his kids were born he was away and he felt guilty and when they went to school and had their little plays and all those things he was away and he felt guilty. So I always thought there was some kind of guilt, you know. I didn't really study analyzing people, but maybe that's why he wrote all those beautiful, weird, haunting, tortured songs, you know.

He had such an air about him. I don't know, he just had something majestic about him. One time we were in a hotel in Nashville, and Jimmy Davis, the governor of Louisiana at that time, came in. And people just kind of looked. He's such a tall, big guy, you know. So stately looking. And it struck me that that's the way I always saw Carter in my mind.

I was involved with them on a personal basis. And their whole family, their mother. I have sat and heard her talk about when they were—well, another thing. She didn't dwell on their poverty or anything, but I've heard Carter say, "We were dirt poor and I didn't know it. I didn't know it because everybody else was just as poor, same condition around there." So I don't think that created his inferior feeling.

But he was so well liked and when Ralph was laid up with that long, long accident, Carter went to the Grand Ole Opry with Bill Monroe. And Bill in one of his good moods one time told me, he said, "You know, Carter came to me trained. He picked up the guitar and stood on that side of the microphone, took his load with them." We used to be in and out of Nashville a lot with them, and others told me that Carter was really liked at the Grand Ole Opry by other performers. Especially Hank Williams. Can you imagine that? They just clicked. They got along really well together.

We were with Carter and Ralph in Nashville for their twentieth year awards. That was 1966. They were guests of honor. It had been arranged through a fan club sort of thing, at one of the major hotels, I can't remember now. A banquet awards deal. And they were guests of honor for bluegrass. Ernest Tubb was for country. He sat on one side and they were on the other. And Sonny Nelson and Roy, they'd just started their bluegrass band and we were there in Nashville to record. That was their first record. They were going to record that night.

So we were there at the banquet and Carter and Ralph had a certificate fixed for Norma Fannin, my vice president, and me. And we took a plaque from the club to give to Carter and Ralph. Carter's was a guitar and Ralph's was a banjo. Just wall plaques. They were nice. And there I was standing at this podium. I was just talking, just giving my good old Stanley spiel. And everybody was there. Buck Owens was sitting right in front of me, and there was Rex Allen. Everybody you could think of from the Opry, they were all there. And who were they, compared with the Stanley Brothers?

And I caught a glimpse of Carter on my left and he was just looking at me and had tears in his eyes and that just destroyed me. Wiped me out. I was mumbling and fumbling and couldn't get off that stage fast enough. It just destroyed me.

Well, at the appointed time Roy and Sonny stood up to go out to the studio to record. George Shuffler, too. He played on that first session for them. And when they got up to go, Carter and Ralph got up too. Now they were guests of honor. And I said, "Where're you going?" "Well, we're going with these boys. They might need us. Going to help them record. They've never recorded before and we're going to go with them."

So they had to split. Boy, they took off, Roy and George and Sonny, they took out in a hurry. And Norma and I drove in a car with Ralph and Carter. Carter drove. And I'll never forget this. This was the last time I was driving with Carter. And we were so lost, Nashville is so confusing. And Carter said, "All the time I've lived here it's always—" Downtown was confusing to him. And we kept going around and kind of ending up back in the same spot, you know. Finally we asked somebody and got on the right road and got out of town. But he said, "Do you think I'll spend the rest of my life just going around in a circle in Nashville?" And it's just stuck in my mind, because boy, how true that was, almost.

So we went out to the studio and Carter went in. Roy's told this many a time. This is my Roy's favorite story, he'd tell you right away. He's told it from the stage, too, a lot of times. They were already in the studio, Roy and Sonny and George Shuffler. And when Carter and Ralph and Norma and I came in, Carter went with hands extended to shake hands, and he said, "I'm Carter Stanley. I'm down here to help these boys any way I can. I'll do anything except play a bass, so don't give me one of those." And I've always just kicked myself for not having them stick a guitar in his hands. That'd been his last session, you know. So he and I sat out in the lobby, or hallway, most of the time, and Carter played on this old antique banjo I have. Sometimes he'd go in, but for the most part Ralph did the A&R on that record.

And so we left and we went to the Black Poodle and two or three places and then we went to the motel—or hotel, we were in a hotel. Carter went to bed. Next day we were there bright and early and Carter looked, oh! He said, "Well, I don't feel that good." And we said, "You want to call a doctor?" "No. Do you always call a doctor when you don't feel well?" So we went out, Ralph and Roy and I think George went with us sometimes. We were popping in and out all over town. We were just doing all kinds of stuff.

And we got so irritated with Ralph because we'd be walking down the street with him and you couldn't walk anyplace because everybody'd stop and say, "Hi Ralph," "Hi Ralph," "Hi Ralph," "Hi Ralph." And they'd want to talk and talk and talk and talk. And I'll never forget it. We'd say, "Well, we're going to leave you if you're going to stay and talk all day." He'd say, "Well, if you go ahead and leave me one more time I'm not going to introduce you to—" Chubby Wise I think it was. I said, "Oh, was that Chubby Wise? I would've loved to've met Chubby Wise." "Well now, you walked off and left me, see?" Anyhow, that night we went to see George Jones over at the Possom Holler, I think. Carter wouldn't get out of bed. We kept going back and checking on him.

So the next morning Roy and I had to leave. Carter looked so thin, and he had just a strap T-shirt, undershirt on, you know, when he was lying in bed. And he had these red blotches on him. And I said, "Carter, why are you—why have you got those?" "I don't know." And now I know. I didn't know then.

And before we got ready to leave he said, "Get my guitar case." It was sitting underneath the edge of his bed. Now George and Carter, boy, they played tricks that you couldn't believe. Their favorite pastime was thinking up something they could play on each other or anybody they could and then they'd have hysterics for a month. So I said, "No, no." Because I didn't know what—I wasn't going to open up his case for him. So I said, "Let George get it out." So George pulled it out for him. And he got out a stick that he was whittling on. And George said, "Smells like cedar. It smells like pencils," he said, "smells so good."

And Carter gave it to me. I said, "Well, what do you want me to do with this?" He said, "I want you to take it home with you in the car and you can whittle on it going home." And I said, "What are you carving?" "Oh God, I'm not carving anything. You're the dumbest person at whittling I've ever met. Don't you know anything about whittling?" I said, "No, not much. I thought you made something." "No, I'm not making nothing," he said. "You whittle like this. Me and George, we drive like maniacs all afternoon to get to the show an hour early so we can sit backstage and whittle and soothe our nerves." So he said, "If you go like this and flick your wrist just right you can make all those shavings go in the same pile." And I have it to this day, that stick. I carried it in my purse up until just a short time ago, years and years and years. It's just worn slick now. It's not much bigger around than a pencil.

But he came to the lobby with us and said goodbye and when I got home the phone was ringing when we walked in the door. And they said, "Carter's not going to live." They had been trying to call, I guess. We'd stopped somewhere. Bean Blossom, maybe. I've forgotten. We stopped overnight and went in the next morning. Carter and Ralph had left Nashville that night and gotten into Kentucky someplace and Carter had actually gone on stage and started hemorrhaging from the mouth. That was—that was it, you know.

I never saw Carter alive from then. They were calling for us to come and I just didn't want to see—I didn't go and I guess I've always regretted that. So when Roy Lee was killed and Ralph called and said, "Roy Lee's been shot"—He didn't say to come but he told me where they were. So Roy and I got bundled up and took off to the funeral home because I always regretted not going to—maybe I should have. But I just didn't want to see Carter, you know. He meant so much to me, and to Roy, too. He left it up to me, but we just didn't want to go. Shouldn't get that involved with people, should you?

The people wrote. They wrote me from all over the world for months. It took a while for that news to circulate, you know. And they sent sympathy cards and letters of all sorts from everywhere. I had boxes I couldn't lift. And I kept telling Ralph, "Ralph, I've got all this mail in my basement. Hundreds of them I opened and thousands of them I didn't open." And he said, "Someday I'll get it." He just couldn't hardly face it all, you know.

And our basement flooded. The only time I ever had water in my basement in my life. Wouldn't you know it? It just soaked those things up. And I thought, well, maybe it's just as well. I don't know. I don't know. It'd just have tortured him some more. So we just threw them out. But if Carter had known that, if he could have seen those letters, he wouldn't have had that insecure feeling. If he could've known how much people loved him, just for what he was, his singing, his—you know?

Lots of that mail was for Ralph to go on. So much of it speculated that Ralph'd never go on, because Ralph is just not the type. You see, Carter was outgoing. He'd come up to you and he just could talk to you from now till sunset about something or other. Where you know how difficult it is for Ralph to talk to his own family sometimes. They're just two different personalities there. So people speculated that Ralph would never go on because of that. Ralph didn't for a little while. He just didn't think he could. They'd just been together, well, all of Ralph's life, because Ralph's the youngest, you know. And he just didn't know if he could possibly go on without Carter. But the mail came in. People wanted him to. And about five weeks, I think, off the road he called up George and they hit it again. Now Ralph was probably far the better businessman than Carter. There's no telling how much money Carter's loaned and thrown away, too. He wasn't conservative in any way. But Ralph, I don't know, he's done real well.

Ralph wanted to do that tribute to Carter. Wendy Smith wrote it. He's a friend of ours. He asked Wendy to put that to words. "Hills of Home" is what it's called now. But Carter had written the original song and he loved that and Ralph knew it and that's the tune he wanted used and set to that with the words. Kind of go through their life together, he told Wendy. And Wendy wrote it, and Ralph hid his eyes and cried the whole time. Finally Wendy went in the dining room, and Ralph and Roy and I were in the living room, and Ralph just couldn't—it was about two years before he could do that on the stage. And in the original version, when Ralph did do it, you can hear his voice break. He says, "Mile after mile after mile," and you can hear him, you know.

It was really hard for him to go on. It was. So you've got to give Ralph so much credit. It just wasn't that easy for him. He wanted to do that Memorial Festival, and he had lots of obstacles thrown in his path. The state police down there, boy are they wicked sons of guns. But it's not just them. It leads back to politics in that county and things I don't understand. He didn't have any encouragement with that festival. That started out as a memorial to Carter. Ralph talked to me about it. He said, "I'm thinking about doing this. What do you think?" And I said, "I think it's a great idea. Who else could better do that than you?"

Larry Sparks had always wanted to sing with Carter and Ralph so badly. I remember one time before Carter died, Larry was staying at our house and he begged me all day long to ask Carter could he sing that night. So Roy, and Red Stanley—a fiddle player, no relation—he was there, too, and they worked out a trio, Roy and Larry and Red Stanley. And all afternoon they were singing these two songs over and over and over. So on the way to the show that night I asked Carter, I said, "If these—if this trio had something worked out real well do you think they might sing it tonight on your show?" And he introduced them on the stage as the Shedhouse Trio and that was the first I ever heard of that. I think it's been well worked, that phrase, you know.

So then Ralph called Larry and he worked with him and after Larry left he got Roy Lee Centers. In my opinion Roy Lee—and I'm taking nothing from Larry because you can't anyhow—but Roy Lee spoke like Carter. I mean, you would hear his voice and you—Ralph told me that when he first was working with Roy Lee sometimes he'd look sideways on the stage just to reassure himself. He just sounded so much like Carter. And he knew all that material.

Jack Lynch's in Dayton, that was a halfway point for Carter and Ralph. Coming in and going back out, they'd stop both ways. They stayed there all the time. They'd call me from Jack's. Jack was on the radio and he had a label going. He was really good to those people. Well, they met Roy Lee Centers there. And Carter and Ralph came into our house and Carter opened up his guitar in the living room, dug his guitar out of the case, and down in there he had a couple of these little records. First time I'd ever even heard of a Ja-lyn record. And he said, "I want you to play these." And I played them. I've got those records to this day. And it sounded so much like Carter I accused it of being him. I said, "You've been moon-lighting. That's what you're doing. You're cheating on King." He thought that was hilarious. They were doing "Will You Miss Me." I said, "I know that's you, Carter." He thought that was so funny. It was Roy Lee, of course.

That was a loss, when he was killed. Wow. Ralph was just dev-astated. We were at the funeral home. Ricky Skaggs was with the Country Gentlemen and Keith Whitley was just drifting around Nashville trying to break into country. And they got to the funeral home, Ricky and Keith did. It was just about the same time we got there. And Roy said to Keith, he said, "Keith, you may have to go back and help Ralph." "Naw, I wouldn't do that," he said. "I don't think I'd go back and work with Ralph again." Ralph called me in a few days at home and he said, "Well, I got me a lead singer." "Who?" "Keith." So the next time we saw Keith, we said, "Hey, you said you never would work with Ralph." He said, "Well, that was before he asked me."

And I guess the final chapter of all this—well, we were in Nash-ville again. Now we don't spend all of our time in Nashville. I detest Nashville really and I have little respect for anything that goes on at Nashville. It's so plastic and phony and it doesn't hold a thing for me. But it did in those days with Carter and Ralph.

And when Ralph was on the Opry the first time he called and we went on down. We went with Keith and Ricky. They were there. And I met Tex Ritter. We were talking about Carter and Ralph and how he knew them and how he respected them and all that. And he says, "I just think that there should be something really done to preserve Carter's image." And Jo Walker called me from the Hall of Fame. He said, "Can you donate something of Carter's?" And I said,

"Well, what can I give?" So I called up Ralph. And he thought about it and thought about it.

Now Larry had been playing Carter's guitar, and someone had tried to steal it. They'd lain on their belly and scooted underneath the tent. They got Melvin's and they thought it was Carter's. Melvin was going a hundred miles an hour after them. They got the guy anyhow, but he meant to get Carter's guitar. So that scared Ralph to death and he'd left it at home after that.

So Ralph said, "Well, gosh—" He had saved every picture, every songbook, every first record, everything that they had had over the years, at his mother's house, the old house. And it had burned. And he said, "What am I going to do with this guitar? If someone doesn't steal it, it might burn." See, in the first place, he'd bought it from Mary, Carter's wife, paid her money and bought that guitar. So he said, "We'll give it to them. That'll be the place." And I kind of encouraged it, too, because that place is fireproof and burglar-proof, as far as I know. It'll always be there. And it's sure damn wealthy enough to keep it there for ever and ever.

So we said, "Yeah. We're going to come and give it at this banquet. We'll bring it." They had arranged at this big banquet that we were going to be there again. It was going to be televised. And Tex Ritter said, "I'm going to be flying in that day." From someplace he'd been playing, Germany or someplace. He said, "What hotel are you going to be in? I'm going to call you there." Well, I thought, it's a likely story. You know all the people you meet and talk to—But he did just exactly what he said. You do meet some people that'll just be straight and honest with you right down the line. And he called and said, "Are you in town there? Things all going along?" "Oh, we're ready to push the button and go."

Roy and I went into Ralph's room to get that guitar, on the way to go to the banquet, and Ralph gave Roy a set of strings and said, "Will you put the strings on it? I think there's a broken string on it." And Roy sat there and wound up the strings on it. Anyhow, they had arranged for Doyle or Teddy Wilburn, I can't remember which one of the Wilburn Brothers, of *all* people in the world, to do the presentation on the air. And he got it so balled up that—Ralph got the trophy of the year and he got back to the table and he didn't know who'd gotten it. I could see it in his face, he didn't know. And I said, "Ralph, who got the trophy?" "Damn if I know. I don't know." I said, "You did." "Well, why didn't he say so? Why didn't you do that?" It was unbelievable. It was the most botched-up thing.

17

Revis T. Hall

"That's all the life I got"

Doc Hall and his wife Bertha spent four of the happiest years of their lives selling T-shirts and other Stanley souvenirs on the Midwest bluegrass circuit in the early eighties. Hall's story is typical in many ways of the hard-core Stanley fan: the mountain (and Old Regular Baptist) roots, the usual migration from the hills for economic reasons, the rediscovery of identity through Stanley's music. In Hall's case it would not be blasphemous to say that this was a kind of conversion, something very much like a genuine religious experience. It had the results that conversion has, too: a changed life, a new and different sense of what is truly important. For the Halls, as for so many other serious Stanley fans, old-time mountain music, especially Stanley's music, became the main focus of existence. Time, money, job—everything else is subordinated to the music.

Stanley fans (and in this the Halls are typical as well) are generally not amateur musicians in their own right, as are so many other bluegrass fans. They are purely appreciators. They are also probably the least philistine group of people in the country. Other forms of art appreciation generally carry with them various forms of nonaesthetic benefits—social prestige for the most part, and sometimes even financial profit. This is not true for the lovers of old-time music: their passion costs them money, sometimes substantial amounts of money, and it certainly does not boost them up the status ladder. They truly love the art for its own sake and nothing more.

Early in 1985 Doc Hall was forced to retire from his nonprofit souvenir business because of the heart trouble that was to bring his life to an end in November, 1986. Before this happened, fortunately, he was able to tell his story, sitting in his trailer on the top of a hill in Roxana, Kentucky, as the music he had given his life to came floating through the windows.

We pulled in here on Wednesday. Took two days to get in. It was just a little bit rainy coming up the mountain there. We didn't have no trouble. The wheels turned loose two or three times. If it'd been dry they wouldn't have spun a bit. You go up and down there a couple of times, you forget it. I'll tell you what, let's face it. You've got to go through the briar patch to get something good. Now that's just the way it is. A little hill ain't going to hurt you because you know what's up here is what you love. No, that hill don't worry me.

I'm a Kentuckian. Bertha, she's from near, between Ironton and Portsmouth, in Ohio. She's a bit of a Buckeye. But she lived right across the river. Well, what started this is, I love bluegrass music. Born in me, I guess. I'm an old-time hillbilly. My dad sat around on the porch, when we wasn't hoeing corn on the hillside or anything, and flipped on that banjo and hummed a little. He couldn't sing for a nickel but he tried.

And then we had Jimmie Rodgers records, great old big ones. And Mom had an old, square RCA Victrola, that you had to wind up, used steel needles, and you had to put it on the record yourself. We'd use a chair and climb up and wind that up to play a Jimmie Rodgers song and stuff like that.

And when I come in out of World War II—in fact, I done some singing in World War II. I never did tell nobody about that. We had a banjo and a guitar and a fiddle in our outfit. We'd sell the beer and stuff out of the PX. We'd create some money, so we'd have us a party in our mess hall. We'd get to drinking some beer and feeling pretty good. So me and a couple of guys, one of them was from Virginia down in here, we'd get up and we'd do some old bluegrass singing. And they got so they wouldn't let us quit. "Hey, more!" And stuff like that.

But I come out and I must have spent fifteen years at a cement plant. Part of it, nine years I think, I was foreman. But I got tired of it, it was about to kill me. And I went from there to driving a truck. I'd dial that old radio in that truck, every station I could get, to hear a little bit of bluegrass. Any way, shape, form, or fashion. Most of it was country. But when they played a bluegrass song, you know, you'd feel like calling them up and thanking them for it.

Well, we went over to Ralph's festival, our first trip over there on the mountain, and I knowed then that that's what it was all about.

But I was getting sick. In '78 they took me out of my truck, about nine or ten o'clock at night. Two or three o'clock in the morning they entered me in the hospital in Portsmouth and that was the last day of work. Never did see my truck no more.

So we went over to Ralph's in '76, '77, '78, and whatever, and we just thought there was nobody like Ralph Stanley and the Clinch Mountain Boys. It was just what I loved. There's some other good bands, don't get me wrong, good people in them, and some good bluegrass people. But—in '79, after I'd had some heart attacks, Ralph was running for a little office down here, treasurer in Dickenson County, and he was going to have some gospel singing in a schoolhouse down there, Wilson Brothers and another band or two. They had the sound system and everything. So we went down there; my son took me down there. I was just barely alive at that time, but I got in the back seat and he throwed a quilt over me. He drove us down there and drove us home again.

But Ralph and them got on the stage and they sung "Amazing Grace." And he underlined it. And about the middle of it an old man come down out of the bleachers and went and got on the stage and he helped Ralph sing it and he underlined the rest of it. And I told my son sitting there, I said, "I've got to go hug him. I know why I love him now." That was it.

Well, it went on and we was everywhere he went, tried to be. And my daughter-in-law over at Indianapolis, she made me a cap, said "Ralph Stanley Number One," because she knew I loved him, you know. So we was over here to Xenia, Ohio, a festival there, Sheriff Bradley put on for orphan kids and stuff. I stepped up to the little camper and Ralph's sitting in a couch there and the deputy sheriff's sitting over there in the shotgun seat.

I stuck my head in and hollered to Ralph, and this deputy turned around and said, "Where'd you get that cap?" I said, "My daughter-in-law had it made for me." He says, "Why don't you sell them?" I looked at Ralph and I said, "Ralph Stanley never gave me no permission to sell anything with his name on it." Ralph looked at me and he says, "You got it now." I said, "Will fifteen percent your royalty be all right?" And he said, "Yup." Well, we went on down here in Kentucky to a festival and Ralph's sitting there against the fence with Jack Cooke, selling records. I said, "Ralph, how about T-shirts, too?" He said, "You got it." I said, "Nobody else?" He said, "Nobody else." So that's what started it.

We didn't make no money. The only time we ever made any money was at Ralph's festival and a couple of more. It was the enjoyment, being with them, that was the pay. You see, the love there overtakes this filthy lucre, don't it? It's good to have this money so you can do it with, don't get me wrong. But the pleasure that you get in your heart—

I loved every minute of it. But now I just got over some heart attacks, and one bad heart failure. Christmas Day in December, Christmas Day night, about 11:30, I died. I know what death's all about. In a way. But we lived up till now. In February I had to turn it back over, because the doctor tells me, no, I can't handle it no more. I've got to get away from it. I can't stand the stress no more. And don't you think that didn't hurt, when I had to tell Ralph. I just kindly turned my head when I talked to him. I couldn't stand to look at him.

But we've enjoyed it. And we thank him, for giving us that little bit of pleasure to work with him. And his wife, we think just as much of her as she was my own sister or Bertha's own sister. She's treated us nice, just as nice as—and the enjoyment, being around her. It's wonderful. Cause I love the way she talks and cuts up and acts the fool. Nobody means no harm or no trouble, we joke and carry on. And I think she's just a nice person. Just can't keep from loving her.

Now we're Ralph Stanley and bluegrass followers. This is the first time we've been to a festival in four years that we could go out here and sit down and listen without worrying about something. We've got some awful good people here, bluegrass people, and we've got some good bands. But there's never going to be nobody in this United States of America that can put on a show like Ralph Stanley does.

And I love him like a brother. I can't help it. That's the way it is. I think he's one of the greatest men that ever was. And has been as far as I can read and go back. Down the line he's been one of the greatest men that ever was. I ain't got the guts enough to say that through a microphone in front of people, cause I go all to pieces. It'd cause me to have a heart attack. But I think the world of him. And my family does, too. We feel like a brother and sister to him and to the whole band, far as that goes.

And I thank the good Lord for letting me be here among the people I love. As long as God lets me live and I'm able to drive that car out there without killing me and her we'll be at the festivals where those boys is at. We'd take our last dollar and go if we had to. You know what I'm talking about? That's the way we feel. That's all the life I got. I love bluegrass, I love those boys, and I want to be with them everywhere I can. That's just the way it is. That's all I can do.

18

Dale Braden

"Basically you hope to break even"

It is the bluegrass festival movement that has kept traditional mountain music alive, at least as a paying proposition, and it is the people who put on the festivals who have made that movement possible. It is essential to make this point forthrightly, because for various reasons these people—"promoters" as they are generally known—tend to have a bad name among people connected with the music, and it is easy to forget how indispensable they are.

In fact, since it is impossible to make a full-time living as a bluegrass impresario, it is really misleading to speak of "promoters" as a class. What we have instead is individual people, sometimes people with access to capital but more often wage earners with almost no capital whatsoever, who love the music enough to want to bring it to their neighborhood.

Sometimes they can have bad luck. An ill-timed rainstorm can wipe out a festival as surely as it can wipe out a farmer's crop, and with equally disastrous results. But at least in that case the reasons for failure are clear. Often they are totally obscure: two festivals can be held in the same county in two successive months with identical lineups and one, year after year, will be a money loser while the other, also year after year, will be an enormous success. And no one can explain why.

The answer, by the way, does not lie in the format of the events. In "Stanley country"—Appalachia and the Midwest—bluegrass festivals tend to be very similar in their arrangements, and visitors from either coast might well find these a little bleak compared to what they are used to. There are virtually no workshops and no special presentations for children or adolescents. The main stage is usually small and spartan. Concession food is predictable and bland, perhaps because many of the participants cook for themselves in their trailers and motorhomes. The only real attraction is wall-to-wall music, six to midnight on Friday (one set per group), noon to midnight on Saturday (two sets per group). Apparently most of the audience likes it that way.

Dale Braden of Norwalk, Ohio, is probably as close to being a "typical" promoter of bluegrass festivals as one can find—though, as he makes clear, he is not at all fond of the term "promoter," or even, for that matter, of the term "festival." He also makes clear the unbelievable amount of hard work that goes into organizing a successful festival, the endless pitfalls that lie in wait for those who wish to engage in such a project, and the selfless love of the music that leads these people to risk those pitfalls no matter what the cost.

I'm from this area, north central Ohio. Born and raised. People tell me I shouldn't be around this bluegrass cause I'm a Buckeye, and so on and so forth. I come from a large family. Thirteen children. Our big thing was listening to Randy Blake on WJJD in Chicago. Every once in a while you'd hear that banjo on there. It was probably Earl Scruggs or somebody in that area. And, you know, I just never get it out of my head. It was country; I don't know if they called it bluegrass at that time. We're talking back late forties, early fifties, when there was no TVs. Run home from school and turn the radio on and you'd listen to "Suppertime Frolic." All the kids did. I got that ringing banjo in my ear and I could never get it out.

And as the years progressed on I learned to play myself. I'd listen to records and whack away at it. Never got very good, for lack of talent or whatever it was. And some of the kids around there played guitars and stuff. Mostly country. Occasionally we'd learn a song that we'd heard on the radio or something.

But when I left school and went in the service, I got stationed in Virginia. This was in '56. And I knew about the type of music and everything. We'd go out to different places. Shipp's Park. Belvedere Beach. Jack Anderson and the Country Boys was a bluegrass band with a steel guitar. That's all it was. Fantastic picker. And we'd go up to Warrenton, Winchester, Washington, D.C., and see Charlie Waller when he was still playing the bars. Buzz Busby. I imagine Red Rector, and, you know, on and on and on.

The Stanleys were at Shipp's Park one time, late '56 as I find out later on, and County Sales sent out one of these Stanley Series albums that was recorded at Shipp's Park and nine chances out of ten I was there. I talked to Ralph about it, after I'd got the album and read the notes.

Well then, when I got out of the service, why, it kind of tapered off for me, cause this was 1959 and bluegrass shows still hadn't started. I came back home and went to work. I was a baker in the service. Come back and got a job where my dad worked in a grain elevator. I got fed up with that and went back into the baking business. Then I moved on to another outfit, did house-to-house sales, then another one and did wholesale. And prices were going up, and I told them, "You can't sell this stuff to these people, they're not going to buy it." And even though I was one of the top four salesmen in the company, I made the decision to leave and go to Ford. And it wasn't six months that wholesale place closed up. I've had pretty good luck that way.

But anyways, up in about 1965, I believe, this first big bluegrass show was put on out in a campground in Virginia. And in 1968 is when we had one in Norwalk. I don't know who organized it, if you want to call it organized. Unorganized organized. It was more like a get-together cause nobody knew who was coming or who was going. Jimmy was there, Jimmy Martin. I believe Ralph picked there. Several name bands. I believe Bill Monroe was there. And this is where I'm getting what I want now. You know, it's, hey, it finally came to me. I don't have to—

Well, that only lasted a couple of years. Then there was something in the newspaper: this woman was going to produce a country show, "Hee-Haw" type, you know, that kind of thing. And I got into it. We did several shows just for charitable organizations. Cousin Clem Shambles is what I called myself, kind of a stand-up comedian, act smart, get people to laugh. I had sawed-off bib overalls, called them the West Virginia hot pants, and I had sweetheart shorts on and we'd do a song, I can't remember the name of it now, but it'd get to a certain point and I'd drop them overalls, see. Just fun. Oh, the people loved it.

Well, in that show was a banjo picker. We'd got together through this newspaper ad. I played some guitar and he played the banjo and we needed somebody else so we hooked up with a fiddle player. And we went all over the country. We'd probably thirty people in the cast. And we had the part where he'd pick "Foggy Mountain Breakdown" or whatever turned him on at that point, see.

And he said to me one day, he says, "You ever go to a bluegrass festival?" And I said, "Yeah, back a couple of years ago they had one out here at the park." He said, "Well, I wasn't around here at that time." He'd come from the Mansfield area. He said, "There's a old-time country music show going on in West Virginia." John and Dave Morris was their names. Ivydale, West Virginia. He did some clawhammer, and he says, "This is the type of music I like. Let's take a trip down there." I was banging away on a mandolin at the time and playing a little guitar. He said, "I know another guy that can play the guitar pretty well. You play the mandolin and we'll get him to play the guitar." So we all packed up one weekend, 1970, about September I believe, went down there. They called it old-time country, but it was actually bluegrass, old style, or that's the way I felt about it, bluegrass old style. Banjo, guitar, bass, fiddle or mandolin or whatever. Played old fiddle tunes, "Billy the Red-Haired Boy," "Cuckoo's Nest."

And from then on it kind of got into my system: hey, there's more to it than just this fooling around, see. So I played with this guy for a number of years, from, oh, '72, '73 to about '76, I guess. Then I went back to Ottawa, where they had the big Ohio National Bluegrass Festival. And the guy that runs the place come up to me and asked me if I'd like to MC. Oh, my heart dropped. You know, I was thrilled to death even being asked, let alone bringing on Ralph Stanley and Jim and Jesse and something like twenty-six bands. Oh man, this is—oh, I'm thrilled to death.

So that's basically how I got started. Doing the MC work and picking a little bit. And I felt that there was more I could do. After watching how this guy produces his show and his ideas, I'd go to the next one and kind of keep an eye on certain things. Why'd he do that? Or, where'd he get that idea from? And different things like that. And some summers I'd work twenty-two festivals. Barely making ends meet, you know, as far as the expenses go. Course I wasn't out there to get rich.

But as we progressed along in the late seventies and early eighties I got to thinking, Wonder how you go about doing this thing, putting one of these shows on? How do they do that? So I talked to different people that I knew and got their ideas. And I said to my wife, I said, "I wonder if we could do that?" Said, "You know, we know quite a bit about this now." We filed things away in our minds. And we didn't realize at the time what kind of money it was going to take. Had no idea how you paid the bands, how you even called them up and got a hold of them and booked them. So you go for more. More research. "How'd you get a hold of that guy?" Said, "I just called him up." And I thought, Hell, you don't talk to these guys. You know, I mean, these guys are big stars. You don't just call him up at his house and tell him to come on over and play for you and stuff like that.

But while I was MCing there at Ottawa, I met Ralph, and Rick and Keith I believe was with him, Roy Lee Centers, some of them guys, and got to know them a little bit. Course I got the nickname Rocky from Ralph. I guess that's no secret to anybody. But that was his way of—he names a lot of people, I guess you know that. I got to know him pretty well, as well as Ralph'll let you get to know him. You know what I'm saying. I don't know everything he does or anything, but I got to be where we could joke back and forth. At least he would call me Rocky, you know, he'd recognize me and speak to me.

Well, from '76 to '83 I worked that big show there. Got to know a lot of people. So I'm starting to get a little bit more brave, starting to think that maybe I do know a little bit about this deal. And this— early eighties—this is when I said to my wife, "Let's see if we can get something together." Well, that's easy, saying. Doing is a whole nother ball game. So we didn't talk much about it for about a year, say latter part of '80 and into the summer of '81. Guy'd mentioned to me, guy I bowled on a bowling team with, he says, "Why don't you call that guy up at RPM and see if you can't get a show going up there?" Cause they all knew I was out playing and MCing and stuff. And I said, "I don't want to call the guy." I said, "If he'd call me then maybe we'd talk."

RPM means Recreation Park and Markets, and then he later changed that to Recreation Park and Music. It was a big horse race track at one time. That didn't pan out and this guy bought it and he didn't know what to do with it. Eventually he did call me, wanted to know if I would help him. Now we're talking summer of '81. Said, "What's the chance of you putting on a show? I can't get things going."

So I told him, "Give me a couple of weeks to see if I can come up with anything." And I thought, Now the park is big enough. It's nice grass. No electric or anything. Course you don't always need electric. It's big enough, you'd get a lot of people in there. Got a nice stage. The stage was there from, he had a rock festival there three years earlier and it didn't work out cause there weren't that many rock people around Norwalk at that time. So everything's there. All I needed to do was, Who am I going to hire? Where do you start? Who do you start with?

My wife spoke up and said, "Well, if we're going to have one"— and this is the exact words she said—"we wouldn't be able to do it without Ralph Stanley." I say, "You're right. Right. But how do we get him? How do we get a hold of him?" I didn't have a phone number on him or anything. And she happened to be looking through the *Bluegrass Unlimited* and she says, "Well, he's going to be down at Cincinnati." November something, either just before Thanksgiving or just after. I forget now. I said, "Well, let's get down there and maybe I can get close enough to talk to him or something. Get some kind of thing going here."

We drove to Cincinnati, Village Tavern. Ralph pulls in with the old milk truck. Charlie and Junior. And I'm still afraid to go up and start talking business with him cause he knows me from the shows but he doesn't know if I am a businessman or if I'm putting him on or anything. So I get nerve enough to get up in that milk truck. He was sitting in there with the heater on, keeping warm. I ask him, I says, "What would be the chances, if I'd put on a show, would you come and play for me?" I thought he'd just say, "Yeah, I'll be there," you know. No. He said, "When are you going to have it?" I said, "Well, we got two dates that I think we can have it." I said, "June." Which that ruled that out cause of Bill Monroe, see. Bean Blossom. He was going to be there. That's only natural. And I said, "How about September?" And at first he didn't seem to think much of it. And then he got his book out. And I kept hinting around, you know, I'd like to know if he'd come and play. I had really had not much of an idea how much he charged, but I figured I could borrow enough money to pay him.

So he fumbled around there and got his book out and looks at page ninety-six or wherever his bookings were and he says, "I got a couple of days in the middle of September, Saturday and Sunday." And I said, "Well, two days, fine. How much you need?" And he quoted me the price. And I said, "Now," I said, "I don't know anything about contracts or anything." See, I have no idea. I said, "I have this piece of paper with the carbon in the middle." So I wrote it on there. Wrote what price he wanted. And I said, "Now this is just an appearance agreement so that you know where you got to be and I know what you're going to get and you know what you're getting." And that was the first band I ever hired in my life. Scared to death. Especially a guy this stature, see?

Now you got the foundation. What do you do from here on? You got to get somebody that can come in and play, not Ralph's music, but somebody that can come in and do their thing and Ralph can do his thing and they don't clash. They complement each other, more or less. Don't know. Have no idea. Boys from Indiana would come up. And I said, "Oh, they're not that well known." But I get to looking through the book and they're better known than I thought they was. I said, "Let's call them up." I believe there was an advertisement in the *Unlimited* with a phone number. It was, his name was Harley Gabbard, I believe. Dayton, Ohio. Call this number for bookings. So I called him and we worked out they'd come in on a Sunday. That was the second band I ever hired. And here I'm a big deal now. I got two bands hired already.

So all right. We got the park. We got the bands, at least two for now. No sound system. That's the next thing. So I was up in a music store and I mentioned it to the guy in the music store. "Oh, we'll do the sound for you," he said. "We'll get that sound for you." I said, "What do you got?" I mean, I don't want no little cracker box. "Oh, we got a big outfit." Well, they did. But they didn't know how to run it. As I later found out that weekend that we had our show.

Concessions: there was another thing. I asked everybody at the Goins Brothers show down at Skeen's Farm. "Oh, that's too far to drive," they said. I looked all over, and not till about three or four days before our show did I find somebody to come in and sell buffalo burgers, or beeffalo burgers I guess they were called. That was a start, what the hell. I run across a guy selling hats. Said what the hell? I can charge him a hundred bucks to come in and set up. Well, he loved that cause he was getting charged anywheres from a hundred fifty to three hundred bucks. I didn't know that. I had no idea. Get him in there and hell, we got two concessions, plus all the bands got records and stuff so, not bad.

Then we hired other local bands. I can't remember exactly who all was on that first show. Opened that gate on a Thursday to let people in. Friday night the local bands did some little shows and then Saturday and Sunday was our big thing.

So when you line up this thing the first thing you do is you get the place, the bands, the sound and keep right on going. But you keep watch on everything and see how it goes and you write everything down. How much did you pay this guy? How many steps did he take to walk across this? I mean details you wouldn't believe I'd write down, so that I could look back and say, Well, here this or that didn't turn out the way I thought it would. Getting into advertising. I'd never done that before. Made up my own flyer. Took it to the printer and printed it up.

See, now we're starting to run into the problems. The health department: you've got to have graywater drains, you've got to have this toilet located so many feet away from the camping area, not next to this and not next to that. I mean, all this stuff starts really hitting us. My neighbor happened to be the chief sanitarian for the county and he wouldn't even give me a break. My own neighbor, next door.

So you run into all these problems. And not expecting to. It was our first show. We made, I wouldn't say a lot of big mistakes, but a lot of little things. Our advertising wasn't that good. We wasn't getting enough flyers out. Different things that we could improve on or wouldn't have happened if we had known ahead of time. So we actually learnt from experience. Trial and error, more or less, you work on it.

Now, here we're at the end of the show. We had seven hundred and fifty-six people the first show. I thought this was fantastic. We're big time now. But, but it didn't pay the expenses. Now where do we go? You're paying them x dollars. And everybody got paid. I borrowed the money to make it. Four thousand bucks. At that time four thousand bucks was a pretty good chunk of money. To cover it, make sure that I got everybody paid.

This was our first show, September of '82. And this list of things that we did, we'd go over it and check each thing: wonder why we did this that way? Maybe we can improve on that. Go down the whole list. After the show we spent a couple of weeks just talking and looking this list over and tried to make improvements. Me and my wife, my family, my brothers and sisters all helped. Working for free. There's no way I could pay them. But they didn't want to be paid anyways. They would've felt insulted. Because they liked the music too.

So I went in and talked to Ralph to hire him back for the next year. And I says, "We didn't do too good." He said, "Well, I can see that there wasn't all that big a crowd." Seven hundred and fifty-six people in a fifty-acre field don't look like very much, see. Now Ralph is not a man for dishing out advice or telling you anything unless you ask him. So I just thought, I'm going to mention something to him. I asked him, I said, "What would you do? Who do you think I should hire?" On a Sunday afternoon, sitting in his bus. He never batted an eye or nothing. He said, "You know what you got to do, Rocky? You got to hire Jimmy Martin." He knows something, see. And I didn't know. I know Jimmy and his music but I had no idea, but he's a pretty good drawing card. So you hire Jimmy Martin next year. So that automatically takes your price up on your, on your paying out, the bands, that takes that up. But, can he, will he be able to? So we get to thinking now. To draw people you have to have these names. "Jimmy," Ralph told me flat out, "Hire Jimmy Martin." As it turns out he was right. No question about that. He was right.

Other things that I did, like schedules for bands coming in. We went out a month ahead of time where we could see somebody who's in the area that was going to play for us that I hadn't seen yet. I had my schedule made up, already had the advertisements in the *Bluegrass Unlimited*. We'd taken our schedule, typed it up and had them run off, and I'd go out to these shows and I'd tell them who I was. Some of them didn't even know me. I'd hand them a schedule and they could hardly believe, here a month away and you already got a schedule. Ralph especially appreciated that, see. Cause he's going from there four hundred miles down the road and he knows he's got to play your show but usually he don't know when cause he has nothing to go by. But he did with mine, see. We made a point to make sure they knew. Then when they pulled in that gate, he pulls in an hour ahead of time or whatever it takes for him to relax a minute and get dressed. That saves him.

And, like when you pay a guy off. If they did two shows today and two tomorrow, the way I worked it is, when they did their first show and they got back to their bus and got changed, I'd give them time to relax and I'd walk in there and hand them that money. Now, he knows, see, hey, this guy means business. He's here to do something for us, he's helping us, I'm helping him, he'll do a good show cause now he's happy, see? He don't have to sweat come Sunday afternoon waiting for his paycheck. This is very important to me. It was always important.

My MCs, you've seen shows where they'll say, "Oh, take a little extra time." Uh-uh. Not at my shows. When these bands come in that gate, they have their schedule. Now he knows that's what time he's supposed to go on. That's the time he wants to go on. I did some of the MC work but I hired a couple of guys and I instructed them, This is the time you're playing by. You get them on and off that stage at that time. Because here we got a guy, he may have to leave right after that last show. He's got his time figured; when he leaves that show, he's got to be at the next one. He's got to have travel time. Don't run him a half-hour, forty-five minutes over. Be on time.

Our organization, which was my family, my sisters, my brothers, my wife, my daughters, my sons, we'd have meetings. We'd go to somebody's kitchen during the early summer and spring. We'd talk all this stuff over. Questions like, what do you wear at the gate? I mean, to some people it doesn't sound like nothing. To me, when you're at my gate, you look presentable. You don't come there with a hole in your pants. People coming in that gate, they look at that big hole in your pants and they say, "Oh, I don't know. Maybe I don't want to be at this place." I don't say you have to dress up with a shirt and tie, but—presentable clothes. I told them, "I want you to look as good after you work four or five hours as them people are coming in with their new clean shave and stuff. I want you to look at least that good." And how they conducted themselves: you don't argue with nobody. If there's any problem, I'm the guy. You don't try to settle things. You refer them to me, you let me make that decision on whether this guy is right or wrong or if he needs something. Let me be the guy. Don't you take the responsibility.

Be nice to people. Treat people like they're your neighbor or your mom and dad. Cause that's the way to keep them there, I believe, to be treated decent, feel safe, bring their grandkids. Cause hey, maybe down the road that grandkid'll come in with two or three people. This all works that way, I believe.

Watching people. I enjoy that part of it. I wonder what she's thinking about? She's looking at something—But I know she's enjoying herself cause she's here. She's contented, she looks contented. So that means, hey, she came to our show because we did everything, maybe not perfect or exact right but somewhere near, that when she leaves she's going to go and maybe tell somebody else. And this is how you start building. People by the gob, "Give me some flyers, give me some flyers, I'll take them to work and hang them up." I don't know if it'd do any good or not, but don't turn the guy down, cause he's got in his head he's going to help you. You need that help. You need every little bit of help you can get.

Be honest with people. Let them know you appreciate them. Run up and hug them. I do that. You've seen me going up to hug somebody, some little guy that I know. He likes that. I mean it's not for, you know, it's because, Hey, good to see you. That's what it's about. I hug Charlie. I don't hug Ralph cause he don't want to be hugged. You don't run up and hug him. But it's love, love in the sense that we're all aiming for the same thing, to have good music, an enjoyable time, whatever.

You clean up the stage area. There's another thing, at our show anyways. The minute that last band left, they went out and cleaned the stage area up. I don't want them people to wake up in the morning and see all that crap out there. They get to thinking, "Hey, boy, this guy, he's a crummy guy. Look at all that crap out there."

Keep the park clean. That means then when she does go tell somebody she'll say, "Boy, this is a clean park. They got some good bands, you have a good time, you feel safe."

And you work with the bands. Help them and they'll help you. Ralph's helped me so many times. Charlie Sizemore. Not so much Jimmy Martin cause I think I only had him two years, '83 and '84. Jimmy's not the type of guy you can sit down and talk a lot of business with to start with. But I need him there to bring people. That's the name of the game. Get the people in the gate.

But like I say I have a job at Ford. This is not my living. I'm doing it because I love the music to start with. But it's not for me. It's for the bands, to make a living, so they can buy groceries for their kids, they got kids. It's for the people that come in here. They want someplace to go, get a clean show, be decent. That's why they come, cause they like to be there. They want to be there with this band and that band.

I called it the RPM Jamboree. Jamboree, not festival. See, I worked for a guy at Cambridge, Ohio, Old National Trail Camp Ground, Ray Farrell. And he always put on his flyers Old National Trail Jamboree. And I asked him, I said, "How's come you put Jamboree?" This is back when I didn't have it all thought out the way I wanted it, see. I said, "Why don't you call it a bluegrass festival?" He said, "You ever look the words up?" No. I never did. So I went home and got the dictionary out. I wanted to find out what the hell this guy's talking about. Did I miss something here? So I looked it up and "jamboree" says in the dictionary "loud music and good times," maybe not exactly them words but that's what it means. So I looked "festival" up. "Festival" is "a celebration of a particular day." I said, "We're not celebrating days." I mean, this is entertainment. Show business. So I started using that word "jamboree." Bluegrass Jamboree. Bluegrass, we know it's that kind of music. Good times. Loud music and good times. So that's basically why I use "jamboree," just from that one little conversation.

The same with "promotion" and "producing." Like a while ago I told Charlie Sizemore, I said, "A producer is the guy that gets all this stuff together." The people that came in here, they put out flyers, that's promoting. The bands get on stage and they say, "Hey, we're going to be at so-and-so next weekend." That's promotion. When we've run an ad in the *Bluegrass Unlimited,* that's advertising promotion. Promoting. Get it out there in front of the people. Promote it. The producer is the guy that gets it all together and tries to make it work. In our case it did work. We didn't make money, but that wasn't my intention, to make money, to start with. Cause I already got a job. I'm not worried about putting beans on the table. I want to see if I can get my ideas across. Produce. Produce and promote.

And years ago the promoters as they called them were not the best-liked people or known as maybe shady characters and so on and so forth and I didn't—this is a classy business. We got brilliant people on this business. You got doctors, probably lawyers, college educated people. They're not a bunch of dummies. They're not a bunch of stupid—hillbillies I guess, that's the only word I can think of right now. They're not. These guys are smart people. Mapmakers. I think Tom Gray is a mapmaker or something. John Starling is a doctor. They're class people, play class music, so why don't we do what we can to make it sound a little classier anyways? Production by so-and-so, or produced by so-and-so. Not promoted by. It just tears it down. So I very seldom ever use "promotion" or "promoter."

Now I know it won't change Ralph's music because you use the word "producer." He's a class guy anyways, so I don't think he needs to do it for class. But like I say my feeling is that as long as we got a little class, we got some class people playing it, we got some class people coming to it, so let's use some little classier words, too.

I want guys, well, like Charlie Sizemore. I use Charlie a lot because I know his situation when he was with Ralph and left. Charlie is one of these class people I'm talking about. And when I found out that he was leaving and he wanted to go back to school and do some picking, try to do both, I told my wife, I says, "Now, there's a guy that'll make it." He has knowledge, training from the master. He's a good guy. He's young. He's doing good. But I think he's going to do better. He's well known. There's the first thing you need to be to start your own band. He's got good clean music, no garbled up garbage. He's working on a sound of his own. He doesn't do the Ralph Stanley sound. He does Ralph Stanley songs, but not necessarily the sound, see. He does them well. But this is the kind of class we need, guys like him.

Don't quit your day job if you're going into the bluegrass producing business, cause you'll starve to death. Basically you hope to break even, or maybe have a couple bucks left over you can throw into next year's show. The idea is you don't want it all coming out of your pocket all the time. So in order to do that you got to get all these people working together and telling them, "Hey, go down to that RPM. That's a good one. That's one of the best." Like

I've heard Ralph say that's one of the best shows he ever played. I appreciate that.

Nineteen eighty-five was our last show. What happened was, I got it pulled out from under me. See, I was in booking Ralph for the following year on a Sunday afternoon. I told the guy that owns the property to come to the camper at six o'clock. I said, "Come on and I'll settle up with you and we'll talk about next year." And nothing was said. So, six o'clock, he comes in and I show him all the ticket numbers to make sure that he knew where I stood, what tickets we sold, what tickets we didn't, got out of sequence or something. They're there. From that number to that number is what we're going to pay you on. I paid him so much a head. And I gave him a slip with the ticket numbers on it ahead of time so that he knew. See? There's no question. That's the way I wanted it to be. It's above the table. So I paid him off and I said, "Now I got Ralph coming back next year and the Boys from Indiana" and he says, "No. No, no." He said, "We ain't having no show next year."

Man. I could've had a heart attack right then and there. This thing, it's not over the hump but it's right there. See, we're getting up around two thousand people coming in there now. And I want to give Ralph a raise now. It's due, he's worked for me four years, and the fifth year—Ralph never asked for no raise but I felt it's about time I tell that man that he's worth more than what I'm paying him. But, no show. He says, "Uh-uh. We ain't having no show." I says, "What do you mean we ain't having no show?" I said, "I got these guys, already talked to them about coming back next year. I've got so-and-so," and I named them off, and I said, Tuesday, we clean up Monday, the park, clean it all up back to where it was originally. Tuesday I'd start calling other people in Nashville and I'd call around different bands that I've heard. I want to talk to them and have them send me a tape or something. I'm—No show. I like to died. And when I walked out of that camper, told my family, you never seen a, it was just like—it hurts me. After all the work you've done. It still gets me. Maybe that's why I don't have another show. But I think, probably the big thing was, I didn't have it in writing where he could say—

I later found out I think what the real reason was. Like I said, from the beginning I kept a record of everything. I wrote everything down. If I loaned you a quarter I wrote it down. Not because I was worried about you paying it back, you must've borrowed it for a reason. You know.

Well, I got called in for an audit. IRS. They wanted to know who paid the bands, how much rent did you pay, something else, I can't remember what it was. Was it the toilets or something? Who paid for the toilets? Or something. So I sat at the table across from that IRS guy and he says, "You got anything on there that ain't supposed to be?" And I said, "I don't think so." He says, "You don't think so?" "No," I said, "no, there's nothing on there that shouldn't be." I got my stack of receipts here. My daughter's an accountant, went to college for it. She's got a ledger, everything down, got my receipts, I got contracts. What the hell am I scared of? I know what I'm doing. I still don't know why he's called me there though, see.

He said, "Did you bring last year's tax returns?" I says, "I wasn't requested to bring them." "Oh. Okay." I could've had them there if I've been requested to bring them. I would've had them there. He thought he was going to stump me or get me nerved up and I'm going to say something that he can nail me for, see. "Who paid the bands?" Bang, bang, bang, bang. "I paid them. I signed the receipts. Here's the contracts." "How much rent did you pay that guy?" "That's it right here." Bam! Laid the receipt right there. On and on. "Where'd you get the money?" I said, "I sold advance tickets, was most of it." "Well, you didn't sell that many." I said, "No." I said, "I sold enough to cover most of the show." I tried not to volunteer anything. I wanted him to ask the questions so I could tell him point-blank. On and on and on.

And he tried his damnedest to find out. He said, "Is this your bank account?" And I said, "No." "Whose bank account is it?" I said, "It's the Bluegrass Jamboree's bank account, special account under my name." I'm dumb and stupid and make mistakes but wouldn't do this thing. You know, this is not my household money we're working with. This is a separate account. He failed to ask me how I got that money in that bank. All he had to do was to say, "How'd you get the money in the bank?" I used some of my personal money and put it in that account. Which there's nothing wrong with that. It's my money. I'm the handler, the guy who, whatever.

Well, this happened, oh, two or three weeks before the show, see. Like I say, 1985 was our last show, and it was the '84 taxes they wanted, see. Eighty-four and '83. So here I get called in couple of weeks before our show, which it turned out to be our last show, for this audit. Not putting two and two together, here *he* had claimed bands on *his* taxes, there was no rent money paid. See, I'm shucking this stuff to this guy, the IRS guy, and he's going to nail *him* now. And I think that's what the whole thing was about. After my audit, he says, "You've got nothing here that I can nail you on." He tried. "I can't nail you on anything."

That's the reason now, the real reason, I think. Now, do I want to do it again? Yes and no. Yes I don't and no I do. If I do I have the family, they've already told me, so I'm not hurting there. I have all this knowledge that we've gained. I've got Ralph and Charlie to help me for sure, plus the other bands that came, Boys from Indiana and so forth, so I'm not worried about that. What I'm worried about is that park again. When I start it up and I get it going, do you throw me out? And pull it out from under me? Do I lose it? Or do we have a permanent thing? That's where the hang-up is. I don't want to come out here and put on a pretty darn decent show and have it pulled out from under me again. No way. No way. I don't want that. It made me look bad. I'm still answering questions about it. And I don't want that to happen no more.

And this guy talked to me a few days ago, about a park. He's supposed to have a fantastic deal, you know. Baloney. I want to check it out. First thing I got to decide, do I want to do it. Here, inside me. Do I want to do it? I don't know. I want to talk to my wife. I want to talk to my family. See what they think. Then I want to go talk to the guy's supposedly got this fantastic park. But I'm thinking about it. I have to. Cause I love this. You know. I mean, it's here, it's in here inside me somewhere. I don't know if it runs through your system, Oh, there's the bluegrass, there it goes, up to your heart, or—I don't know how that works. It's there. I enjoy it, I love it. But the hitch is the park. I don't want to get that thing going two or three or four years and, st, gone. It hurts. It really hurts. I don't want that.

I like to walk into a place and have somebody say, "Oh, hey, there's old Dale. Boy, a nice guy, you know." That's the way I want to be known as. I don't want to be known as that *permoter* that didn't pay his bands and got throwed out of some place because he didn't do right or so on and so forth. When I come in, I want them to say, "Hey, Dale, how're you doing? Here's a beer, have a beer." I don't want to be known as a grouch or the guy that couldn't put on a bluegrass show because he didn't know how. I want to be known as the guy that put the one on at Norwalk RPM and made a success of it.

So there you go from the top to the bottom again. Get all that stuff in order. Organize. And in the end when you get to that last can that wasn't picked up and somebody's stumbled over it, shouldn't have been there to start with if we did our job and picked it up before he got there and stumbled over it—So you eliminate all the griping and groaning, or a lot of it. You can't satisfy everybody. I want to be known as the guy that kept that park clean. Or the crew that kept the park clean. I didn't do it myself. But you work at it and you work hard. And the people don't know that. That we spent all night cleaning up that stage area and emptying them garbage cans before they got up. They don't know that. We were real quiet, going around and picking stuff up. They come out in the morning and it was like nothing went on here. I want it to be that way. My sister, little things, going around and checking the toilet paper in the crappers. That's not a very pleasant job. But there's people that complimented us about that. That's what I wanted them to do. I want to know that they're happy.

Little things. We got all the big stuff. The bands and all that other crap. No, it's the little stuff that really helped us a lot. "Can I park over by so-and-so?" Go ahead. If there's a place there park there. I don't care. You're happy there, go there. I don't want to have to say, "You be there, you be there." They don't want that. They come in, "I want to go back under that little sprout of a tree that was there last year." Go. I don't care, if there's nobody else there. Make it as convenient as you can. That's the people that promote it for you.

Like I say, I love it, and the basic reason was, that I had some ideas and I wanted to see if they'd work. I think they did work. With help, you know. It wasn't all me. But get that banjo ringing for me. Let me hear that fiddle whining. Oh, ooo, I want it. I love it. Nice people. It's all, it's all fun.

It ain't me. I want you to understand, it ain't I. We had a lot of help doing this thing. And I can't give them enough credit for the almost precision things that they did to help me. My family, and a lot of people. That's what it takes. It's not me or I, it's us, we. And then at the end you stand back and say, We did it. That's the payoff.

19

Frank Neat

"If I was buying a banjo that's the one I'd buy"

The buying and selling of musical instruments in the bluegrass world is often, to be honest, handled in such a way as to give horse trading a good name. Every musician knows stories of people who have made it their life's work to "discover" and buy instruments from ignorant owners at far less than their true value, or to sell counterfeit "antique" instruments to gullible enthusiasts at outrageous prices. And the marketing and endorsement of new instruments is likewise often a very questionable business.

It therefore comes as more than a breath of fresh air—it is almost a shock to find that the Stanleytone banjo (the name is a play on Gibson's "Mastertone" marque) is a genuine value for the money, as good a banjo as one can find on the market today. Since Ralph Stanley plays each Stanleytone on the road until he sells it, it is a uniquely special souvenir. But it is also a superbly crafted, custom-made professional instrument. Some endorsers wouldn't dream of doing anything more with the instruments they lend their names to than being photographed with them. Ralph Stanley not only uses the Stanleytone on stage but has even played it in recording sessions.

In the typically personal, hand-to-hand way that Stanley does business, prospects try out the Stanleytone while sitting on the steps of the Clinch Mountain Boys' bus, and buyers take the banjo directly from Ralph Stanley's hands. There is no need for certificates of authenticity or signed labels, though Stanley would no doubt be happy to autograph the banjo for any buyer who might wish it. The Stanleytone is guaranteed for life by word of mouth, and so far there have been very few complaints indeed.

The man responsible for this praiseworthy state of affairs (besides Stanley himself) is Frank Neat of Dunnville, Kentucky. Neat got into the business of making Stanleytones almost by accident, after making a banjo for Stanley when his old Gibson was stolen (temporarily) some years ago.

Though Neat spends most of his days working in a modest shop behind his house on a country road three miles out of Dunnville, he can often be seen at festivals in the Kentucky area, wearing a black satin jacket with "F. Neat Banjo Repair" sewn on the back. He is soft-spoken, courteous, and astonishingly young-looking for a man who has five grown children. He has the calm, confident appearance of the true craftsman, one who is in the enviable position of doing exactly what he wants and knowing that he is one of the best in the world at doing what he does.

Frank Neat doesn't advertise; he doesn't need to. One of his most spectacular creations, a one-of-a-kind banjo he built (with funds provided by a group of fans) to mark Ralph Stanley's fortieth anniversary as a professional musician, appeared on the front cover of *Bluegrass Unlimited* in February, 1987. News of his work for Stanley has spread by word of mouth, and he now has all the business he can handle, including maintenance and customizing work for some of the most particular and demanding professionals in the field. Even nonmusicians will understand the reasons for his impeccable reputation as they listen to him talk shop in the following pages.

I was raised in Kentucky. I left there when I was about nineteen, I guess, and moved to Indiana. I lived south of Indianapolis about eighteen year and then I moved back to Kentucky. But originally I'm from Kentucky.

I started trying to pick banjo when I was about thirteen and never did do a whole lot with it. But when I moved to Indiana I got with some groups up there and we played staff band at Bean Blossom in the sixties for three year. We was playing staff band when Ralph and Carter did their last show there. That one particular Sunday we was booked someplace else, but we played just about every Sunday there for three years.

Then I got acquainted with Jim Faulkner, that lived in Indianapolis. At that time he was building necks and replacing the tenor necks out of some of these old Mastertones. Well, I bought a RB-800 Gibson and he took it and done some work on it and whenever I got it back course the first thing I had to do was tear it apart and see what he had done. So I started going up to his place and I'd help him out. I went with him to Scruggs's house one time and got to spend the afternoon with Earl—he knowed Earl, you know—and then we went down to Lexington where J. D. was playing in the Holiday Inn and spent some time down there together. And he's really the one that got me started.

I started doing the same thing he was doing, replacing the tenor necks in the old Mastertones. And then it got to where the Master-tone Gibsons was getting scarce and they was so many people building necks so I started building a few banjos along, you know, nothing much. I'd mostly get parts from Stewart MacDonald or wherever I could get them and assemble them.

And then when Ralph was over at Bean Blossom he got his old Granada stole over there, see. I don't know much about that, except someone brought it back in and told him that they picked a guy up walking down the road with it and bought it for fifty dollars. Ralph told me he just paid them the fifty dollars and was tickled to death to get it back.

But at that time I asked him about building him a banjo because I knowed that he played raised heads and all that. So he said, "Well, I don't know why you haven't already built it." That's the answer he gave me.

So I built one up and put his name up the fingerboard on it and the only thing he told me, he said, "Just make it a small neck and make it just as bright as you can." So I made it a raised head and put his name on it and he took it and played it maybe six months or something like that, off and on. He never did play it a lot because it had his name on the fingerboard and it will mess you up, you know, on the positions if you don't get used to it. Yeah, in fact I think he sold it.

But anyway he called me one day and asked me if I'd be interested in building some banjos and he said he'd sell them. He said we'd call them a Stanleytone and he left everything else up to me. You know, how they was built. So we started out just building the chrome first and then he thought we ought to get into building a gold one, too, one that would be a little more expensive, so we started building them.

I was working there in Indiana second shift in a factory and I thought, well, if I move back to Kentucky I can live cheaper, you know. Want to do this full-time. And that's what I done. I'd have been just as well off to stay in Indiana, though. Yeah, as far as living any cheaper, I couldn't, but anyway if Ralph hadn't been selling banjos for me I wouldn't have never quit my job. I'd worked at a factory there eighteen year. Working for Arvin Industry. We was building mufflers and tail pipes. And I had in enough time so that I could phase my retirement.

And I've been doing this full-time since '80. I've bought some land there in Kentucky and went down in '79 and built a house and built a shop, you know. I went back and worked until March of '80, I guess it was, and quit and come down.

I've just a simple setup. I've got a band saw, drill press, and turning lathes and I've got my own fretsaw. Now I do have a little different scale than Gibson's got, for the frets. The one I've got I like better. Seem like it notes out a little truer. And I've got my own fretsaw set up for that. And then, you know, just simple tools, sander and stuff like that is what I've got. My own pearl. You know, I never could cut it the way they recommend cutting it. I have to cut mine different. I put mine in a vise and cut it.

They's sometimes people will come in. Course I'm out in the country. Dunnville is about three mile and eight-tenth but it's only a small town. A bank and two or three grocery stores, a post office. But I'm fifteen mile from Russell Springs, and then Liberty and Columbia's pretty close. But normally when anybody comes they want to buy something. I don't have many people just coming in to look and see what I'm doing. J. D., he comes down and spends the day with me once in a while, cause we're working on this Gold Star thing with him right now. I'm building him a neck for it. I guess he likes the shape necks I build, you know, the way I build them.

Well, like I say, Ralph, he come up with—he said we'd build the banjos and put "Stanleytone" on them and then he left it up to me, you know, to put my name on it. And we built up some. Then he decided to put his name up on the peghead too. He was down at the house one day and he told me he believed they'd sell better, to put his name up there. So we started putting "Ralph" up there and put—I've wished that I just put my last name on there, just "Neat," you know, instead of putting the "F" on there and then Neat. Little bit late now.

With the Stanleytones, what I try to do is get a good fit on all the hardware. It's basically the neck. I like to get a real good fit on fitting the neck to the body. And if I have to I'll take it out and recut it two or three times to get it right. I like for the right angle to be on the neck where I don't have to pull the body very much one way or another. Although you know if you'll pull it just a little bit it'll stay in tune better because it don't have as much give to it.

But I don't like to pull it much. Just, you know, to get the right action on the strings. But mainly what I try to do is just get a good fit on all the parts.

For the rims I use three-ply hard rock maple. Jimmy Cox in Maine makes those. And the resonator, he makes those. The flanges come from Stewart MacDonald, cause they make a good bronze flange. And the tension hoops comes either from Stewart MacDonald or from Maine, Jimmy Cox. They're both made about the same. And then I get the tone rings from Woodhaven Industry in Oregon, Illinois. He'll make tone rings for a lot of different people. He makes them for First Quality.

The keys are Schaller. I get them out of Germany. I've used Stewart MacDonald keys on some of them, too. Either Stewart Mac-Donald or the Schaller. Schaller, they've got the gold-plated but a lot of times you get them and they've got great big screws you know, tension screws? They have those great big screws and I don't like that much. I don't think they look that well.

A good case—I can find the cases, you know, but really good cases, they are hard to come by. The best ones I've found come from Saga Instrument Company out there in California. I think I get the same case that they put the J. D. Crowe Gold Star in. The best case they build, you know, is what I'm getting. I've only been using these probably about the last year and a half, something like that. And they's a case company at Elkhart, Indiana, that you can get cases out of. I've got cases through First Quality Banjo and if I get in a pinch for a case I can call him one day and I'll have it the next.

Right now I'm using the Vega strings. I have used Stew Mac strings on them and I have used that string Ralph endorses too. They're all—well, one will argue one way and one some other you know but—anyway, right now I put Vega strings on them.

I normally will thin the bridges down on them before I send them to him. Because the bridge is just a five-eighths maple and ebony bridge and I get them from Germany. And I'll normally sand them down, thin the top of them before I put them on there.

How are they selling? On the gold we've got I believe sixteen more of it and on the chrome I'd have to look in my books to see. I'm not sure. But I believe it's up around thirty-three of those I've built. We've sold more gold than we have chrome, just a few, because the last couple of years seem like he's been pushing the gold a little bit more and I haven't been making as many chrome. For a long time I was here up around seventeen or eighteen on chrome and just one or two on gold.

But I'd a lot rather build the chrome ones than I would the gold anyway. The gold ones are nice, you know, they're pretty to look at and all that but boy, they've got a lot of trim, just nothing but trim on them. They're basically made out of the same thing.

It will vary sometimes, how they sell. Like this past winter Ralph hadn't sold anything. He sold a couple back last fall when he was out in California and then he hadn't sold anything till just here lately. They was one winter that he sold two a month. In I believe '83 and '84, either that or '84 and '85, one. Anyway, he started in December and he sold two in December and two in January and two in February and two in March. It kept me hopping just to keep them made.

But with Ralph you never know when he's going to sell one. He might have three and you won't know that he's sold anything until he's completely out. And so I try to keep him one all the time if I can but then they's times when he'll get without, too. Cause like I say he might have three and if he sells them all out and then don't tell you, why then he comes up here all at once and telling you he's out of banjos and you don't have one built and so—He'll sell them, though. If he's only got one he'll sell it, someone wants to buy one.

Once in a while I'll ship them to Ralph. But normally, he goes through Lexington on his way if he's going west. I'll meet him there in Lexington and take him up a couple, cause I live only about seventy-five miles south of Lexington. Then sometimes if I've got one ready and he's going to be at a festival and I'm going, well then I'll take it there. But if he gets out, you know, where I have to meet him somewheres, why we meet in Lexington. Normally there at Holiday Inn right beside Route 75. It's handy for him and it's handy for me too.

But I have shipped them to him, you know. He told me last night that this one he got, I guess it was last week, was the only one he ever got that wasn't in tune when he got it. I lowered the strings down on it before I sent it. I normally just tune it up and send them out. He says most of them is in tune when he gets them.

You know, the biggest part of banjo pickers likes flathead, but as far as the raised head I think the Stanleytone's about as good a raised head as you can find. I built it basically like Gibson built them in the thirties. That's what I tried to do. Of course I put a smaller neck on them than Gibson cause Ralph, he insisted on a small neck.

But Ralph, he seems to like the Stanleytones awful well. He keeps telling me he wants one of each for himself, you know, one of chrome and one gold. You know, there'll be some of them that he likes better than he does others. They's no two banjos exactly the same, you know. They don't sound the same. But then as I build them I find some that I like better than I do others, too. And the ones I like Ralph don't necessarily like better. So I guess it's your own personal taste.

But I feel like that they're as good a banjo really as you can buy on the market today. Not because I build them and not because Ralph sells them, but if I was buying a banjo that's the one I'd buy. I work on Gibsons and I work on Gold Stars and all that and I know basically how they're all built and I know that they's none of them that they take a whole lot of pride in the way they fit them together.

The banjos I build for Ralph are really just a small part of what I do now. I build quite a few flathead banjos, too. I do finish work for First Quality Banjo, check his necks and do finishing work for him. I do finishing work for Doug Hutchins down here and then I do finishing work for Jimmy Cox up in Maine. A lot of times I work twelve hours a day. Keeps me pretty busy.

I work for Sonny Osborne. I do all the work on Sonny's Granada, refrets and—which that's a big compliment for Sonny to just leave the banjo with you, as much as he thinks of it. I do J. D. Crowe's work now. And then of course I do all of Ralph's and Tom McKinney's, I do all of his work. Rual Yarborough, used to pick banjo with Bill back a few years ago, I do work for him. I do work for a lot of good banjo pickers but that's the only ones I can name that plays professional. They found out about me through Ralph, mostly. Course as Ralph would advertise the Stanleytones he'd tell who'd built them. That's helped me a whole lot.

But I love to build necks. I'd like to get to where that's all I had to do, is just to build necks, you know, so I could get enough of that to work. That and build the rest of these Stanleytones. I like to build banjos but that don't thrill me the way building necks does.

I make all that wood, you know, cut it all down and everything. I've got a planer that will do that. To start with I had to buy all that, you know. I bought it in the walnut and the maple, already cut down to eighth of an inch. But it's pretty expensive that way so I said, Well, I'll take care of this. So I got me a planer and I do all that, cut all that down.

The ebony wood I use for fret boards, I get most of that from Martin Guitar Company. The maple I get right down there close to where I live. Everybody down there looks for good nice maple and walnut for me. And course when I lived there in Indiana they's three walnut veneer mills right there in town where I lived and I got a lot of walnut there. I've got walnut to last from now on, I guess. But the maple, I'll pick that up round down there where I live.

I normally will cut it and let it air dry four or five years, something like that. I'll cut it down and get it sawed into four-by-fours and then let it dry maybe a couple of years and then saw it into neck blanks and let it lay for—I've got some there, the dates on them whenever I've cut them up and I like to let them lay about two year.

And then course after that I cut them in two and laminate them. So in all of them that I've built I've not had to—yeah, I did rebuild one neck for a guy one time, but that was just, you know, in his own mind. I fixed the neck. It was bowed a little bit and I fixed it. But he still wasn't satisfied so I just built him a neck for that.

And they been three of them that they've broke. Two of them I fixed back and the last one belonged to a guy in Canada that Ralph had sold a banjo to and his insurance covered that and he wanted a new neck built for it, so I built him up a new neck. But the three that's been broke, they've let them fall out of music stands, you know, hit it just right and they break up at the peghead.

But they're strong. The lamination, see, makes them stronger. And then of course I put a three-sixteenths adjustment rod, truss rod in through them too. But I guess I've been lucky, I haven't had any of them to twist or anything where I couldn't straighten them. And I haven't had to work on but very few of them.

On the necks that I build, whenever I cut them out into blanks, I'll take a four-by-four and I'll cut four necks out of it. And sometimes they'll be one that'll twist and if it does I don't do anything with it, just use it for scrap. The ones that stays straight is the ones that I use. And then I'll saw them down the middle and take this side and put it over on that side, kind of back to back. You know, maple, it wants to twist a lot of times. Instead of just crooking one way or another it'll twist. But if you do that, well then, one piece, if it tries to twist, will pull it one way and the other piece will pull it the other way. So it seems to work out pretty good.

And then whenever I laminate the necks I'll take the first piece of wood and glue it and let it sit there and dry. And I'm a nut about using a lot of C-clamps. Whenever I clamp one I normally have got like twenty clamps on one side of the neck, you know. And then I'll put the other piece on the other side and let it set and dry. I take about two days to laminate one neck, you know, to get it glued up together. Then I let it lay and dry maybe for a couple of weeks before I do anything with it.

I use Elmer's carpenter's glue to laminate them with. And then on the fret board I use just a regular white glue, just Elmer's white glue. It holds good, and if you ever want to take the fret board off then you can get it off, and seems like it works awful well. A lot of guys, they like to order glue from other places and all that but I've tried different glues and I've actually glued wood together and tried to pull it apart and I've found the carpenter's glue holds about as good as anything you can get. And then it's handy. You can pick it up in any grocery store.

For the finish I use a Sherwin-Williams lacquer, gloss lacquer. I use a sealer, Sherwin-Williams sanding sealer, and I'll normally spray about six coats of that on it. And then I put around eight coats of lacquer over that. I'll spray it in sealer and let it dry overnight and sand it and then I'll put around four coats of lacquer on it and let that dry the next day and then sand it and then put about four more, and then I have had to put two more on that you know. Depending on how it—well, really it depends on the weather. A lot of it does. But I've used lacquer from everywheres just about, and that's about as good as I've ever found.

Now this special banjo for Ralph's fortieth year, I'm building it gold. The neck'll be laminated. It's in five pieces, because he wants it small and that's the only way that you can get the neck to hold. You know, the last time he talked to me on the phone he said—well, the way he brought it around, he said, "I don't want to get personal, but this banjo that you're building me, I want you to make sure it's got a small neck in it." And the last gold one I sent him, seem like it had a little smaller neck than normal and he told me last night, he said, "That's the shape. That's the way I want the neck." I turn the necks out by hand, you know, and it's almost impossible to get them all the same size. I'll measure them and saw them out and then—you know, they'll vary a little bit in sizes.

And I've got some walnut there that's just like a fiddleback maple except it's walnut and it's got the stripes. And I'm a-building the neck out of that. I've got a resonator that's the same stuff, you know, that's fiddleback walnut.

And I'm going to put the abalone trim around it plus the white binding. And it'll have about the same engraving that the gold ones has got, except this one's going to have a two-piece flange instead of a one. It'll be more like his old one. And then the tailpiece'll probably be a Kirshner because I wanted "1946-1986" put on that, engraved on the tailpiece. On the armrest I wanted "40 years of bluegrass music" engraved on the armrest. And then up on the peghead it'll have "1946-1986." And on the inside of the rim I'll take stencils and write out what it is in there, you know, who it was made for and who it was made by, you know, made for Ralph from his fans and friends. Ralph sort of wanted that on the resonator, but that's so much inlaying on the resonator till you'd never get all that done. And it'd be too much pearl, you know, it'd look like it was all pearl if you done all that.

And I'm going to just finish it out natural, walnut color's the way it'll be. I think he'll like it all right. The only thing that's got me worried is the vine inlay going up the fingerboard. He'll be able to play it but Ralph looks at the positions instead of the position dots you know and—although he can play it if he'll take a little time and look at it and see how it's laid out.

You know, I'm not doing the inlay on this one. I'm getting another guy to do it, because I've seen this inlay that he's done before. It's got a flower vase down about where the Stanleytone box is. It's a vase, you know, and the flower comes out, the vine's a-coming up. It's got some leaves on it and then at each position they's a rose made out of abalone. It's laid out in the positions so you can go by the abalone and play it.

Up on the peghead, it's got a rose up there out of abalone and it's got this bird, like a hummingbird with its bill running down that abalone—you have to look at it, you know, to really appreciate what this guy can do, inlaying it. He lives in Leitchfield, Kentucky. Bryan England's his name. But I've got the neck ready to send to him right now. It normally takes him a couple of weeks to do that. And then I'm putting the fiddle-shaped peghead on it. I know Ralph likes that. I can have it ready in a month from now if I need to. I haven't been pushing it. I've been taking my time on it.

Ron Chacey's doing the engraving on the hardware. He does the engraving on these others, so he's doing the engraving on it, you know. It should come out sounding just about like the Stanleytone sounds. I think Ralph will like it.

20

Richard Underwood

"Ralph's got a certain timing that just sends me"

The world is becoming more urbanized every day. This observation is of course a cliché, and it is equally commonplace for lovers of traditional culture to lament the trend. It should not be forgotten, however, that most people move to the city because they want to, because they find opportunities for development and enrichment there that they could never find in the places they come from. The Germans had a word for it: "Stadtluft macht frei"—city air makes you free. And it would be ridiculous as well as immoral for a traditionalist, especially an outsider, to insist that people remain in poverty and isolation in order to provide him with occasional entertainment.

But still, the question gnaws at us: can traditional culture survive modern urbanization? Specifically, can someone who is born and raised in a city (or a suburb, which amounts to the same thing) successfully and convincingly perform and contribute to the old-time music?

Many artists and fans of bluegrass and traditional country music would argue that the answer is no. Hank Williams put it powerfully if bluntly: "You have to step in a lot of mule shit before you can sing country music."

But if this study has one thesis to make, it is that old-time music is an art. However unconsciously, its successful practitioners have made themselves what they are through study, hard work, and individual choice. They were not born great. It stands to reason that even a city dweller, given an unusually high degree of imagination, goodwill, talent, and energy, could learn the art of old-time music and put it across convincingly to its original audience.

The strongest argument for this notion is the history of a bluegrass band called the Johnson Mountain Boys. What made audiences and critics so delighted with this group in the first place was the fact that they were young and yet strictly traditional, at a time when young bluegrass performers, whatever their origins, seemed intent on taking the music away from tradition. But what makes them even more interesting in retrospect is the fact that though they are essentially suburbanites from the Maryland/D.C. area they somehow seem to have managed to approach the music from the inside. Excellent urban revivalists have existed before: the New Lost City Ramblers (who were close enough to tradition to have shared a stage with the Stanley Brothers without blushing during their European tour of 1966) come to mind. The Ramblers could produce a sound that was virtually indistinguishable from the pre-war string band recordings they used as their source. But they were essentially preservationists, museum curators of a sort. It was clear to their audiences (or to this member of their audiences at any rate) that they were operating from outside the tradition, and it could be argued that this was why they were so highly successful at communicating with their urban college audiences.

The Johnson Mountain Boys, on the other hand, operated from inside the tradition. They worked the standard circuit: the muddy (or dusty) made-over farm lots that house the festivals held every year around the area marked by U.S. 23. They were accepted by the standard audiences: they had to be, or they would not have found work along this circuit. Though musically conservative, they were highly creative; they did not sound like Flatt and Scruggs or the Stanley Brothers but like the Johnson Mountain Boys. They were (until their recent disbandment) active, successful, money-earning proof that old-time music, as an art, is strong enough to survive the onslaught of urbanization.

Richard Underwood played banjo and sang for several years for the Johnson Mountain Boys. He did not learn music from his parents. He first heard the banjo on a television program, and he learned to play from a city-based teacher, through formal lessons which featured written tablature. But his banjo playing and his singing have an undeniably authentic sound. His story bodes well for the future of traditional art in general, and of Ralph Stanley's art in particular.

I was born in Washington, D.C., on July 14, 1956. Just a pretty typical suburban family. It wasn't a country thing or anything like that. There wasn't a whole lot of music around the house. My father had always liked country music, including bluegrass, but he never went out to the shows, and didn't have a record collection or anything like that to speak of.

I guess I heard the banjo quite a few times, growing up as a kid, because I know I remember my father watching the Porter Wagoner show with Buck Trent just about every week. But I had absolutely no interest. To me it was only something to make fun of, to be honest. I guess it was something that kids weren't supposed to be into. It was all right for your parents to be into, but you weren't really supposed to be into it.

I kept that attitude pretty much up until the time I was, say, fourteen or fifteen, and all of a sudden I saw the Earl Scruggs Revue on public TV. And maybe I was ready for them at the time, because Earl had the sons with him with the long hair and electric bass and electric guitar and drums, but when I started watching the show it was interesting because it wasn't the drums or the electric guitar or the electric bass, which was what I was used to from listening to hard rock, but it was the sound of that banjo and Josh's dobro and Vassar's fiddle that captivated me. And for the first time in my life I think I wanted to learn to play an instrument. And I knew it was going to be something acoustic like a dobro or a banjo.

My parents helped me find a banjo teacher, who was kind of an unusual fellow in that he was a young black guy who lived in the city and who was a real bluegrass nut. He was kind of a Flatt and Scruggs man, which was real good, and he was a real good teacher, had a lot of patience, and got me started learning almost all Scruggs stuff. The first year I learned almost all Earl's stuff. This guy's name was Earl Williams. He was basically into three players: he was into Scruggs, Crowe, and Ralph. And that was banjo playing to him. So the first year was a real Scruggsy year.

We had tabs. We didn't use tabs the way we do them now. He had kind of a personalized style of just writing the string with the fret above it. Kind of a simplified tab. But a written tab, yeah, because, you know, we're talking about starting just a stone beginner at this point, so I needed something. I know a lot of people look down on tab, and I don't think that tab is a real good way to learn for people that are fairly advanced and can probably get real close to a record or something without it. Because it is a laborious and slow way. But for a stone beginner, I think it's going to be real hard for a lot of people to stick with it and get anywhere with the banjo if they don't rely on some kind of written system. Everybody doesn't need it, but I think for a lot of people that are starting out it's a pretty useful tool these days.

Now the Johnson Mountain Boys were together before I got into it. There was a band, not as we know it, but there had been a band, Dudley Connell being the only original member at this point, but with various people. It was pretty much just another little local Washington band. And I had worked with just about all of the members, I guess. I worked with Buzz Busby from time to time, when Buzz would get a job and needed a band. And Dudley worked with us, I remember, and Dave McLaughlin did, back when he was playing. Dave had played fiddle with the band originally, and left, and Gary Reid, who works for County Records, played bass with us. So we all met basically through that pretty much, I think.

Now I had played with some other bands besides Buzz, two or three other bands where it was for money but certainly not full-time. It was a barroom kind of thing on the weekends. It was nothing real serious. I wanted to do more with music at the time but didn't really think I ever would be able to for a lot of reasons. But in '79, they asked me if I wanted to play with them full-time. I had to think about it. It wasn't a full-time proposition; it was just to play in a weekend band at that point, a hundred and fifty dollars a night or something for the band.

And so I thought about it a little while and I decided to, because I really wanted to play and they were playing the kind of bluegrass that I really liked. I guess Eddie Stubbs had just started with the band right before I did, and a month later Larry Robbins came, to play bass with us. And then about two years later Dave came back to play mandolin. As for our style, and this business of being a reincarnation of the early fifties, I really think we never even thought about that in the early days. There was a lot of things we were doing that we really never thought about. We just thought, well, this is the way you do it.

When other people started picking up on it and it started appearing in print and things like that a few times, then we probably became aware of some of the things that people were thinking and they were saying. But there wasn't really ever any kind of philosophy of any kind. Because, thinking back about '79 and '80, we didn't really even intend to be a full-time band. I myself would never have believed, if someone had told me in, say, the summer of '79, when the band formed pretty much as we know it now, that we'd ever be able to go full-time and make a living, because I didn't think that there was that much interest in traditional bluegrass. Not the kind of stuff we were doing. But about that time period, I think the pendulum was swinging back.

As for how we feel now, I guess it's a complex thing. Certainly there's a debt, we feel a debt toward the pioneers in traditional bluegrass. But we also very much want to be our own thing. And I think it's helped us a whole lot to feel that way. It helped us to write a good bit more of our own material and to look for real obscure material instead of doing the greatest hits of Flatt and Scruggs and the Stanleys and Monroe. Of course those are good songs but it's hard to improve on a lot of them, because they were done quite well, and it probably wouldn't ever get us anywhere, doing a whole lot of it. But I think we probably have our own sound right now more than we ever have and I think that'll continue.

Now with the banjo, somewhere along the line, '79, '80, something like that, I started playing more like Ralph in the sense—I've never sat down with the records to speak of and tried to learn anything note for note. It's frustrating, and there's really no point to it, other than if there's a particular song and you just want to learn that. Some people really love to learn. I like to take short cuts to learning, so if I can get real close and it sounds almost identical then that's good enough for me.

But I started using the index finger to lead with, instead of the thumb like Scruggs would do. Did I know what I was doing? Well, I knew it sounded different. I knew that the accenting and the timing sounded a bit different and it sounded more like Ralph. And I liked the way he sounded.

I know that Scruggs tells you to use the thumb, and to this day I haven't really rejected it. Some nights I have a hard time because I'm up there and there's certain songs like "Train 45" or, say, "Granite Hill," that Dave wrote, and depending on how I feel I'll play it different. And that's probably not a good way to be, because I'm sure Earl knows how he's going to do it. He's going to lead with the thumb, and Ralph, I'm sure, is going to lead with the index finger, and they probably never go through what I'm going through. But I like both of them so much, you know. I hear a Scruggs record and I love that and I hear the way Ralph does it and I love that. So I like to be able to switch back and forth, and on some songs I'll look for a thumb type effect and on others, I guess I'm looking more for that index feel.

Now the difference between Ralph and Earl, I guess that's a hard thing to say because you have to think of it in the context of the band. Ralph plays the perfect banjo for Stanley music. Earl played the perfect banjo for Flatt and Scruggs music. It's just that feel for what they're doing. They both have the perfect feel and they've both mastered it. I guess it's real hard to explain, other than obviously the index lead that Ralph uses is different than the thumb lead that Earl uses.

They're both fairly melody oriented. As a matter of fact, Ralph is probably more melody oriented on taking his breaks than Earl was, because Earl was almost more cliché Scruggs lick oriented than really following the melody as closely as he could. Which is neither good nor bad, because it sure sounded good the way he did it. But Ralph really seems to hit those melody notes pretty much right down the line on most songs when he takes a break. Bring the index finger all the way up to the fourth string and things like that.

As for the change in Ralph's timing over the years, I can't pinpoint it. I haven't sat down and listened to those records side by side, and that would help maybe to pinpoint it if you really listened carefully. It's a smoother sound rhythmically now. And a lot of this isn't just coming from Ralph. It's coming from the other guys. It's coming from the Clinch Mountain Boys. Obviously Charlie doesn't play the guitar the way Carter did. For one thing, Carter used a thumb pick, and everybody who's come along since with Ralph has used a flat pick. So it's a different guitar style. It has to be. It's a different way of playing it. It has to sound a bit different. Mechanically, it's a different way. I think that has a lot to do with it.

And I think I hear the same kind of thing in Monroe, too. I think these guys have just been around so long, you know, you got to learn something. Ralph's got a certain timing that just sends me. I think it's great. Like the way they'll do "Let Me Walk Lord by Your Side." We did the Early Bird Show at the Opry two or three years ago and I heard them do that. He's just got this rolling beat that's so nice. And a lot of it's coming from the banjo. It's that fast waltz time and they're just so smooth with it. I can't really describe it technically other than that I like it a whole lot.

And I asked Ralph about it, I said, "Is that, is that—" you know, talking about the timing and how it changed, trying to say it in a subtle way, not that your timing's a lot different, or it's improved, or whatever, but, "Was that something you could hear?" you know, for a long time, and he said, "Yeah." And I always wanted to get back to him on that and pick his brain a little bit as to what the mechanics are maybe a bit more.

He certainly is playing a part with the rolls and stuff, that accenting the timing that he's doing with the banjo. But there's four other guys up there that have a big part to do with it, too. He's got two guitars now and when a lot of those records and stuff were cut in the old days it was a mandolin instead of the second guitar. And there was somebody else playing bass that probably had a lot different style than Jack's playing. It's really an interaction of all five instruments so much.

One thing I'm not sure of and I shouldn't even say it, but it might be interesting to check tapes of shows or the records or whatever if you really want to get into that thing. It sounds to me like some of his slower material is a little bit faster than it would have been in the days of the Stanley Brothers. And I've always felt that you can get a bit better timing on that kind of thing. I don't particularly think that real slow, real drug songs lend themselves well to bluegrass instrumentation. They certainly don't for a banjo. And, like the two-finger backup. That stuff is hard as hell to play if a song is really being drug real slow. And I think he's doing some of that stuff just a hair faster. Just enough to make it more comfortable to do some decent banjo backup.

And I think Ralph's as unique on his singing as he is on his playing. It's probably the most unique voice in bluegrass. I'm sure in both cases, playing and singing, it's just the way he feels it. And there'll never be another person who feels either the instrumental or the vocal end of music quite like he does. To say he is very, very unique is definitely a great understatement.

21

Junior Blankenship

"I have no other priorities"

Lead guitarist Hillard Blankenship, Junior, was probably the least overtly colorful of the Clinch Mountain Boys during his decade-long era with the band but at the same time one of the best-liked. Most fans will of course remember him for his tasteful and elegant guitar breaks to Ralph Stanley's songs, his blistering instrumental solos ("Bill Cheatham" more often than any other), and the sweet tenor vocal solos he would take, once per set in the usual Stanley pattern, with such traditional favorites as "Little Cabin Home on the Hill."

But an even more vivid memory, from a fan's point of view, would be of Junior Blankenship standing by a festival campfire late at night, playing his guitar and singing "On the Other Hand" or some other recent country hit. This sort of activity on the part of professionals used to be a standard feature of the early bluegrass festivals; there is a good deal less of it now, but Junior kept the tradition alive. There was no ego involvement here: if he knew a song, he would sing it: he was there to please. And if an amateur musician happened to be hanging around with an instrument, Junior Blankenship, unlike so many other accomplished musicians (amateur or professional), would welcome him into the circle, encourage him to play something, and do his best with his self-effacing backup work to make what was being played sound as good as possible.

And his best was always very good indeed. Quiet, retiring, friendly, and supremely generous, Junior Blankenship was a self-confident professional to his fingertips, an excellent example of why bluegrass lovers believe that "their" kind of music is something different from any other.

To the distress of many fans and against the strong warnings of at least one of his best friends in the music business, Blankenship left the Clinch Mountain Boys in 1989. As yet he has been unable to establish an independent career.

———————

I was born February the eleventh, 1960, at the old Grundy Hospital, Grundy, Virginia. We were living in Virginia then, but my dad was up in Wichita, Kansas, working. He worked there for eight year. He came back home after I was born. We went up to Kansas and stayed for eight year and then came back down to Virginia to live and we've been there ever since.

None of my family never did really pick that much, other than Dad. My daddy's brother doesn't pick anything. My daddy, he played the mandolin a little bit. He played the guitar before he played the mandolin. And that kind of helped me, you know, in a prospective way, to kind of pull me toward music. And he helped me a whole lot. He sure did.

He showed me several chords, you know, the major chords of music. That's all he showed me. He said, "Now son," he said, "this is it. You take this and do what you can with it. This is all I'm going to show you." He didn't want to push it on me. He just wanted, you know, to lay it there and say, "If you want this you can have it. If you don't, you don't have to take it." And I chose it and I thought it was a good choice and I enjoy what I'm doing right now. I thank the Lord for Dad and Mom guiding me along that way.

My dad played with a group called the Rocky Mountain Boys. They've played quite a few festivals. Not really big festivals. Well, Ralph's, they played Ralph's festival. That's about the only really big festival that they ever played. But when I come up through my musical years I started with Dad's group and we played up through till I got about sixteen, seventeen years old.

And Ralph rung up a call one day and said, "How'd you like to work for me?" and I said, "Sure enough." What the heck, you know. I'm going to jump on it. And I jumped on it and I love his music and there just ain't nothing like it you know. It's just down home.

I used to stand there at the top of the hill at Ralph's festival—that's no joke, I did. I used to stand there a many a time and I'd look down there and Dad'd be beside me or something you know, pretty close to him and I used to say, "Dad, one of these days I'm going to be right down there. It'd tickle me to death to get to play with that man." And my dream come true and I just—you know, it shocked me, really it did, when he called me. It really shocked me. But it tickled me to death.

How it happened, my dad, he'd been over at Clintwood one day, Clintwood, Virginia, not far from where I live. And Ralph was at the courthouse one day in Clintwood, and Mason Little, who helps Ralph with the festival, he's really responsible for getting my job. He's the man got me my job, you know. I walked up and I asked Mason several, severals of times, "Mason, what would it take to get a job with Ralph, get to pick with him and sing with him?" He said, "Junior," he said, "just sit back and ride a little. I'll see what I can do."

Well, after Keith quit, Ralph talked to Mason. I reckon somewhere or another it come about. Anyway, Daddy met with Ralph in the courthouse over there one day for some reason. I don't know why. I think Daddy was over there reading deeds or something and Ralph was over there for—I don't know, and they walked up and they spoke to one another and Ralph asked Dad, said, "Hillard," said, "I'd like to get Junior to go to work for me. Would you mind?" You know, which I was working with Daddy. He said, "You can do more for him than I can." So I took off. And I've enjoyed it and I love it.

When I was about fifteen, we played Ervinton High School, right there where Ralph was raised. You know, he went to that school, I think. Well, he did go to the old high school there. Used to be the old high school set just above there, before they put the new one in. But—well, actually him and Carter both did. And we played a little 4-H talent show there one time.

And Ralph happened to be a judge, which I did not know. I did not know who was judge and I didn't even know Ralph at the time. I was just young and I didn't know who Ralph Stanley was at the time, just seeing him sitting in a crowd. I did not know. I knowed his music and I loved it but I didn't know who he was if I stepped over him. And we went up there and we done the show and everything and Ralph was one of the judges and we won first place.

Well, we went from the county into a state competition—me and Keith O'Quinn and his brother Kyle O'Quinn. Kyle played the mandolin, Keith played the banjo, and I played the guitar. And there were just the three of us. We won first place at the county, we won first place in the state, and we went on to—well, not the state, we went to the district, then went to the state. And we won all of them and those awards now are still down in my high school where I graduated. They're still in the showcase.

I enjoy any kind of traditional music, you know. I like people like J. D. Crowe. J. D. does a good job. And the Country Gentlemen, they're a good traditional group. There're just so many good groups it's just hard to pick all of them. It is.

Around home I fish a lot. I love to fish. I love the outdoors. And I fish a lot and pick a pile of ginseng you know down home. Make a little money digging a little root here and there. You know, I like to get away from it for a while. You're traveling on the road so much. I mean sixty-five, seventy percent of your time you're on the road, you know, and the rest, the forty percent you want to be relaxed a little while. You know, it kind of gets to burn on your mind. You're just like family on the road. Somebody'll kind of get a little itch onto you sometimes and you—but you rub that off, you know. It comes off after a while.

But it's just a good life. I love it. I'm home through the week, you know, like Monday, Tuesday, Wednesday, and Thursday. Might leave on a Friday. We start picking on Friday night, Saturday night, Sunday, maybe sometimes Monday. Or sometimes we'll leave on a Thursday night, Wednesday night. Course time I get home I enjoy it. Me and Mom and Dad—I'm the only kid in the family—and so it's pretty nice.

Ralph is a fine person, wonderful person. I really like him and enjoy traveling with him. I mean he just makes you feel at home, you know. There's so much you can say about him. I mean that's so good and you just can't beat a man like that. He's just so good to us and I enjoy working for him. And I hope to work for him for, you know, from now on. I sure do. Another forty years? Well, I'd like to stand there beside him that long. I really would. No doubt about that.

I have nothing else to do. I have no other priorities. So I enjoy just being with anybody that I can. I have no other plans. Not for now. Maybe, possibly, cutting me a album a little later, but you know there's a awful lot to—get things worked out, you know, get started with it. I'm looking forward to doing it. But no other plans. Unless something drastically happened. I may have to go driving a truck tomorrow. You never know.

22

Charlie Sizemore

"You're so terribly indebted to somebody like that"

"I've been questioned and quizzed constantly by people who don't understand why I'm going to school," Charlie Sizemore recently told a friend. "And if I liked to fish, they certainly wouldn't say, 'Well, what's the end—?' You know, or if I liked to hunt or if I liked to mountain-climb or if I liked to bike ride or marathon race, that would bring no question. But I constantly have to justify to people why I go to school. And that amazes me.

"When we would play a college, I remember, when I was working with Ralph, I would get out and walk around on the campus and pretend as if I were in school. I really wanted to go. But inevitably the question is, 'Well, you're going to school. What are you going to be?' And many people simply cannot get away from the idea of seeing school as a means to an end rather than just an end in itself, which I think it certainly is. I'm not preparing for anything. I pretty much expect to be what I am, which is a guitar player, just be a guitar picker."

Charles E. Sizemore, of course, is much more than just a guitar picker. Several times he has been saluted by record reviewers as being one of the best lead singers in bluegrass today. Throughout his nine-year tour of duty with the Clinch Mountain Boys he was unfailingly hard-working, loyal, and supportive above and beyond the call of duty. He has been equally hard-working, and equally well received, since he left Ralph Stanley's band and started his career as an independent musician in 1986.

At the same time he has always in one way or another been a student. He graduated early, and second in his class, from his high school in Salyersville, Kentucky, despite a very full extracurricular work schedule, musical and otherwise. During his ensuing nine years with Ralph Stanley he studied singing, he studied the music business, and, informally and on his own, he studied the history and politics of Kentucky. (The latter activity inevitably brought on a bit of ribbing, since the sight of a sideman reading a hard-cover book in a band bus is not a common one.) After he left the Stanley band in 1986—appropriately enough, the last album on which he appeared with Stanley was the 1986 Winterhawk Scholarship Album—his studies became more formal; he earned the degree of bachelor of arts, majoring in political science, from the University of Kentucky early in 1991, and has recently signed up for a master's program at Middle Tennessee State University. He may well one day match his old mentor's honorary doctor's degree with an earned doctorate of his own.

Impatient with organized religion, Sizemore has a conscience that would be the envy of the most dedicated Christian. It could have cost him—though it did not—his coveted position with Ralph Stanley when (at the age of seventeen) he met Ralph's initial job offer with a refusal to break the unwritten rule that says a sideman owes his employer two weeks' notice before leaving a band. And it made his eventual departure from the Clinch Mountain Boys protracted, awkward, and at times unbearably painful, as his ambition fought with his loyalty and gratitude, and his employer had to contemplate over an extended period the impending departure—or desertion, as it seemed at the time—of a young man who by then had become almost as much an adopted son as a valued sideman.

After a year or so, not surprisingly, the dust cleared, and Sizemore and Stanley were restored to mutual affection and admiration. And when Ralph glanced up at Charlie at a recent reunion show and cheerfully remarked that he seemed to have grown since they'd last shared a stage, the old master was once again demonstrating his instinctive and acute penetration—along with, in this case, an unwonted flair for metaphor.

I was born in Richmond, Kentucky, and moved to Salyersville when I was about a year old. That's where my parents were from. I was born November 23d, 1960. My daddy was in school down at Eastern Kentucky University there in Richmond at the time. He's a high school teacher. He doesn't teach music. He's a history teacher but he's a music lover, you might say. He's a big Stanley Brothers fan. He doesn't much like anything else so when I was growing up that was all that was allowed in the house and that was about all I listened to and I learned to like it.

My grandfather was an old-time drop thumb banjo picker. Of course my daddy is too when he wants to play that way. He picks the guitar a little and plays the banjo quite a bit. He taught me a few chords on the guitar. I got interested in it when I was about twelve, I guess. I started listening to mostly those Stanley Brothers records and tried to figure out just what they were doing.

A fellow named Lum Patton had a band round there where we lived. He liked to play Stanley Brothers music and of course my daddy was the same way. So when I was about thirteen I started working in their band, the Half Mountain Boys. We worked quite a bit. We didn't make much money but it was good experience for me. I was just learning how to play the guitar and that's when I really became seriously involved in it, when I was about that age.

I spent three years in that band. Then I was offered a job in 1976, in the fall I guess of 1976, with the Goins Brothers, playing lead guitar. Though I played the banjo on the first show I did with them. It was a matinee show. I played the banjo and I also played— it was either the Boxing Bear or the Boxing Gorilla, I'm not sure.

You see, school kids probably know and care very little about music, and a Boxing Bear or a Boxing Gorilla or a ghost or something like that will attract kids to a matinee show. And Curley Lambert, who was the mandolin player in the band, had been the Boxing Bear to that point, as I understand it. He boxed Big Wilbur, who was Melvin Goins. They would play a few songs and then have the little Boxing Bear routine. I played a little bit of banjo at the time and Melvin knew that and he called me one day and told me he wanted me to play a school with him. It was in Blaine, Kentucky, and I played the banjo. We played "Old Macdonald Had a Farm" and "Froggy Went A-Courting" and all that stuff and then later on in the show I put on—it was hot in that gym, too—I put on a Boxing Bear costume and proceeded to beat up on Big Wilbur. And that was my introduction into show business.

During my stay with the Goins Brothers, which was a little over a year, I guess, I played lead guitar with them. During that time I became acquainted with Ralph Stanley, who I had met when I was just a child. He knew who I was and was somewhat acquainted with my family. And Ralph as I understand it was needing a lead guitar player, and he'd heard me play and apparently thought I could do the job and I was real excited about the possibility of going to work with Ralph Stanley, playing lead guitar.

He first talked to me about it in October of 1977. He asked me when I got out of school. I said, "I graduate early. I'll get out in December." He said, "Do you have a car?" I said, "Yes, I do." He said,

"Well, I may be needing a guitar player and I may be giving you a call about that time." But things didn't work out exactly that way because Keith Whitley, who was lead singer in the band at that time, left in November and went to work in J. D. Crowe's band. And on November 19th of 1977 we were booked, the Goins Brothers, which I was still a member, was booked to play a double show with Ralph in Greenfield, Indiana.

I knew something was up. I suspected that Ralph was perhaps going to approach me about going to work then, playing lead guitar. Anyway, when I came in Ralph asked me, would I care to sing a song on stage with him. I said, "Well, of course not. Be glad to." He said, "Well, come back here and let me sing a song with you, see what you sound like. Bring your guitar." I said, "Okay."

And he brought Jack Cooke back and we went back in between a little partition that separated the bathrooms from the auditorium. And we stood back there and we sang a couple of songs. I think we sang "I Hear a Choo-Choo Coming" and I noticed he was looking very intently at my rhythm guitar playing and I knew it was getting to be serious at that time. I said to myself, "Something's in the wind; I know it." And we sang another song.

Anyway, he called me up on stage and I sang a song or two with him. "I'll Just Go Away," I believe. And Ralph asked me to go to Myrtle Beach with him that weekend. He asked me that in the bathroom. I was in the bathroom and Ralph walked in and he looked over at me and said, "Do you think you could go to Myrtle Beach with me this weekend?" And bear in mind, I hadn't been offered the job. My assumption was that this would be a trial run for me, that I would go down to Myrtle Beach and after that weekend Ralph would decide whether or not I indeed would have a job.

I couldn't go to Myrtle Beach with him and I told him that, because it's understood, even if it's not written, that when you join a band you must give the band a two weeks' notice when you leave. And it really wasn't a difficult decision for me because I knew that I wouldn't leave Melvin's band without giving Melvin the required notice but it really—I went home that night thinking that perhaps I may have not done the correct thing because Ralph told me he would call me and of course, you understand when somebody says, "I'll call you," that means nine times out of ten that they're not going to call you.

But he did call me. He called me that Monday afternoon. And he hired me even though I couldn't go to Myrtle Beach with him that weekend. And although I had the job as of that Monday I didn't go to work with Ralph until—I think I played one weekend with Melvin because he wasn't working the weekend after that. So I played one more weekend with Melvin and I went to work with Ralph on the twenty-ninth, if I'm not mistaken, and our first show was in Pikeville, Kentucky. It was during the week, and that weekend I went with him to North Carolina and then we went to New York, I guess the following week. So, although I was still in school at the time I went to work full-time with him when I started, which if I'm not mistaken was the twenty-ninth of November.

It was completely different from working with Melvin. It was a lot of pressure. When Ralph hired me I was sixteen years old and I was acutely aware of the position that I was stepping into. I'd followed Ralph's band, I'd listened to his singers, and I think I had a pretty good understanding of Ralph's music. I knew exactly what I expected Ralph's band to sound like and I think I had a pretty good idea of what he would like his band to sound like. And I felt a lot of pressure. I was replacing Keith Whitley, who was an excellent singer and extremely popular among Ralph's fans. And I think it would in many ways have been better for me had I not gotten into that position at the age I was. Because it was tough trying to fill that position when I obviously in my mind wasn't qualified to do it. Eventually, I think, I got to the point where I could do the job and do it I think fairly well. But I know at the time I was hired I always had this feeling that I had no business there, in that job, that somebody else could've done it better at the time. Although I don't know who that person would've been.

But it was a lot of pressure for me in the first years and I worked really hard at trying to be a good singer. And I'd never felt that type of pressure before. I didn't feel it in Melvin's band because I was playing lead guitar and I was completely comfortable with what I was doing and I was completely confident that I was qualified with what I was doing. But in the case with Ralph's band, I was working right at the edge of my confidence, I believe, and although that can be interesting and exciting at times it also can put a lot of pressure on a young man.

I think I learned, in terms of music, working with Ralph, I learned how to sing. I was not a singer when I joined the band. I think I could hopefully call myself a singer when I left the band. It's not that Ralph ever sat down—although he did occasionally, but he's not the type to sit down and say, "I would like for you to sing this way or that way," because it's impossible to teach someone how to sing. Or in my opinion it is. But the fact that I was singing with Ralph during the time I learned how to be a singer had a tremendous influence on me. In terms of my phrasing I still phrase a lot like Ralph. Because it's ingrained in me. I can't get away from that. Even though I think I don't sing now like I did when I was singing with Ralph. But I still find myself phrasing a lot like Ralph.

To me the most important thing about singing is phrasing. Naturally you want to sing on pitch, and I think it helps a singer to have an agreeable voice, something that's pleasant to hear. But other than that the most important thing is learning how to phrase a song. I think that comes by practice, just comes by singing. If you'll listen to the Stanley Brothers' Mercury records, that's what made Carter Stanley such a great singer. It was phrasing. And Ralph too. No matter what the words are in a song, or no matter what speed you sing a song, it never appears to, well, I don't know, it don't strain him to get the words in. It's just easy. The words just flow into a song. If that makes any sense.

The phrasing on some of the songs on the *Snow Covered Mound* album was really strange. Like the "Troublesome Waters." I remember I had a sheet of paper and I invented little symbols to tell me how to phrase, and while we were rehearsing I would go and I would write it down. So that way when we came to sing it I could phrase with Ralph on it.

Anyway, I learned a lot about how to get on stage and face an audience and probably the most important thing as far as singing is concerned—which is basically what I did with Ralph; I played rhythm guitar but my job was to sing and hopefully sing well. But I think what makes Ralph Stanley unique among singers is that he sings a song—and I know this sounds clichéd, but it's the truth— he sings a song like he means it. He convinces you that he means what he sings. And that's a good singer to me. And hopefully when I sing a song I've chosen a song that I can sing and convince the people that I'm not just up there going through the motions and stuff. But more importantly that people will feel when they hear me sing a song that they believe me. And I learned that from Ralph. He would even bring that to my attention sometimes, because Ralph wanted me to really feel a song if I was singing it and I did.

And this brings a lot of things to mind. Of course if you're not a good singer you're not going to convince anybody of anything. But I believe there are a lot of people who are technically good singers that will never get the heart of an audience because they're simply not believable singers. There're lots of people that I'm sure are good singers that I wouldn't walk across the road to listen to. I'm sort of like Chester Marshall, I'd rather hear Ralph Stanley clear his throat and tune his banjo than, you know, two-thirds of what's going on in music. I'd rather hear somebody who actually is a convincing singer even if he is a little off-key. Which I am occasionally.

But while I'm going on here, the most important thing I learned from Ralph, and I have trouble convincing people of this some-times, the most important thing I got from Ralph is not that people learned who I am, even though that was important. It's not nearly as important as a lot of people think it is that people know who you are, that they recognize you as Ralph Stanley's lead singer. That's a blessing but believe you me, it can be a curse at times, too, because they've seen you in that role and they expect you in that role and it's difficult for them to accept you outside that role. So therefore that has a down side to it as well.

But the most important thing that I learned from Ralph, or the most important thing I got from Ralph, is some kind of a resolve, a determination, because I've seen it in Ralph so much, that when everything's piled up against you, in the face of all kinds of adver-sity, to just go forward. And I think about this occasionally in my band. Because I've had quite a few ups and downs since I've left Ralph's band, and I'm frequently asking myself, "Well now, how would Ralph handle this?" And the thing that immediately comes to mind is, Ralph would simply do what is necessary and then go forward. As I've seen him do time after time after time.

Even when I break down on the road, as I have in my old, worn-out van, I find myself thinking, "Well, in this instance, what would Ralph do?" And knowing that Ralph's been through what I'm going through right now in trying to keep a band or trying to book a band and trying to make a living playing music—what I've done simply pales in comparison to what Ralph has been through. And I think if I have got a third of the resolve and the determination that Ralph has I'll be successful in this music, because when it's all said and done that's what separates the people who are successful from the people who aren't successful. Believe me, talent is not unique. There's tons of talent. But it is those that go forward even when the circumstances aren't the most pleasant that eventually are able to succeed in this music.

I can think of a ton of things that Ralph has been through. Of course, being broken down on the road is one thing. One thing I never saw Ralph faced with was band changes, when I was in the band. And I've had band changes in my band and I never saw it in Ralph's. But I saw how he handled it when Keith Whitley left the band. It was, at the point at which Keith left, that was history, and then it was time to go forward and, you know, bring Charlie on board, let's go from here. I remember that.

I remember Ralph sitting up all night one night. We were playing in Scioto Furnace, Ohio, and we had to be in Louisiana the next day. Jack Cooke, who did a lot of the driving when I first started in the band, since I wasn't allowed to drive, I was too young, Jack wasn't there and Ralph had to do most of the driving that night. And the lights went out and I saw him drive all night with the parking lights to get to the show. And he didn't seem to be too upset about it. He determined that how he could get to the show was drive with the parking lights on all night. And he did that. He drove fifteen miles an hour all night long. And daylight came eventually and we were able to make it to the show.

Another time, in the motor home, we broke down when we were on our way from Coushetta, Louisiana, to Elizabethton, Tennessee. And he sent me and Curly Ray—I guess we were his trusted lieutenants at the time; I hadn't been in the band long, but he sort of vested a little bit of confidence in me at the time—he sent me and Ray and we flagged down a truck and went to a truck stop and got a wrecker and was coming back and we were sitting up there. That's the first time I've ever ridden in an eighteen-wheeler. It's an experience, sitting way up there. And we looked and there was Ralph a-coming and they had the—I think they still had the lid up on the motor home and he was going about fifteen miles an hour and it was hitting on about three cylinders and Ralph was driving and he said, "Boys, we don't need that wrecker," and he paid the wrecker seventy dollars and up the road he went and the fire a-flying and Ralph a-driving, that determined look on his face. Just a-going right on. Ralph exemplifies that more than anybody I've ever met. It's just unreal what a single-minded determination he has. If he can't get Carnegie Hall he'll book the damn Texaco station. That's rare.

And I never heard Ralph complain. It is difficult, but I never heard Ralph complain about it. He's gone on stage sick before. He's gone on stage when he shouldn't have been on stage. And I have very little patience with people that say this is a terrible business, and what an awful thing has been thrust upon me to have to make a living playing bluegrass music. My suggestion to those people who want to grunt and gripe and complain about it is they're not under a court order to do it and they certainly don't have to. I wouldn't do it if I didn't like it. And I would suggest to anybody that feels otherwise just to get out of it. But I never heard Ralph complain about anything. And Ralph didn't have any patience with people who did complain. And I seem to have acquired that trait.

I met my wife Robin—I don't remember when I first met her. According to her, she got my autograph when I was playing with the Goins Brothers at Scioto Furnace, Ohio. And that would've been in May of 1977. I met her around bluegrass festivals and we stayed in touch off and on and all this and, ah, you know how the story goes, eventually got serious and got married in, in—December. When did I get married? I got married in—what year was it? Eighty-six? No, hell, no, it was away back, wasn't it? I got married in—I was twenty-three, I just turned twenty-three. I was born in 'sixty. I got married in 1983. I've been married almost six years. Gosh. Yeah, it's 'eighty-three. I got married on December 17th, 1983. Sure enough.

Before we were married Ralph and Melvin Goins—I was playing with Ralph at the time of course—concocted the idea, knowing that I'm a fairly serious person and have not a great deal of tolerance for foolishness, came up with the idea of bringing Robin out on stage and having her serenade me. And they certainly did and they succeeded in making me about half mad and about half embarrassed at the same time. Oh, everybody had a wonderful time with it, except me, of course. But I'm not sure that was in her favor or against her as far as how it contributed to our becoming married and all that.

Patrick was born October 23d, 1986. And Audrey, my little girl, she'll be a year old in October. She was born in October, 198—8? I guess. Damn. Getting old. 1988. My mother is a midwife and she assisted in the birth of both of my kids. Audrey, she's no trouble at all. I could just have her around all the time. Now the boy's another matter. We take turns watching them, me and Robin. We're just sort of bumping into each other every now and then. Shake hands in the hallway. A funny thing for an eastern Kentucky boy to be doing? Yeah, well, the times they are a-changing. Everybody ought to take it up, I'll tell you. I just like to experience things, I guess. I don't like to have missed out on anything. I don't know.

Let me tell you something. The music business is fine, and good grades in college are important, I guess. But my number one priority in life is to be a good father. And I really want to be one. And I intend to be one. And I'll be one in spite of hell. Every free minute I have I spend with my kids. I don't go to parties. I don't have any kind of a recreation thing I do. I don't belong to an independent league ball team any more or any of that stuff. I spend every minute I can with my kids. Because as more and more demands are placed on my time by the music business, especially recently, I know that I'm going to be away from them a lot. So I really want to be close to my kids. And I try hard to be close to them.

I don't want to sound like a martyr here, you know. I don't mean that. I don't mean that I'm sacrificing. But it's a matter of priorities and my priority is to be a good father and give my kids—another cliché—I want them to have all the advantages I didn't have. And I've pretty much worked from scratch, myself. I've never had a great deal of encouragement or never been told I should do this or I should do that since I was twelve, thirteen years old. I don't remember ever showing my report card to anybody. If I got good grades it was simply because I thought it was necessary that a student get good grades. And I would like for my kids to be able to not struggle through college. I mean, I'd like to send them to a—but maybe there's something to be said that if you have to really work hard for something that it's more important to you. Cause I see a lot of kids down at U.K. that have all the resources available to them that should be out hoeing tobacco like I was doing when I was a teen-ager or throwing hay on a cart or something. I think that would be good for them.

I left Ralph—I would like to be able to explain this in one sentence, this is why I left Ralph, period. But I can't do that. It's much more involved. There were several reasons I left the band. One— and these aren't in the order of importance—I'd been in the band nine years and I was bored. I seem to have a short attention span or something, I don't know, but I seem to get bored very easily and to be frank I was bored the last few years I was in the band.

I didn't want to leave the band because I'd grown up in the band. It was like family to me and in that sense I didn't want to leave. But I was wanting to do something different, whatever. I wanted to go to school and I tried several abortive attempts at the time to go to school and work with Ralph at the same time and I soon saw that that was impossible. So that was another reason.

And I thought I had something to offer musically, whatever that means. I'd begun to get my own ideas about music and I'd been writing songs for a while and I felt like I was being—this isn't a complaint, mind you—but I felt like I was being held back, creatively speaking, by being in Ralph's band. Not that I wanted to impose any of my ideas about music on Ralph. We agreed pretty much on his music and I—Ralph is the ultimate authority on his music, and we had very little disagreement about how his music should sound. But it's just that I felt like I wanted to just do something different for a while.

I stayed longer than I should have. And I think it wasn't fair to Ralph and it wasn't fair to myself. I told Ralph, and we spoke about this, it was no secret, I told Ralph that I would stay with him at least five years and I would make no commitment beyond that. I think I owed him that. And, like I say, in the last couple of years I played with Ralph, I really don't think that I was as involved mentally in what was going on in the band as I should have been.

I think he was aware of it. He'd been aware of it for years. But I think that's part of the price of being a bandleader, that everybody's not going to be enthused about what they're doing for ever and ever and sometimes you have to accept that that's going to be the case. But anyway, like I said, in fairness to Ralph and in fairness to me I probably should have left the band sooner because I simply was not—I lost my enthusiasm for the band. And at that point I should have recognized it and left the band instead of trying to delude myself into thinking that I could continue in the capacity I was in.

Look, if it weren't for Ralph I wouldn't even be in this business. I'm sure I wouldn't. He just put me in a situation that I either had to learn to sing or go to the house, you know. If it weren't for that I probably wouldn't even be in it. He gave me a good paying job when I was just a very young man and he gave me every opportunity in the world.

You're so terribly indebted to somebody like that. I swear I remember getting off the stage back then and I'd say, "Ralph, I can't sing." But Ralph never would say, "Look at Roy Lee Centers, how good he could sing." He never did give me any of that stuff. He'd always say, "Yeah, you're doing fine. You'll make it. You just need a little time."

And to me that's worth more than anything, I mean, looking back on it. It always will amaze me why on earth Ralph wanted to hire me but I'm sure glad he did. I've got a lot of faults but ingratitude is not one of them. I never took that job for granted and I never took all that Ralph did for me for granted.

It was awful for me. It was a terrible time. Because in a way and in a big way I didn't want to leave the band because it was—I mean, other than the things that immediately come to mind. My wife was pregnant at the time, and Ralph's—that was a good job, a good-paying job, and I really had nothing in store for me when I left. It's not like I moved from point A to point B. I mean, I moved from point A to point zero and then started. And I knew that's what was in store for me.

Had I been a little more naive about this business it probably would've been easier for me to have left, but I understood completely what I was getting into when I left Ralph's band. And I've had very few surprises since I've left Ralph's band in terms of the difficulty of putting together a band from scratch, trying to come up with a sound that you're satisfied with and then trying to make a living doing it. Brother, that is no small undertaking. So really in a big way I didn't want to leave Ralph's band, but I just simply knew it was necessary that I leave. I felt when I left I was doing exactly what I should have done and I'm convinced of that now. I was almost certain then. But I'm convinced of it now, that I did the right thing. And I don't quite know how to put it, but—and this is another cliché. Man, I can drop them like you wouldn't believe—but there was no challenge there. And this is challenging, what I'm doing now. It's extremely challenging. And it's taxing and all that stuff. And that's probably—and even when it was difficult for me to work with Ralph it was a challenge when I decided that I wasn't qualified for the job. At least I had something to work toward, you know. Getting qualified.

There was some, not a great deal, but there was a little bit of tension between Ralph and me in the last few months I worked, because he knew I was leaving the band. Ralph don't talk a lot, but he isn't dumb. He's shrewd. He knows what's going on. Ralph knew I was leaving I'm sure at least six months before I left the band. And I sort of had him hanging because I'd never spoken to him about it and he was unsure of what was going on. And in a way I had myself hanging a little bit because I didn't know, I wasn't a hundred percent sure of anything. But immediately after I gave Ralph my notice, it seem like the air was cleared and everything was fine.

We were playing in Maryland somewhere, I forget where, when I gave my notice. And it was on Sunday and as is usually the case, there were people on and off the bus all day. And I knew that was the day I wanted to give Ralph my notice because school started approximately two weeks from then and that's when I wanted to leave the band, so I could start college. And Ralph was sitting on the bus. As I remember he wasn't sitting in the big captain's chair he has up there, whatever, the big lounge chair, he was sitting over in the passenger's chair, against a window, and I walked on the bus and I didn't go sit down. I stood at the door so I could sort of face him and he glanced over at me a time or two but never did really look me squarely in the eye.

And I said, "Ralph, the Milan festival's the week after next and I'd like for that to be my last day. That would give you your two weeks' notice." And he said, "Yeah, yeah, okay," and he was sitting there looking out the window, and of course I went through the formalities, you know, "I've enjoyed working for you and I've certainly appreciated the job, and I've tried to do a good job as well as I knew how to do it." He said, "Yeah, you've done a good job" and we got into a discussion of who—Of course he wasn't surprised, in fact he said, "Yeah, I knew you were leaving," and he'd been thinking about lead singers and we had a discussion about who should be my replacement. And he said—apparently he'd forgotten when I was in fact leaving—he said, "How long do you want to work now?" So he was kind about it. In effect, he was saying, "Now that I know you're leaving you can stay as long as you want. I'm not going to kick you out." He said, "How long do you want to work?" And I repeated that I would like to work through the Michigan festival and that would give me time to start college. He says, "So you're going to college?" And I don't think he was surprised with that either. And I said, "Yeah, I'm going to start school." And that was it. There was no more discussion of it.

Until the night after the Milan festival we were pulling out in the bus and I think Ralph and me both were a little reluctant to go to bed. Ralph was sitting in his chair and I was, as I frequently did, I was standing down in the well in front of the bus so I could see that the driver was awake and watch the road well. I did that especially when Ralph was sitting in his chair, rather than sit behind Ralph so I couldn't see the road signs and couldn't see the driver. And we sat there a long time and talked. Talked more to Ralph that night probably than I did in the previous nine years, I don't know, but we talked about just little foolish stuff.

And then he got up and went to the back and sent for me and I went back to the back, as was the custom. He sent to each band member and he paid them. When I got up and I walked back he was standing there and he said, "I'll probably be asleep when you get off the bus in the morning." He said, "Here's your money. You done a good job." And we shook hands and I went back to the front of the bus and that was all. That was it.

Very uncomfortable. It was a very uncomfortable situation, I think for Ralph, and I didn't feel comfortable either because I probably would liked to have hugged his neck at the time but of course, hell, we wouldn't do nothing like that. We just shook hands and said, "Well," like we were going home after a fishing trip or something, I don't know.

Notes on Sources

Chapter 1: The First Forty Years

For Stanley's own account of his life see Chapter 5. The "Forty more" line comes from one of the author's two formal interviews with Stanley; see the Bibliography under J. Wright (1984). The folksinger Walt Michael is profiled by Ledgin (1991). For Ralph Stanley's influence on musicians beyond the boundaries of "Stanley country," see, for example, Menzel (1988). For the liner notes on "Big Tilda" see Lomax ([1960]).

Appalachian religion, including Harrison Mayes, is the subject of a sympathetic and fascinating study (with remarkable photographs) by Dickinson and Benziger (1974). The world of the Stanleys' youth is brilliantly re-created in the short stories of Ball (1988); the anonymous book-jacket introduction to this collection describes the high rate of illiteracy and military enlistment in the area. On Appalachia in general Batteau (1990) is an excellent antidote to romanticism.

The "Farm and Fun Time" broadcasts are covered by Tottle (1987a and b, 1988a and b) and Wilson (1972); the Columbia sessions by D. Green (1980) and Reid (1982). There is a brief, up-to-date note on the Shouns automobile accident in Rosenberg (1981). The Stanley Brothers' experiences in Live Oak, Florida, are covered in detail in Reid (1985). The important Wango recordings are discussed by McCeney (1975), Reid ([1984]), Vernon (1973), and Williamson (1976). The positive evaluation of the Brothers' last appearance at Bean Blossom was made by Norman Carlson on a recording distributed by the Stanley Brothers Tape Club (1966); see also Reid ([1982]). The phenomenon of small record companies has been explored by Carlin (1976) and Tribe (1977). The bluegrass consumer revolution of the sixties is one of many topics thoroughly covered by Rosenberg (1985). For Stanley's (apparent) move toward a more archaic style see, for example, Rinzler (1974).

The sidemen have been the subject of a long string of articles, as follows—Cline: Kuykendall (1981), Stanton (1975a); Cooke: Brower (1987a); Shuffler: Gould (1977); Sparks: Cook (1977), D. Green (1972), Rancke (1986), Roemer (1982), Vernon (1983); Centers: McGinnis (1974); Whitley: Hershey-Webb (1977), Stanton (1975b); Sizemore: Morris (1986); Skaggs: Hatlo (1980, 1985), Oermann (1981), Price (1974), Tottle (1977).

The quotations from the early Bean Blossom sets are taken from a private tape provided by Don Hoos of Evanston, Illinois. Stanley's belief that "That Beautiful Woman" tells a true story emerged in conversation with the author at a festival in Indiana (July 1991). The sources for the quotations about Stanley's singing are the following: "Unmistakably rural," Malone (1968); "Almost sepulchral voice," Malone and McCulloh (1975); "Finest traditional singer," Malone and McCulloh (1975). "Bright Morning Star" is sung at an early mountain funeral in a novel by L. Smith (1983). On Scruggs's banjo being "a better style" see J. Wright (1984) and Shrubsall (1975). The "pioneering interviewer" was Bartenstein (1972).

For accounts of the Smith Ridge festival see Boyd (1972), Bowden (1987), Kent (1984), and Pinsley (1974). On the temporary removal of the festival to Kentucky see Williams (1985). Stanley replied that he was "not crooked enough" when asked by the author if he was still in politics (J. Wright 1984). The Lincoln Memorial University classes are described by Mitchell (1977).

Chapter 2: J. E. Mainer

Mainer recorded the tape on which this chapter is based in Concord, North Carolina, January, 1969. A portion of the chapter first appeared in *Banjo Newsletter* 13.11 (1986): 12–13. See also Carlson (1967), Tarantino (1983), Tribe (1975).

Chapter 3: Ruby Rakes Eubanks

Interviewed in Romulus, Michigan, June 14, 1987. Ruby Eubanks died on November 20, 1992.

Chapter 4: Benny Steele

Interviewed in Roxana, Kentucky, May 25, 1985.

Chapter 5: Ralph Stanley

This chapter is a composite; it includes (with permission) material from Bartenstein (1972), Rinzler (1974), Henderson (1976), Tottle (1981b), Brower (1987b), J. Wright (1984), an unpublished interview conducted in 1966 by Mike Seeger and supplied by Gary Reid, and a follow-up interview conducted in Roxana, Kentucky, on May 22, 1987, with the help of Jack Mansfield. Previously published in a slightly different form as Stanley (1988).

Chapter 6: Joe Wilson

Interviewed in Washington, D.C., December 27, 1985. A portion of this chapter first appeared in *Banjo Newsletter* 15.5 (1988): 12. See also Snyder (1986), Wilson (1986).

Chapter 7: George Shuffler

Interviewed (by telephone) in Valdese, North Carolina, March 21, 1985. A very welcome rainstorm, after a long drought in the area, helped to contribute to Shuffler's volubility. A portion of this chapter first appeared in *Banjo Newsletter* 12.12 (1985): 14–15 and 13.1 (1985): 17–18. See also Gould (1977).

Chapter 8: Lester Woodie

Interviewed in Smith Ridge, Virginia, September 28, 1986. See also Erbsen (1980).

Chapter 9: Melvin Goins

Interviewed in Smith Ridge, Virginia, May 26, 1984, and Whitmore Lake, Michigan, July 19, 1985; the chapter is a composite of these two interviews. A portion of it first appeared in *Banjo Newsletter* 12.1 (1984): 22–23. See also M. Godbey (1983), Tribe (1974).

Chapter 10: Larry Sparks

Interviewed in Martinsville, Indiana, July 5, 1985. A portion of this chapter first appeared in *Banjo Newsletter* 13.3 (1986): 17. See also Cook (1977), D. Green (1972), Ranke (1986), Roemer (1982), Vernon (1983).

Chapter 11: Curly Ray Cline

Interviewed in Chicago, Illinois, March 9, 1985. A portion of this chapter first appeared in *Banjo Newsletter* 12.9 (1985): 17–18 and 12.10 (1985): 19–20. See also Cheatham (1980), Kuykendall (1981), McDonald (1988), Stanton (1975a). For the mystique of eastern Kentucky foxhunting see Arnow (1949).

Chapter 12: Jack Cooke

Interviewed in Roxana, Kentucky, May 25, 1985. A portion of this chapter first appeared in *Banjo Newsletter* 13.6 (1986): 14–15. See also Brower (1987a).

Chapter 13: Ron Thomason

Interviewed at Thomason's home in Thackery, Ohio, June 28, 1985. A portion of this chapter first appeared in *Banjo Newsletter* 13.5 (1986): 19–20 and 16.7 (1989): 10. See also Menius (1985), Thomason (1971), S. Wright (1980).

Chapter 14: Jack Lynch

Interviewed in Roxana, Kentucky, August 30, 1986.

Chapter 15: Dick Freeland

Interviewed (by telephone) in Asbury, West Virginia, December 1, 1985. See also Dallman (1975), Vernon (1973a).

Chapter 16: Fay McGinnis

Interviewed at Whitmore Lake, Michigan, July 20, 1985. See also Carlson (1987), Smolka (1985). For the "Mountain Echoes" television program see J. Wright (1987).

Chapter 17: Revis Hall

Interviewed in Roxana, Kentucky, May 24, 1985.

Chapter 18: Dale Braden

Interviewed in Greenwich, Ohio, August 10, 1990.

Chapter 19: Frank Neat

Interviewed in Roxana, Kentucky, May 23, 1986. A portion of this chapter first appeared in *Banjo Newsletter* 14.1 (1986): 19. See also J. Wright (1982 and 1989).

Chapter 20: Richard Underwood

Interviewed in Roxana, Kentucky, May 24, 1985. A portion of this chapter first appeared in *Banjo Newsletter* 13.10 (1986): 12–13. See also Henry (1984), Rhodes (1981).

Chapter 21: Junior Blankenship

Interviewed in Milan, Michigan, August 18, 1984. A portion of this chapter first appeared in *Banjo Newsletter* 12.6 (1985): 24–25.

Chapter 22: Charlie Sizemore

Interviewed in Medaryville, Indiana, August 5, 1989. A somewhat longer version of this chapter, in which Sizemore goes on to discuss his subsequent career, appears in *Bluegrass Unlimited* 25.1 (1990): 24–32. See also Morris (1986). For the Winterhawk Scholarship Album see Snyder (1987).

A Note on Recordings, 1967–86

The following list is a record of a truly remarkable achievement: for-ty-five albums, over 550 songs and tunes, recorded through a period of twenty years. This amazing figure surely makes Ralph Stanley one of the most extensively recorded artists in any kind of music. One main impetus behind this ceaseless effort is strictly commercial: to provide the Clinch Mountain Boys' relatively small but fanatically loyal follow-ing with new albums to buy as the band makes its regular annual round of the festival circuit. The pattern has become as firmly estab-lished as a baseball team's spring training or the late John O'Hara's Thanksgiving Day novels: a recording session in the winter, usually in December and usually lasting one day, which results, if all goes well, in a new release to be introduced at the Memorial Festival in May.

While the band members are reluctant to articulate any deeper or higher motive to their recording work than this, the fact is that keep-ing the fans happy, on the one hand, and finding the right music and performing it in the right way, on the other, are basically synonymous. And every now and then in the studio, when the band is struggling with a particularly hard take, Ralph Stanley will make a remark like "Boys, this record's going to be around for a long time" that betrays his realization that, rather than simply stamping out souvenirs, he is in fact leaving a legacy. And while no one would claim that all of the cuts on all of these records are of equal value, taken as a whole the level of that legacy has been very high indeed.

The list covers the first twenty years of Ralph Stanley's ongoing solo career and coincides, in its arbitrarily chosen cutoff date, with Charlie Sizemore's departure from the band. Throughout this period long-play-ing albums were the main medium for the publication of Stanley's ma-terial, and almost invariably a single recording session yielded a single album. Cuts were generally pressed in the order in which they were recorded; there have been, to my knowledge, no unreleased cuts and virtually no preserved outtakes. The albums were cut live, rather than by stacking tracks, and they were created independently: Dick Freeland was only the nominal producer during his tenure with Rebel, and after his time there were no separate producers at all. Since Curly Ray

Cline's numbers, which are based on his recordings, have been an integral part of the band's stage performances, his albums have been included in the list as well.

Accounting for the origins of this enormous body of material is not an easy task. Urban folk musicians are generally very anxious to give their audience a full description of their sources, since they see this as a way of guaranteeing authenticity. In fact, folksinger Tom Glazer enjoys describing how John Jacob Niles, who of course was a sophisticated, trained musician, would even go so far as to invent vernacular sources for material he had composed.

Professional bluegrass entertainers, on the other hand, are just the opposite. They are reticent about their sources and suspicious of inquiries about them—understandably enough, given the ferocious battles about song-stealing that marked the early days of the music. The investigator, faced with the artists' endlessly vague memories, can only importune so much; one must then rely on educated guesswork, guesswork based on earlier recorded material. But such guesswork has its pitfalls.

An experience I had in the mid-eighties will serve to illustrate these difficulties. I had found a song called "Omie Let Your Bangs Hang Down," sung by Gaither Carlton of Deep Gap, North Carolina, on an album (County 717, *More Clawhammer Banjo Songs and Tunes*) which is popular among urban revivalists but virtually unknown among Appalachian bluegrass musicians. Following the pattern established by such Curly Ray Cline classics as "Blue-Eyed Verdie" (which of course is a version of "Black-Eyed Susie"), I rewrote it, using the name of Mrs. Ray Cline, as "Verdie Let Your Bangs Hang Down," changing the first verse into a chorus and making one or two other minor alterations.

A few months later I played the song for Ray Cline at the Memorial Festival on Smith Ridge. Unbeknownst to me a fan named Evelyn Tussey taped the song while I was playing it and gave the cassette to Cline. Soon after this Ray was saying that he was going to use the song on his next album, and not long after that he was saying that he was going to have me sing it on the record.

On April 2, 1986, I was in the Maggard Studio in Big Stone Gap, Virginia, watching Ralph Stanley record the album that was later to be titled *Lonesome and Blue* (Rebel REB-1647), and when the session was over Cline asked me if I was going to return to the studio in a month or so, when he would be recording his next album. I replied that my schedule was crowded and I wasn't sure I'd be able to make it. So we decided to record the song then and there; I borrowed Ralph Stanley's banjo, the Clinch Mountain Boys learned the tune and the chorus in an astonishingly short time, and after a false start or two we successfully recorded the song on the first take.

The rest of the Cline album was recorded in May, and when Jack Lynch published it under the title *The Deputy* (Nashville Country C-

101) I cheerfully signed a form statement claiming complete responsibility for the words and music of "my" song, whereupon it was credited to me in the liner notes.

A year or two later I came upon an old album by J. E. Mainer which featured a song called "Tabby Let Your Hair Hang Down." I played the record and lo and behold, there was "Verdie," note for note and almost word for word. I mentioned this to Cline the next time I saw him, and he looked at me with a perfect poker face and said, "Yeah, that'll happen sometimes."

If I had not known the facts of this case I would surely have said that J. E. Mainer was the "source" of "Verdie Let Your Bangs Hang Down." And it is perfectly possible that despite the help of experts like Professor Ivan Tribe of Rio Grande College in Ohio I have made similar mistakes in the outline that follows. So: *caveat emptor.*

Ralph Stanley's first source for music was of course his family. He recalls his mother playing such banjo standards as "Cripple Creek" (recorded on albums 5 and 12 in the list), "Shout Little Lulie" (21), and "Old Joe Clark" (41), and his father singing "Man of Constant Sorrow" (11 and 18) and "Pretty Polly" (11 and 18). And he remembers his parents and neighbors singing such hymns as "Amazing Grace" (7 and 29) and "Village Church Yard" (16) in the Old Regular Baptist church in nearby McClure.

Ever since his solo career began Ralph Stanley has rerecorded a good deal of earlier Stanley Brothers material, in part because the original records were out of print and in part because even when they were in print he was not sure of his legal right to sell them. Almost all of these songs were written by Carter Stanley; they include (among many others) "The Darkest Hour" (36), "The Fields Have Turned Brown" (22), "Let Me Walk Lord by Your Side" (15), "Lonesome River" (8 and 21), "Riding That Midnight Train" (11 and 20), "Sharecropper's Son" (1 and 27), "White Dove" (8, 11, 15 and 26), "Who'll Sing for Me" (20), and "Wonderful World Outside" (1).

Among prewar groups and performers, the Monroe Brothers are the probable source for "All the Good Times Are Past and Gone" (11), "Long Journey Home" (2 and 11), and "Roll in My Sweet Baby's Arms" (12 and 40). The Carter Family provided "East Virginia Blues" (2 and 12), "Gold Watch and Chain" (21), "I Wonder How the Old Folks Are" (20), "Jimmie Brown the Newsboy" (36), "Will the Circle Be Unbroken" (19), and "Will You Miss Me" (13). From Molly O'Day came "The Drunken Driver" (37), "Poor Ellen Smith" (2), "Snow Covered Mound" (4 and 34), and "Traveling the High Way Home" (29). Brother duets were naturally an important source; cf. "Brown's Ferry Blues" (28: Delmore Brothers), "Knoxville Girl" (2: Wilburn Brothers), and "Somebody Loves You Darling" (44: Wiley and Zeke Morris). "Going round This World" (2) was learned from Lily May Ledford and "Maple on the Hill" (18) from Wade Mainer.

In his youth Curly Ray Cline enjoyed a close association with Fiddling Arthur Smith, who became the source for a substantial number of his songs and tunes, including (for instance) "Adieu False Heart" (45), "Blackberry Blossom" (28), "Fiddler's Dream" (30), "Peacock Rag" (23), "Sugar Tree Stomp" (25), and "Walking in My Sleep" (9 and 11), as well as Ralph Stanley's "Bound to Ride" (12 and 21).

Occasionally modern (i.e., postwar) country and southern gospel musicians provide material that is appropriate for the archaic Stanley sound. Examples include Buck Owens ("Act Naturally": 40), the Louvin Brothers ("Are You Afraid to Die": 29, "The Family Who Prays": 39), Hank Williams ("I Saw the Light": 11 and 33, "Six More Miles": 13), Loretta Lynn ("Everybody Wants to Go to Heaven": 39), Johnnie and Jack ("What about You": 20), Ferlin Huskey ("Wings of a Dove": 38), George Jones, one of Ralph Stanley's favorite singers ("Old Old House": 31), and the Dixon Brothers ("Wreck on the Highway": 34).

Most notable among Stanley's relatively more modern sources has been Bill Monroe. On stage the Clinch Mountain Boys have featured Monroe's versions of "John Henry" and "Molly and Tenbrooks," and their albums include well over a dozen other songs either written by or associated with Monroe, such as "Blue Moon of Kentucky" (11 and 44), "Footprints in the Snow" (31), "Little Girl and the Dreadful Snake" (31); "On and On" (20); "Put My Little Shoes Away" (31); "Uncle Pen" (11); and "Walk Softly on This Heart of Mine" (37).

Over the years Stanley's sidemen and their families have provided a good deal of material, which they either wrote themselves or unearthed for the band. "Love Please Stay" (1) came from Melvin Goins; "What Kind of Man" (4) from Larry Sparks; "Don't Ask Me Why" (18) and "Take Me Back" (14) from Roy Lee Centers; "Standing by the River" (16) from Ricky Skaggs and "All I Ever Loved Was You" (18) from his mother Dorothy; "Looking for the Stone" (24) and "Zion's Hill" (24) from Keith Whitley; "Henry Brown" (31), "Power of Love" (31), "There'll Be None on the Other Side" (29), and "They Won't Believe" (24), among others, from the Marshall Family, especially Danny Marshall; "My Lord Will Send a Moses" (39) from the Cooke Family; and "Melody of Love" (37) and "Dip Your Fingers in Some Water" (34) from Charlie Sizemore, who found the latter song and wrote a second verse for it. The Blankenship connection, Junior and Senior, brought "I've Got a Mule to Ride" (37) from the Rocky Mountain Boys.

Other songwriters (and suppliers of traditional material) often tend to be personal friends of Stanley's. For instance, Osburn Thorpe, deputy sheriff of Dayton, Ohio (and previously chief deputy of Breathitt County, Kentucky), supplied (e.g.) "Darling Brown Eyes" (6), "I Was Born a Rambler" (3), and "She Ran Away with Another Man" (3). Gene Duty, a resident of Detroit who originally came from Council, Virginia, was the source for (e.g.) "Rock Bottom" (14), "That Beautiful Woman" (1 and 27), "That Lonesome Old Song" (13) and "What a Price" (29).

Jack Lynch completed Duty's "In Memory of Carter Stanley" (3) and also furnished "Bonnie and Clyde's Hop" (2). Wendy Smith, another Michigan musician, was responsible for "Daughter of Geronimo" (14), "Hills of Home" (6 and 24), "Lonesome" (1), "River Underground" (14), "Shot-Gun Slade" (13), and "Sweet Sally Brown" (1). Landon Messer of West Virginia, a fine traditional singer who seldom misses a Memorial Festival, supplied "Hemlock and Primroses" (1 and 27), while his friend and sometime stage partner Lowell Varney wrote the autobiographical "Sixteen Years" (43) and "When You Go Walking after Midnight" (43). From Bill Grant, festival entrepreneur of Hugo, Oklahoma, came "Medicine Springs" (6: named after a landmark near his home) and "Stairway to Heaven" (10). Curt and Hope Randolph of Viola, Illinois, not only raised the boar hog which led to Curly Ray Cline's best-known album cover and song; their daughter, Candi, also wrote "How Could I Dream Such a Dream" (36), "Jealousy" (36), "The Letter I Never Mailed" (36), "Who's in Your Heart" (44), and "Your Worries and Troubles Are Mine" (36) for Ralph Stanley. The varied talents of John B. Preston of eastern Kentucky are revealed by the comic "Smarter Than the Average Idiot" (41), the admonitory "Red Wicked Wine" (44), and the extraordinarily ancient-sounding "I've Just Seen the Rock of Ages" (29), while Preston's brother Ronnie wrote "Walking up This Hill on Decoration Day" (32), which has an equally traditional flavor and could serve as a theme song for the Smith Ridge festival. Randall Hylton is a songwriter and solo performer who has successfully pitched three excellent songs at Ralph Stanley: "It's a Hot Night in August" (44), "Room at the Top of the Stairs" (44), and "Two Men a Praying" (42). Finally, Ralph's wife Jimmie wrote "Fallen Tears" (27), "I Only Exist" (6), and the hair-raising gospel song "When I Bid You All Adieu" (39).

Stanley's instrumentals are generally original, or original reworkings of traditional melodies. Titles tend to be serendipitous, as with the earlier "Hard Times" (11 and 21), which commemorates the difficulties the Stanley Brothers were having earning a living at the time of its composition. The band was in California when the tune of that name (6) was written. "Old Time Pickin'" (13 and 21) was named after the old-time banjo Stanley borrowed from Fay McGinnis to play it on. "Lisa's Joy" (18) was named after Ralph and Jimmie Stanley's elder daughter, Lisa Joy Stanley, and "Row Hoe" (1) was named after a famous fighting cock.

(Abbreviations—b: banjo, f: fiddle, g: [rhythm] guitar, lg: lead guitar, m: mandolin, bs: bass.)

1. King 1028: *Brand New Country Songs by Ralph Stanley* (Sharecropper's Son, Hemlock and Primroses, That Beautiful Woman, Poor Rambler, Lonesome, Lost Train / Row Hoe, Wonderful World Outside, Sweet Sally Brown, Love Please Stay, I'm Better Off Now That You're Gone, You Never Could Be True). Cincinnati, Ohio: 5/19/67; 10/24/67. b: R. Stan-

ley, f: C. R. Cline, lg: L. Sparks, g: M. Goins, m and harmonica: Earl Taylor, bs: Jim McCall.

2. Jalyn JLP 118: Ralph Stanley: *Old Time Music* (Knoxville Girl, John Henry, Poor Ellen Smith, East Virginia Blues, Long Journey Home, Going round This World / Chicken Reel, Mississippi Sawyer, Bonnie and Clyde's Hop, Billy in the Low Ground, Cackling Hen, Going Down Town). Dayton, Ohio: 8/67. b: R. Stanley, f: C. R. Cline, lg: L. Sparks, g: M. Goins, m: Curly Lambert, bs: J. Lynch.

3. Jalyn JLP 120: *The Bluegrass Sound of Ralph Stanley* (In Memory of Carter Stanley, Lonesome Road Blues, She Ran Away with Another Man, I Was Born a Rambler, Twenty One Years, Sally Goodin / We'll Be Sweethearts in Heaven, Sweetest Love, Blue Eyed Ellen, Baby Girl, Your Saddle Is Empty Old Pal, Carter's Songs). Dayton, Ohio: 2/14 and 2/15/68. b: R. Stanley, f: C. R. Cline, g: L. Sparks, m: Frank Wakefield, bs: J. Lynch.

4. King 1032 (= Starday SK 1032): Ralph Stanley: *Over the Sunset Hill* (Jesse James Prayed, Going up Home to Live in Green Pastures, What Kind of Man, I Want a Clear Record, Prepare Me O Lord, I Wanna Go Home / A Little Soldier for Jesus, Over the Sunset Hill, Snow Covered Mound, I'll Be with Dad and Mother, Thou Long Expected Jesus, Be Ready to Go). Cincinnati, Ohio: 2/21/68. b: R. Stanley, f: C. R. Cline, lg: L. Sparks, g: M. Goins, bs: G. Shuffler.

5. Old Homestead OHS 90142 (= Melody MLP 17): *Curly Ray Cline (The Old Kentucky Fox Hunter) and His Lonesome Pine Fiddle* (Kentucky Fox Race, Black Mountain Blues, Mocking Bird, Cripple Creek, Golden Slippers, Sweet By and By / Curly Ray, Sourwood Mountain, Wednesday Night Waltz, Orange Blossom Special, Red Dog, What a Friend). Hamilton, Ohio: 2/15/69. f: C. R. Cline, b: R. Stanley, g: L. Sparks, bs: M. Goins.

6. King KSD 1069 (= Starday SK 1069): Ralph Stanley: *Hills of Home* (Hills of Home, Darling Brown Eyes, My Long Skinny Lanky Sarah Jane, Coosy, Midnight Storm, Let's Go to the Fair / Dark Hollow, Dug-Gunn Shame, The Kitten and the Cat, California, I Only Exist, Medicine Springs). Nashville, Tenn.: 7/14 and 15/69. b: R. Stanley, f: C. R. Cline, lg: L. Sparks, g and m: Jimmy Martin, bs: Jim McCall.

7. Jalyn JLP 126: *The Working Man: "Curly" Ray Cline and His Lonesome Pine Fiddle* (The Braying Mule, Callaway, Back Up and Push, Never Alone Waltz, 8th of January, Amazing Grace / Pretty Little Indian, Dan's Dream, Rockhouse, Bill Cheatham, Chitlin' Cooking Time in Cheatham County, Oldtime Religion). Dayton, Ohio: 1/1/70. f: C. R. Cline, b: R. Stanley, g: Roy Lee Centers, bs: G. Shuffler.

8. Jalyn JLP 129: *Ralph Stanley and the Clinch Mountain Boys Featuring Keith Whitley and Ricky Skaggs* (We'll Be Sweethearts in Heaven, Mother No Longer Awaits Me at Home, White Dove, Our Last Goodbye, Lonesome River, I Love No One but You / The Angels Are Singing in Heaven Tonight, It's Never Too Late, Loving You Too Well, Too Late

to Cry, Little Glass of Wine, I Long to See the Old Folks). Dayton, Ohio: 1/9/71. g: Keith Whitley, g and b: Roy Lee Centers, f and m: Ricky Skaggs, f: C. R. Cline, m: R. Thomason, b: R. Stanley, bs: J. Cooke.

9. Rebel SLP 1498: *The Lonesome Pine Fiddle Sound of Curly Ray Cline: Chicken Reel* (Chicken Reel, Soldier's Joy, Walkin' in My Sleep, Yodelin' Waltz, Dixon County Blues, Old Rugged Cross / Irish Washerwoman, Raggedy Ann, Blue-Eyed Verdie, Leather Britches, Carroll County Blues, I'll Fly Away). Clinton, Md.: 1/14/71. f: C. R. Cline, b and tambourine: R. Stanley, g: Roy Lee Centers, bs: J. Cooke.

10. Rebel SLP 1499: Ralph Stanley: *Cry from the Cross* (Cry from the Cross, You're Drifting On, Will He Wait a Little Longer, Bright Morning Star, Death Is Only a Dream, Come On Little Children / Take Your Shoes Off Moses, Stairway to Heaven, I Am the Man Thomas, Step Out in the Sunshine, Sinner Man, Two Coats). Clinton, Md.: 2/22 and 2/23/71. b: R. Stanley, f: C. R. Cline, g: Roy Lee Centers, lg: Keith Whitley, m and f: Ricky Skaggs, bs and hands: J. Cooke, bs: Ed Ferris, hands: Cliff Waldron.

11. Seven Seas SR 690/1 (= Rebel REB 2202): *Ralph Stanley in Japan* (How Mountain Girls Can Love, Leather Britches, Sitting on Top of the World, Love Me Darling Just Tonight, Clinch Mountain Backstep, Uncle Pen, Memories of Mother / Little Maggie, Listen to the Mocking Bird, Riding That Midnight Train, Baby Girl, Sourwood Mountain, I Saw the Light / Orange Blossom Special, Blue Moon of Kentucky, Long Journey Home, Pretty Polly, Daybreak in Tokyo, All the Good Times Are Past and Gone, How Far to Little Rock / Rank Stranger, Walking in My Sleep, Man of Constant Sorrow, I Hear a Choo-Choo Coming, Old Country Church, Hard Times, White Dove, Old Time Pickin'). Tokyo: 5/5/71. b: R. Stanley, f: C. R. Cline, g: Roy Lee Centers, bs: J. Cooke.

12. Birdree PMC 6004: Ralph Stanley: *John Henry* (John Henry, Pretty Little Indian, Little Birdie, Cripple Creek, East Virginia Blues, Little Glass of Wine / Somebody Touched Me, Sally Goodin, Working on a Building, Roll in My Sweet Baby's Arms, Bound to Ride, Mississippi Sawyer). Tokyo: 5/6/71. b: R. Stanley, f: C. R. Cline, g: Roy Lee Centers, bs: J. Cooke.

13. Rebel SLP 1503: Ralph Stanley: *Something Old—Something New and Some of Katy's Mountain Dew* (Brand New Tennessee Waltz, Six More Miles, Cluck Old Hen, A Little Boy Called Joe, Going to Georgia, Gloryland / Shot-Gun Slade, Will You Miss Me, Old Time Pickin', Katy Daley, That Lonesome Old Song, Prettiest Bed of Flowers). Clinton, Md.: 2/23 and 7/30/71. b: R. Stanley, f: C. R. Cline, g: Roy Lee Centers, m: Ricky Skaggs, lg: Keith Whitley, bs: J. Cooke.

14. Jessup MB 108: Ralph Stanley: *Michigan Bluegrass* (Are You Proud of America, Rock Bottom, Another Song Another Drink, Take Me Back, You're Going Away, Hulla-Gull / Let's Keep Old Glory Waving, River Underground, Ain't It Hard, Daughter of Geronimo, Buckwheat,

Keep My Love with You). Jackson, Mich.: 8/30/71. b: R. Stanley, f: C. R. Cline, g: Roy Lee Centers, m and f: Ricky Skaggs, lg: Keith Whitley, bs: J. Cooke, bs: Lyn Hall.

15. Jessup MB 129: Ralph Stanley: *Gospel Echoes of the Stanley Brothers* (Let Me Walk Lord by Your Side, In Heaven We'll Never Grow Old, Wings of Angels, The Darkest Hour Is Just before Dawn, Working on a Building, Master's Bouquet / Leaning on Jesus, White Dove, Shouting on the Hills of Glory, A Few More Seasons to Come, Daniel Prayed, My Main Trial Is Yet to Come). Jackson, Mich.: 10/3/71. b: R. Stanley, f: C. R. Cline, g: Roy Lee Centers, m: Ricky Skaggs, lg: Keith Whitley, bs: J. Cooke.

16. Rebel SLP 1508: Ralph Stanley: *Old Country Church* (Old Country Church, My Lord's Been Walking, I Hold a Clear Title, Standing by the River, Ten Thousand Angels, Village Church Yard / Honey in the Rock, Give Me the Roses While I Live, Green Pasture in the Sky, These Men of God, Hide Me Rock of Ages, When I Get Home). Clinton, Md.: 12/10 and 12/11/71. b: R. Stanley, f: C. R. Cline, g: Roy Lee Centers, m and f: Ricky Skaggs, lg: Keith Whitley, bs: J. Cooke.

17. Rebel SLP 1509: Curly Ray Cline: *They Cut Down the Old Pine Tree* (They Cut Down the Old Pine Tree, Mississippi Sawyer, Sweet Thing, Lonesome Pine Breakdown, Lost Girl, Pass Me Not Oh Gentle Savior / Farmer's Girl, Sally Goodin, Tennessee Waltz, Big Daddy Blues, Pike County Breakdown, Precious Memories). Clinton, Md.: 12/12/71. f: C. R. Cline, b: R. Stanley, g: Roy Lee Centers, lg: Keith Whitley, m and f: Ricky Skaggs, bs: J. Cooke.

18. Rebel SLP 1514: *Ralph Stanley and the Clinch Mountain Boys Play Requests* (Man of Constant Sorrow, Maple on the Hill, Flood of 57, Pretty Polly, Clinch Mountain Backstep, Don't Ask Me Why / Little Maggie, All the Love I Had Is Gone, I'll Remember You Love in My Prayers, All I Ever Loved Was You, Lisa's Joy, God Gave You to Me). Clinton, Md.: 8/31/72 (and 2/24/71, 6/30/71). b: R. Stanley, f: C. R. Cline, g: Roy Lee Centers, m and f: Ricky Skaggs, lg: Keith Whitley, bs: J. Cooke, bs: Ed Ferris.

19. Rebel SLP 1515: Curly Ray Cline: *My Little Home in West Virginia* (My Little Home in West Virginia, Lost Indian, Big Taters in the Sandy Land, Maiden's Prayer, Lost Train Blues, How Great Thou Art / Flem Jones, Take Me Back to Tennessee, Natural Bridge Blues, Arkansas Traveler, Pike County Waltz, Will the Circle Be Unbroken). Clinton, Md.: 10/13/72. f: C. R. Cline, b: R. Stanley, g: Roy Lee Centers, g: Mike Johnson, bs and tambourine: J. Cooke, bs: Ed Ferris.

20. County 776 (= King Bluegrass KB 522): Ralph Stanley: *On and On* (Going to Paint the Town, What about You, On and On, Cumberland Gap, Loving You Too Well, Who'll Sing for Me / Love Me Darling Just Tonight, Poison Love, Riding the Midnight Train, I Wonder How the Old Folks Are, Bill Cheatham, Nobody's Love Is like Mine). Lexington, Ky.: 2/18/73. b: R. Stanley, f: C. R. Cline, g: Roy Lee Centers, lg: Ricky Lee, bs: J. Cooke.

21. Rebel SLP 1530: Ralph Stanley: *A Man and His Music* (Shout Little Luly, Little Birdie, Hard Times, Gold Watch and Chain, Train 45, You Know I'll Be Lonesome / John Henry, Old Time Pickin', Bound to Ride, Rocky Island, The Orphan Girl, Lonesome River). Clinton, Md.: 3/22 and 3/23/73. b: R. Stanley, f: C. R. Cline, g: Roy Lee Centers, lg: Ricky Lee, m: John Duffey, bs: J. Cooke.

22. Rebel SLP 1522: Ralph Stanley: *I Want to Preach the Gospel* (I Want to Preach the Gospel, Going up Home to Live in Green Pastures, Fields Have Turned Brown, Rank Stranger, Dark and Stormy Is the Desert, Angel Band / Brighter Mansion, I'm Going That Way, Who Is That, I Want to Make Heaven My Home, Great High Mountain, Rose among the Thorns). Clinton, Md.: 3/22 and 3/23/73. b: R. Stanley, f: C. R. Cline, g: Roy Lee Centers, lg: Ricky Lee, m: John Duffey, bs: J. Cooke.

23. Rebel SLP 1531: Curly Ray Cline: *Fishin' for Another Hit* (Crawdad Song, Kansas City Railroad, Peacock Rag, Lee Highway, I Wear the Banner, Peace in the Valley / Dance All Night with Your Bottle in Your Hand, Whistlin' Rufus, Girl Don't Pay Me No Mind, Garfield March, Trouble among the Yearlings, Midnight Waltz). Clinton, Md.: 12/21/73. f: C. R. Cline, b: R. Stanley, g: Roy Lee Centers, lg: Ricky Lee, bs: Ed Ferris.

24. Rebel SLP 1544: Ralph Stanley: *Let Me Rest on a Peaceful Mountain (Hills of Home)* (Hills of Home, My Lord's Gonna Bless Me, You Better Sit Down and Pray, Looking for the Stone, Children Go Where I Send Thee, Baptism of Jesse Taylor / They Won't Believe, Zion's Hill, Turn Back, Thank You Mom, Take a Walk, Purple Robe). Clinton, Md.: 3/25 and 3/26/75. b: R. Stanley, f: C. R. Cline, g: Keith Whitley, lg: Ricky Lee, bs: J. Cooke.

25. Rebel SLP 1545: Curly Ray Cline: *Why Me Ralph?* (Why Me Ralph, Rickey Allen, Whispering Hope, Alabama Jubilee, Sugar Tree Stomp, When They Ring Those Golden Bells / Money in the Bank, Crazy Blues, Chinese Breakdown, Florida Blues, Wild Horses, Sweet Bunch of Daisies). Clinton, Md.: 3/26/75. f: C. R. Cline, b: R. Stanley, g: Keith Whitley, lg: Ricky Lee, bs: J. Cooke.

26. Rebel SLP 1554/55: Ralph Stanley: *Live! At McClure, Virginia* (Includes many artists; cuts featuring Ralph Stanley are: I Hear a Choo Choo, I'm on My Way Back to the Old Home, Stone Walls and Steel Bars, Cotton-Eyed Joe, Nobody's Love Is like Mine, White Dove, I Just Think I'll Go Away, Can't You Hear Me Calling). McClure, Va.: 5/23, 5/24, and 5/25/75. b: R. Stanley, m: Bill Monroe, f: Leslie Keith, m: Jimmy Martin, et al.

27. Rebel SLP 1562: Ralph Stanley: *Old Home Place* (Old Home Place, Hemlocks and Primroses, My Deceitful Heart, Poor Rambler, If That's the Way You Feel, Sharecropper's Son / Bootleg John, Devil's Little Angel, That Beautiful Woman, Fallen Tears, Home in the Mountains, Lonesome without You). Silver Spring, Md.: 2/16/76. b: R. Stanley, f: C. R. Cline, g: Keith Whitley, lg: Dan Marshall, bs: Ed Ferris.

28. Rebel SLP 1566: *It's "Bread and Water" for Curly Ray Cline (Clinch Mtn. Boy Jailed!!!)* (Pikeville Jail, Blackberry Blossom, Turkey in the Straw, Uncle Ward's Hornpipe, House of David Blues, Just a Closer Walk with Thee / Brown's Ferry Blues, Katie Hill, Twinkle Twinkle Little Star, Waltz for Dad, Tennessee Wagoner, When the Saints Go Marching In). Wise, Va.: 11/11/76. f: C. R. Cline, b: R. Stanley, g: Keith Whitley, lg: Renfro Profitt, bs: J. Cooke.

29. Rebel SLP 1571: Ralph Stanley: *Clinch Mountain Gospel* (Over in the Gloryland, Star of Bethlehem, Oh Death, There'll Be None on the Other Side, Mother's Not Dead, Jesus Saviour Pilot Me / Traveling the High Way Home, I Just Saw the Rock of Ages, Amazing Grace, What a Price, Are You Afraid to Die, I Am Weary). Lexington, Ky.: 5/12/77. b: R. Stanley, f: C. R. Cline, g: Keith Whitley, lg: Renfro Profitt, m: Dan Marshall, vocal: Chester Marshall, bs: J. Cooke.

30. Rebel SLP 1577: Curly Ray Cline: *Who's Gonna Mow My Grass?* (Who's Gonna Mow My Grass, Yodeling Waltz, Durham's Bull, Booger Man's Dream, Boil Them Cabbage Down, Fifty Year Ago Waltz / More Pretty Girls Than One, Flop-Eared Mule, In the Land Where We'll Never Grow Old, Fiddler's Dream, I Like the Old Time Ways, Family Bible). Wise, Va.: 1/5/78. f: C. R. Cline, b: R. Stanley, g: C. Sizemore, lg: J. Blankenship, m: Dan Marshall, bs: J. Cooke.

31. Rebel SLP 1579: Ralph Stanley: *Down Where the River Bends* (Down Where the River Bends, Put My Little Shoes Away, Footprints in the Snow, Henry Brown, Just Dreamin', I'll Just Catch a Train and Ride, The Old Old House / The Power of Love, Dream of a Miner's Child, I Wanna Sing a Song for Carter, Cuttin' the Cornbread, Little Girl and the Dreadful Snake, Pretty Woman, Hometown). Lexington, Ky.: 3/29/78. b: R. Stanley, f: C. R. Cline, g: C. Sizemore, lg: J. Blankenship, m: Dan Marshall, vocals: J. Cooke, bs: John Johnson.

32. Rebel SLP 1590: Ralph Stanley: *I'll Wear a White Robe* (What Is It for a Saint to Die, I'll Wear a White Robe, Just over the Stars, I'm in a New World, Oh Lord Remember Me, No Sorrow Can Reach Us There / Old Time Religion, Life's Other Side, Who Rolled This Stone Away, Walking up This Hill on Decoration Day, Mountain Preacher's Child, Oak Grove Church). Crum, WVa.: 3/9/79. b: R. Stanley, f: C. R. Cline, g: C. Sizemore, lg and m: J. Blankenship, bs: J. Cooke.

33. Old Homestead OHS 90138: Curly Ray Cline: *Boar Hog* (Boar Hog, Oklahoma Stomp, Grey Eagle, Faded Love, Turkey Call, He Won't Accept Excuses / Rubber Dolly, Won't It Be Wonderful, Dill Pickle Rag, Today Has Been a Lonesome Day, I Saw the Light, Under the Double Eagle). Wise, Va.: 3/10/79. f: C. R. Cline, b, g, and turkey call: R. Stanley, g: C. Sizemore, lg: J. Blankenship, bs: J. Cooke.

34. Stanley Tone RSR 1154 (= Rebel REB 1613): Ralph Stanley: *Snow Covered Mound* (Wreck on the Highway, Troublesome Water, God Who Never Fails, On Heaven's Bright Shore, Dip Your Fingers in Some Water, Snow Covered Mound / Keys to the Kingdom, Will They Miss

Me, Go Down Moses, Guide Me O Thou Great Jehovah, Tarry with Me O My Saviour, Harbor of Love). Crum, WVa.: 2/27/80. b: R. Stanley, f: C. R. Cline, g: C. Sizemore, lg: J. Blankenship, harmonica: Chester Marshall, vocal: Dave Marshall, bs: J. Cooke.

35. Blue Jay LPA 201: Ralph Stanley: *Hymn Time* (Won't You Meet Me There, He Washed My Sins Away, New Home, Keep It White, Going Home with Jesus, I'll Be Ready to Go / I Can Try, He'll Carry You Through, That Old Cross, Blue Jeans and Old Faded Shirt, He Is All I'll Ever Need, Waiting for That Mansion). Big Stone Gap, Va.: 7/10/80. b: R. Stanley, f: C. R. Cline, g: C. Sizemore, lg: J. Blankenship, bs: J. Cooke.

36. Rebel REB 1601: Ralph Stanley: *The Stanley Sound Today* (Lonesome Here without You, Your Worries and Troubles Are Mine, Could You Love Me One More Time, Jealousy, How Could I Dream Such a Dream, Tennessee Truck Driving Man / The Letter I Never Mailed, No Schoolbus in Heaven, Dixieland, Jimmie Brown the Newsboy, Sitting on Top of the World, The Darkest Hour). Ashland, Ky.: 2/4/81. b: R. Stanley, f: C. R. Cline, g: C. Sizemore, lg: J. Blankenship, bs: J. Cooke.

37. Rebel REB 1606: Ralph Stanley: *The Memory of Your Smile* (Highway of Regret, Melody of Love, I've Got a Mule to Ride, Who Will Call You Sweetheart, Bad Case of the Blues, Little Glass of Wine / City Lights, Walk Softly on This Heart of Mine, What I Wanted Most, The Drunken Driver, The Memory of Your Smile, Bury Me under the Pines). Big Stone Gap, Va.: 12/17/81. b: R. Stanley, f: C. R. Cline, g: C. Sizemore, lg: J. Blankenship, bs: J. Cooke.

38. Old Homestead OHS 70047: Curly Ray Cline: *The Old Kentucky Fox Hunter Plays Gospel* (Just over in the Gloryland, Little Black Train, Wings of a Dove, Battle Hymn of the Republic, Lonely Tombs, Why Me Lord / Me and Jesus, Take a Little Time for Jesus, Swing Low Sweet Chariot, I'm Gonna Eat at the Welcome Table, When the Saints Go Marching In, What a Friend). Big Stone Gap, Va.: 12/17/81. f: C. R. Cline, b: R. Stanley, g and lg: C. Sizemore, lg: J. Blankenship, bs: J. Cooke.

39. Rebel REB 1619: Ralph Stanley: *Child of the King* (My Lord Will Send a Moses, Model Church, When I Bid You All Adieu, I'd Be Willing to Run All the Way, Willing to Try, Everybody Wants to Go to Heaven / I'm a Child of the King, One Greater Than David Is Here, I Wonder If Mother Knows, The Family Who Prays, It Must Have Been Jesus, If I Could Crown You Mother). Big Stone Gap, Va.: 3/30/83. b: R. Stanley, f: C. R. Cline, g: C. Sizemore, lg: J. Blankenship, bs: J. Cooke.

40. Rebel REB 1627: Ralph Stanley And Friends: *Live at the Old Home Place* (Swinging a Nine Pound Hammer, I Ain't Wost, Mr. Stanley Sing On, Roll in My Sweet Baby's Arms, The Stanleys Will Sing Again, Act Naturally, Don't Step over an Old Love / Next Sunday, Darling, Is My Birthday, Waiting for a Train, On Heaven's Bright Shore, I Don't Want Your Rambling Letters, Amazing Grace). McClure, Va.: 5/27, 5/

28, and 5/29/83. b: R. Stanley, f: C. R. Cline, g: C. Sizemore, lg: J. Blankenship, g: Buddy Moore, bs: J. Cooke, et al.

41. Tin Ear 33010: Curly Ray Cline: *Smarter Than the Average Idiot* (Cacklin' Hen, Billy in the Low Ground, Step It Up and Go, Kentucky Waltz, Watermelon Hangin' on the Vine, Just a-Hangin' / Down Yonder, Smarter Than the Average Idiot, Patty on the Turnpike, Death Came Creepin' in My Room, Fly on the Baby's Nose, John Hardy). Chicago, Ill.: 1/27 and 1/28/84. f and hunting horn: C. R. Cline, b, triangle, and vibraslap: R. Stanley, g and b: C. Sizemore, lg: J. Blankenship, m and washboard: Hillard Blankenship, bs, washboard, and tambourine: J. Cooke.

42. Rebel REB 1637: Ralph Stanley: *I Can Tell You the Time* (Oh Daniel Prayed, I Want a Clear Record, Sometimes I Sing, The Man in the Middle, Thy Will Be Done, Victory in Jesus / He Will Set Your Fields on Fire, The Little Old Church by the Road, Two Men a Praying, Over There, I Can Tell You the Time, Jerusalem My Happy Home). Big Stone Gap, Va.: 2/6/85. b: R. Stanley, f: C. R. Cline, g: C. Sizemore, lg: J. Blankenship, bs: J. Cooke.

43. River Tracks RTS 1097: *Ralph Stanley Sings Sixteen Years* (Cotton-Eyed Joe, That Happy Night, Don't Wake Me Up, I Lived in Her World, After Midnight, Say Won't You Be Mine / Sixteen Years, Dickenson County Breakdown, Back to the Mountains, In Despair, This Weary Heart You Stole Away, Little Willie). Crum, WVa.: 3/6/86. b: R. Stanley, f: C. R. Cline, g: C. Sizemore, lg: J. Blankenship, bs: J. Cooke.

44. Rebel REB 1647: Ralph Stanley: *Lonesome and Blue* (Mountain Rosalee, Lonesome and Blue, True Blue Bill, Red Wicked Wine, Take Me Home with You Tonight in a Song, Room at the Top of the Stairs / Who's in Your Heart, Somebody Loves You Darling, Old Richmond Prison, Blue Moon of Kentucky, It's a Hot Night in August, So Blue). Big Stone Gap, Va.: 4/2/86. b: R. Stanley, f: C. R. Cline, g: C. Sizemore, lg: J. Blankenship, bs: J. Cooke.

45. Nashville Country C-101: Curly Ray Cline: *The Deputy* (Up Jumped the Devil, Waltz of the Wind, Smokey Mountain Rag, Old Joe Clark, I Wonder Why, Cotton-Eyed Joe / She'll Be Coming around the Mountain, The Bee, Adieu False Heart, Sugar Foot Rag, Fire on the Mountain, Verdie Let Your Bangs Hang Down). Big Stone Gap, Va.: 4/2 and 5/7/86. f: C. R. Cline, b: R. Stanley, g: C. Sizemore, lg: J. Blankenship, b: John Wright, bs: J. Cooke.

Bibliography

Arnow, Harriette Simpson. 1949. *Hunter's Horn.* New York: Macmillan.

Artis, Bob. 1975. *Bluegrass.* New York: Hawthorne Books.

Ball, Bo. 1988. *Appalachian Patterns.* Atlanta: Independence Publishers.

Bartenstein, Fred. 1972. "The Ralph Stanley Story." *Muleskinner News* 2.3:6–18.

Batteau, Allen W. 1990. *The Invention of Appalachia.* Tucson: University of Arizona Press.

Blake, Cully, and Mike Leary. 1972. "Muleskinner News Visits Ralph Stanley." *Muleskinner News* 2.3:2–5.

Booth, Mark W. 1981. *The Experience of Songs.* New Haven: Yale University Press.

Bovee, Bob. 1988. "The History of Early Recorded Country Music: Grayson and Whitter." *Inside Bluegrass* 14.2:6–8.

Bowden, Bobbi. 1987. "Smith Ridge or Bust." *Bluegrass Unlimited* 22.1:40–42.

Boyd, Richard. 1972. "2nd Country Music Day to Honor Brothers." Bristol *Herald Courier* 5/26.

Brower, Barry. 1987a. "Making the Blend: The Jack Cooke Story." *Bluegrass Unlimited* 21.7:55–57.

———. 1987b. "Ralph Stanley: Keeping It Right Down and Simple." *Bluegrass Unlimited* 21.8:13–16.

Burton, Thomas G., ed. 1981. *Tennessee Traditional Singers* (Ambrose N. Manning and Minnie N. Miller on Tom Ashley, Charles K. Wolfe on Sam McGee, F. Jack Hurley and David Evans on Bukka White). Knoxville: University of Tennessee Press.

Campbell, John C. 1921. *The Southern Highlander and His Homeland.* New York: Russell Sage Foundation.

Cantwell, Robert. 1972. "Believing in Bluegrass." *Atlantic* 229.3:52–54, 58–60.

———. 1976. "The Lonesome Sound of Carter Stanley." *Bluegrass Unlimited* 10.12:10–16.

———. 1984. *Bluegrass Breakdown: The Making of the Old Southern Sound.* Urbana: University of Illinois Press.

Carlin, Robert. 1976. "The Small Specialty Record Company in the United States." *JEMF Quarterly* 12:63–73.

Carlson, Norman. 1967. "J. E. Mainer and His Mountaineers." *Stanley Brothers International Fan Club: The Stanley Standard, Memorial Issue* 2.2:32–34.

———. 1987. "The Stanley Brothers Fan Club and a Twenty Year Bluegrass Odyssey." *Bluegrass Unlimited* 21.7:29–34.

Cheatham, Russ. 1980. "Charlie and Lee Cline and the Lonesome Pine Fiddlers." *Bluegrass Unlimited* 14.8:18–22.

Coelho, Dennis. 1977. Review of Rosenberg (1974), *Journal of American Folklore* 90:218–19.

Cohen, John. 1975. "Ralph Stanley's Old Time Mountain Bluegrass." *Sing Out!* 23.6:2–3, 6, 8.

Cook, Thomas. 1977. "Larry Sparks: 'I'm Givin' It All I've Got.'" *Bluegrass Unlimited* 12.2:14–18.

Dallman, Jerry. 1975. "Introducing Dick Freeland (of Rebel Records)." *Pickin'* 2.2:19–20.

Daniel, Wayne C. 1985. "Fiddlin' John Carson: The World's First Commercial Country Music Artist." *Bluegrass Unlimited* 20.1:40–43.

Davis, Ed. 1975. "Arthur Smith." *Muleskinner News* 6:9–11.

Dickinson, Eleanor, and Barbara Benziger. 1974. *Revival!* New York: Harper and Row.

Erbsen, Wayne. 1980. "Lester Woodie: Coming up the Hard Road." *Bluegrass Unlimited* 14.9:41–48.

Ewald, Wendy, ed. 1979. *Appalachia: A Self-Portrait.* Frankfort: Gnomon Press.

Ewing, Tom. 1976. "Earl Taylor: One of the Bluegrass Greats." *Bluegrass Unlimited* 11.3:10–14.

Fox, Jon Hartley. 1983. Review of Wright, *Discography, Bluegrass Unlimited* 18.5:36.

———. 1985. Review of Reid, *Discography, Bluegrass Unlimited* 20.1:49.

Freeland, Charles R. 1971. "An Era of Ralph: It Started in January 1967." *Ralph Stanley 1971* [souvenir book for tour of Japan], 38–41.

Godbey, Frank J. 1977. "Bluegrass, Bluegrass . . . : A Television Series." *Bluegrass Unlimited* 12.5:9–11.

Godbey, Marty. 1982. "The Lost Fiddler: Art Stamper." *Bluegrass Unlimited* 17.5:24–27.

———. 1983. "The Goins Brothers." *Bluegrass Unlimited* 18.2:16–23.

———. 1984. "Wendy Smith and Michigan Bluegrass, " *Bluegrass Unlimited* 18.10:30–35.

Gordon, Douglas. 1976. "The Stanley Tradition in American Music." *Pickin'* 3.1:34.

———. 1979. "Ralph Stanley: Traditional Banjo Stylist." *Frets* 1.9:14–21.

Gould, Ron. 1977. "The Shuffler Family: Foothills Gospel." *Bluegrass Unlimited* 12.5:31–34.

Green, Archie. 1965. "Hillbilly Music: Source and Symbol." *Journal of American Folklore* 78:204–28.

Green, Douglas B. 1972. "Larry Sparks." *Bluegrass Unlimited* 7.6:7–8.

———. 1980. Liner notes to Rounder Special Series 09 (The Stanley Brothers and The Clinch Mountain Boys, *The Columbia Sessions*, vol. 1), Rounder.

Greene, Clarence H. 1983. "Fiddling Steve Ledford." *Bluegrass Unlimited* 17.11:63–66.

Harrell, Bill. 1970. "Carter Stanley Memorial Award." *Bluegrass Unlimited* 4.12:19.

Hatlo, Jim. 1980. "Ricky Skaggs: Bluegrass Prodigy Comes of Age." *Frets* 2.8:16, 18, 20–21.

———. 1985. "Ricky Skaggs: Nashville's Latest Star Paid His Dues in the Trenches of Bluegrass." *Frets* 7.3:30–32, 37, 43–45.

Henderson, Tom. 1976. "Ralph Stanley Interview." *Muleskinner News* 7.1:8–11.

Henry, Murphy. 1984. "Richard Underwood." *Banjo Newsletter* 11.10:4–7.

Hershey-Webb, David. 1977. "Keith Whitley: The Thing to Me in Music Is the Feeling in a Song." *Muleskinner News* 8.1:6–9.

Humphrey, Mark. 1983. "Life and Death in Three-Part Harmony." *L.A. Weekly* 4/29–5/5:26.

Hylton, Randall. 1983. *How to Write and Sell Bluegrass Songs*. Nashville: RJH Publishing Company.

Kent, Jim. 1984. "Portrait of a Film: Ralph Stanley's Bluegrass Festival." *Bluegrass Unlimited* 18.11:16–22.

Kephart, Horace. 1922. *Our Southern Highlanders*. New York: Macmillan.

Knight, Julie. 1985. "Pioneer Banjo Man: Hoke Jenkins." *Bluegrass Unlimited* 20.3:24–31.

Kochman, Marilyn. 1984. *The Big Book of Bluegrass*. New York: Quill.

Komoriya, Nobuharu. 1971. "Ralph Stanley Goes to Japan." *Muleskinner News* 2:18–19.

Kuykendall, Pete. 1981. "Curly Ray Cline." *Bluegrass Unlimited* 15.11:32–37.

Ledgin, Stephanie P. 1991. "Walt Michael: Beyond the Hammered Dulcimer." *Sing Out!* 35.4:2–7.

Lomax, Alan. [1960]. Liner notes to Atlantic 1347, *Southern Folk Heritage Series: Blue Ridge Mountain Music*, Atlantic.

Malone, Bill C. 1968. *Country Music U.S.A.* Austin: University of Texas Press.

———. 1979. *Southern Music American Music*. Lexington: University of Kentucky Press.

Malone, Bill C., and Judith McCulloh, eds. 1975. *Stars of Country Music*. Urbana: University of Illinois Press.

McCeney, George B. 1975. "Don't Let Your Deal Go Down: The Bluegrass Career of Ray Davis." *Bluegrass Unlimited* 9.12:28–34.

McDonald, Janice Brown. 1988. "Why Curly Ray, Ralph?" *Bluegrass Unlimited* 23.3:24–26.

McGinnis, Fay. 1974. "Roy Lee Centers." *Ralph Stanley International Fan Club Newsletter* Fall, 1974, 1–5.

Menius, Arthur. 1985. "Dry Branch Fire Squad's Quest for Lonesome." *Bluegrass Unlimited* 20.1:14–20.

Menzel, Marv. 1988. "Laurie Lewis and the Grant Street Band." *Inside Bluegrass* 14.2:4–5.

Mitchell, Larry. 1977. "'Dr.' Ralph Stanley." *Pickin'* 4.7:4–14.

Morris, Paul. 1986. "Charlie Sizemore: A Lonesome Voice from the Hills." *Bluegrass Unlimited* 20.11:28–30.

Moser, Vicki. 1985. "Randall Hylton: Bluegrass Songwriter." *Bluegrass Unlimited* 20.4:46–49.

Obrecht, Jas. 1986. "Acoustic Roots: Fiddlin' John Carson." *Frets* 8.6:57.

Oermann, Robert K. 1981. "Ricky Skaggs Remembers the Stanley Brothers." *Bluegrass Unlimited* 15.11:26–29.

Pinsley, Elliot. 1974. "Clinch Mt. Block Party." *Pickin'* 1.11:10–12.

Plonsker, Mike. 1975. "Bluegrass: People and Pickin': A Film." *Bluegrass Unlimited* 9.9:25–26.

Price, Steven D. 1974. "Ricky Skaggs: Portrait of a Young Bluegrass Musician." *Pickin'* 1.1:18–19.

———. 1975. *Old as the Hills: The Story of Bluegrass Music.* New York: Viking Press.

Pugh, John. 1983. "Carlton Haney: True Great." *Bluegrass Unlimited* 18.3:22–25.

Rancke, Charlie. 1986. "Flying Sparks: Traditional Bluegrass Flatpicking." *Frets* 8.6:34–37.

Reid, Gary B. [1982]. Liner notes to Stanley Series 1.4, Copper Creek.

———. [1984]. Liner notes to County 753, The Stanley Brothers: *Uncloudy Day* (= Wango 103), County.

———. 1984. *Stanley Brothers: A Preliminary Discography.* Roanoke: Copper Creek Publications.

———. 1985. "The Stanley Brothers in Florida." *Florida Bluegrass News* 1.2:6–7.

Reid, Gary B., and Marian Leighton. 1982. Liner notes to Rounder Special Series 10 (The Stanley Brothers and the Clinch Mountain Boys, *The Columbia Sessions, 1949–1950,* vol. 2), Rounder.

Reid, Gary B., and Mosie Reid. [1981]. Liner notes to Stanley Series 1.1, Copper Creek.

Rhodes, Don. 1977. "Arthur Smith: A Wide and Varied Musical Career." *Bluegrass Unlimited* 12.1:20–23.

———. 1981. "Band on the Run: The Johnson Mountain Boys." *Bluegrass Unlimited* 16.6:12–17.

Rinzler, Ralph. 1974. "Ralph Stanley: The Tradition from the Mountains." *Bluegrass Unlimited* 8.9:7–11.

Roberts, Glenn, Jr. 1977. "The Marshall Family." *Bluegrass Unlimited* 11.12:16–24.

Robertson, Archie. 1950. *That Old-Time Religion.* Boston: Houghton Mifflin.

Roemer, John. 1982. "Larry Sparks Partial Discography." *Bluegrass Unlimited* 17.2:55.

Rosenberg, Neil V. 1974. *Bill Monroe and His Bluegrass Boys: An Illustrated Discography.* Nashville: Country Music Foundation Press.

———. 1981. "Thirty Years Ago." *Bluegrass Unlimited* 16.1:13.

———. 1985. *Bluegrass: A History.* Urbana: University of Illinois Press.

Sayers, Bob. 1976. "Leslie Keith: Black Mountain Odyssey." *Bluegrass Unlimited* 11.6:13–17.

Senter, Ginger R. 1988. "Dickenson County Honors Ralph Stanley." *Bluegrass Unlimited* 23.2:73.

Shapiro, Henry D. 1978. *Appalachia on Our Mind: The Southern Mountains and Mountaineers in the American Consciousness, 1870–1920.* Chapel Hill: University of North Carolina Press.

Shrubsall, Wayne. 1975. "Teach-In: Ralph Stanley's Banjo Style." *Sing Out!* 23.6:7–8.

Smith, Lee. 1983. *Oral History.* New York: Harper and Row.

Smith, Mayne. 1965. "An Introduction to Bluegrass." *Journal of American Folklore* 78:245–56.

Smolka, Ron. 1985. "Roy and Fay McGinnis: Mountain Echoes on the Sunnyside." *Bluegrass Unlimited* 20.6:55–57.

Snyder, Eugenia. 1986. "Joe Wilson: A Bluegrasser at the Helm of the NCTA." *Bluegrass Unlimited* 20.10:77–82.

———. 1987. "Putting Something Back into Bluegrass." *Bluegrass Unlimited* 21.11:80–84.

Spaulding, Arthur W. 1915. *The Men of the Mountains.* Nashville: Southern Publishing Association.

Spottswood, Richard K. 1976. "Carl Sauceman: The Odyssey of a Bluegrass Pioneer." *Bluegrass Unlimited* 11.2:10–17.

———. 1987. "Country Music and the Phonograph." *Bluegrass Unlimited* 21.8:17–23.

Stafford, Tim. 1987. "Rock Me in the Cradle of Bluegrass: Bluegrass Music in the Tri-Cities Region of Upper East Tennessee." *Bluegrass Unlimited* 22.4:18–24.

Stanley, Ralph. 1988. *It's the Hardest Music in the World to Play: The Ralph Stanley Story in His Own Words,* ed. John Wright. Chimacum, Wash.: Beaver Valley Press.

Stanton, Kathleen. 1975a. "Curly Ray Cline." *Pickin'* 2.3:10–17.

———. 1975b. "Keith Whitley: Music: It's Everything to Me. The Feeling's Down Deep." *Pickin'* 2.10:4–9.

Tarantino, Ellen Nassberg. 1983. "Wade Mainer: Profile of a Country Gentleman." *Bluegrass Unlimited* 18.5:26–28.

Thomason, Ron. 1971. "Ralph Stanley and the Clinch Mountain Boys." *Bluegrass Unlimited* 5.11:5–6.

———. 1979. *Lonesome Is a Car up on Blocks.* Springfield, Ohio.

Tottle, Jack. 1974. "Don't Wait for Them to Buy—Sell It: John Duffey and His Music." *Bluegrass Unlimited* 9.5:8–13.

———. 1977. "Ricky Skaggs: Clinch Mountain to Boone Creek." *Bluegrass Unlimited* 11.7:8–16.

———. 1981a. "The Bristol Country Music Foundation: Music, Memories and a Museum." *Bluegrass Unlimited* 15.10:14–17.

———. 1981b. "Ralph Stanley: The Stanley Sound." *Bluegrass Unlimited* 15.11:14–21.

———. 1987a. "WCYB: Bristol's Farm and Fun Time." *Bluegrass Unlimited* 22.4:25.

———. 1987b. "For Most of Their Brilliant First Decade, Bristol Was Home: The Stanley Brothers." *Bluegrass Unlimited* 22.4:27–29.

———. 1988a. Liner notes to Rebel REB 854, *Live Again: WCYB Bristol Farm and Fun Time,* Rebel.

———. 1988b. Liner notes to Rebel REB 855, *The Stanley Brothers on WCYB Bristol,* Rebel.

Tribe, Ivan M. 1974. "The Goins Brothers, Melvin and Ray: Maintaining the Lonesome Pine Tradition." *Bluegrass Unlimited* 8.11:11–18.

———. 1975. "J. E. and Wade Mainer." *Bluegrass Unlimited* 10.5:12–21.

———. 1976. "Curley Lambert: Bluegrass Evergreen." *Bluegrass Unlimited* 10.8:12–15.

———. 1977a. "Jimmie Skinner: Bluegrass Composer, Record Retailer." *Bluegrass Unlimited* 11.9:34–37.

———. 1977b. "Sing Your Song Jimmy: The Jimmy Williams Story." *Bluegrass Unlimited* 11.12:28–32.

———. 1980. "The Masters Family: A Major Influence on Bluegrass Gospel." *Bluegrass Unlimited* 14.9:30–35.

———. 1983. "Lowell Varney and Landon Messer: Traditional Bluegrass from the Big Sandy Country." *Bluegrass Unlimited* 17.11:56–60.

———. 1986. "The Prater Brothers: Youthful Bluegrass Traditionalists." *Bluegrass Unlimited* 20.10:30–31.

Tribe, Ivan M., and John W. Morris. 1980. "Bill Napier: Creative Instrumentalist." *Bluegrass Unlimited* 14.7:20–23.

Tribe, Ivan M., and Deanna Tribe. 1975. "Lee Allen: Rooted in the Stanley Tradition." *Bluegrass Unlimited* 9.10:37–38.

[unsigned]. 1974. "Roy Lee Centers: 1944–1974." *Bluegrass Unlimited* 8.12.

[unsigned]. 1978. "Leslie C. Keith (1906–1977)." *Bluegrass Unlimited* 12.8:5.

Vernon, Bill. 1973a. "Ralph Stanley in the Studio." *Muleskinner News* 4.5:6–7, 31.

———. 1973b. Liner notes to County 738, *The Stanley Brothers of Virginia,* vol. 1 (= Wango 106), County.

———. 1983. "Larry Sparks." *Bluegrass Unlimited* 17.10:13–18.

Wernick, Peter. 1976. *Bluegrass Songbook*. New York: Oak Publications.

Whisnant, David E. 1983. "Charles Dudley Warner and Social Change in the Southern Mountains: A Note on Serendipitous Discovery." *JEMF Quarterly* 19.70:69–75.

Wilgus, D. K., ed. 1965. "Hillbilly Issue." *Journal of American Folklore* 78:195–288.

Williams, Bruce. 1985. "Two Big Music Festivals and Thousands of Fans Are Coming to Letcher." *Tri-City News* 1/23.

Williamson, Tony. 1976. Liner notes to County 754, *The Stanley Brothers of Virginia*, vol. 4 (= Wango 105), County.

Wilson, Joe. 1972. "Bristol's WCYB: Early Bluegrass Turf." *Muleskinner News* 3.8:8–12.

———. 1982. "Sidelines in American History, Part 1: When Bluegrass Bands Needed Lightning Rod Salesmen." *Bluegrass Unlimited* 17.4:40–42.

———. 1986. "Is G Always for George?" *Bluegrass Unlimited* 20.8:33.

Wolfe, Charles. 1973. "Man of Constant Sorrow: Richard Burnett's Story." *Old Time Music* 9.2:6–10, 9.3:5–11.

———. 1978. "The Odyssey of Arthur Smith." *Bluegrass Unlimited* 13.2:50–57.

Wright, John. 1982. "The Stanleytone." *Banjo Newsletter* 10.1:7–8.

———. 1983. *Ralph Stanley and the Clinch Mountain Boys: A Discography*. Evanston: Lonnie Mason.

———. 1984. "Ralph Stanley Today." *Banjo Newsletter* 11.3:5–10.

——— [ed.]. 1985. *Ralph Stanley and the Clinch Mountain Boys: Old Time Songs*. Chimacum, Wash.: Beaver Valley Press.

———. 1987. "Mountain Echoes." *Banjo Newsletter* 15.2:15.

———. 1989. "Resurrection." *Banjo Newsletter* 16.5:15.

———. 1990. "Charlie Sizemore: 'You Do What Is Necessary and Then Go Forward.'" *Bluegrass Unlimited* 25.1:24–32.

Wright, Sharon. 1980. "The Dry Branch Fire Squad." *Bluegrass Unlimited* 14.7:12–15.

Index

JOHN WRIGHT has been a regular columnist in *Banjo Newsletter* since December, 1980; he has also written for *Bluegrass Unlimited* and *Precious Memories: A Journal of Gospel Music*. He has produced a banjo book for Ralph Stanley and a souvenir songbook for Curly Ray Cline, as well as liner notes for albums by the Stanley Brothers, Ralph Stanley, Curly Ray Cline, Charlie Sizemore, and Dave Evans. He is a member of the International Bluegrass Music Association, BMI, and the Democratic party of Evanston. In his day job he is John Evans Professor of the Latin Language and Literature and chairman of the Classics Department at Northwestern University, and a member of the American Philological Association and the Society of Fellows of the American Academy in Rome.